CW00801430

Transnational Railway Cultures

Explorations in Mobility

Series Editors:
Gijs Mom, Eindhoven University of Technology
Mimi Sheller, Drexel University
Georgine Clarsen, University of Wollongong

The study of mobility opens up new transnational and interdisciplinary approaches to fields including transport, tourism, migration, communication, media, technology, and environmental studies. The works in this series rethink our common assumptions and ideas about the mobility of people, things, ideas, and cultures from a broadly understood humanities perspective. The series welcomes projects of a historical or contemporary nature and encourages postcolonial, non-Western, and critical perspectives.

Transnational Railway Cultures

Trains in Music, Literature, Film, and Visual Art

Edited by
Benjamin Fraser and Steven Spalding

berghahn
NEW YORK • OXFORD
www.berghahnbooks.com

First published in 2022 by
Berghahn Books
www.berghahnbooks.com

Library of Congress Cataloging-in-Publication Data

A C.I.P. cataloging record is available from the Library of Congress
Library of Congress Cataloging in Publication Control Number: 2021037217

British Library Cataloguing in Publication Data

A catalogue record for this book is available from the British Library

ISBN 978-1-78920-918-1 hardback
ISBN 978-1-78920-919-8 ebook

Contents

Illustrations

Figures

Map

Introduction

Benjamin Fraser and Steven Spalding

Transnational Railway Cultures accomplishes two interlinked goals: it shifts the cultural study of trains into a transnational mode, and it prioritizes representations of the rail experience in a wide range of humanities texts. This volume's ten chapters investigate the dual role of trains as both artistic symbols and social realities as they figure into avant-garde music, poetry, fiction, travelogues, film, and visual art from selected spaces across the globe. The chapters cover railway cultures in and across Argentina, Catalonia, China, England, France, Germany, India, Italy, Mongolia, Russia, Scotland, South Korea, Spain, and the United States, with each chapter dealing with at least two if not three of these areas. Contributors to the volume themselves hail from a variety of global contexts, including Argentina, England, India, and the United States. The result is an ambitious volume that appeals to a global readership and forges a new line of interdisciplinary and transnational scholarship on the cultural representations of the railroad.

Steering readers toward brief summaries of the individual chapters that make up this book, the present introduction sets the coordinates for our journey. Throughout highlighting various and sundry texts devoted to the scholarly study of train travel, we begin by acknowledging two key points of reference. *The Railway Journey,* by Wolfgang Schivelbusch ([1977] 1986), and *The Machine in the Garden,* by Leo Marx (1988), have both been privileged in the cultural study of trains. These books—and the subsequent studies that have relied on them explicitly and implicitly—included compelling analyses of the changing social relationships that have long accompanied locomotive power. Each theorist, in his own way, humanizes and broadens what might otherwise be a dry, historical, or instrumentalist accounting of the contradictions and consequences inherent in technological shifts.

Wolfgang Schivelbusch's *The Railway Journey: The Industrialization of Time and Space in the 19th Century* ([1977] 1986) is a primary touchstone for this book. Though it has sometimes been seen in purely historical terms, his study is increasingly a point of origin for twenty-first-century cultural and transnational investigations of the train. Schi-velbusch's oft-repeated insights into the machine ensemble and the compartment forge the coordinates for understanding a new social consciousness that arises with the railway. Undoubtedly, the expansion of a physical infrastructure for railway transportation is made possible by, and further develops, a new fusion of social space, temporality, and technology. As his study explored, this machine culture reshapes human social relationships in profound ways. New fears and anxieties emerge from the experience of train travel and the press coverage of crashes; new illnesses such as railway spine and railway brain began to capture the public's attention.[1] Connections of the railroad with death were heightened through popular discourse, such that "the threat of being run over while bound to the train tracks preoccupied a transnational cultural imagination from the mid-nineteenth century onwards" (Aguiar 2011, 154). Visions of increased speed and the realities of space-time compression forced a recalibration of the tropes of closeness and distance and the social forces of alienation.[2] In these broad arguments and the human scope of his book, Schivelbusch arguably established the foundation for contemporary cultural studies of trains (Spalding 2014, 42).[3]

While some readers may be tempted to see the geographical scope of *The Railway Journey* in terms of the national histories of Austria, England, France, Germany, and the United States, we underscore that it is unquestionably a transnational contribution. Schivelbusch identifies a coherent and relatively nimble set of insights regarding what is at once a new material and social technology. In the process, he reveals the general contours of what we call a transnational railway culture. As supported by subsequent research, this notion of a railway culture has proved versatile enough to be applied to spaces around the world.[4] It is important that there is room in the historian's account for the machine culture of rail technology to take on the nuances present in distinct sociocultural, national, regional, local, and imaginative and artistic contexts.[5] Whether explicitly or implicitly, then, each chapter of this volume owes greatly to the cultural and transnational study of the railway as initiated by Schivelbusch.

The crucial importance of the humanities in any evaluation of the legacy of the railway was notably emphasized in a work that constitutes the second touchstone for the present effort: *The Machine in the Garden: Technology and the Pastoral Ideal in America* (Marx [1964] 2000). In that book, scholar Leo Marx took on the writings of canonical authors including Emerson, Thoreau, Hawthorne, Melville, Twain, James, Adams, Norris, Hemingway, and Faulkner. Marx's success, it has been noted, "probably owes much to his border-jumping, interdisciplinary method as a literary scholar who made a point of addressing wider cultural concerns, and in particular technological issues" (Meikle 2003, 155). As Colin Divall and Hiroki Shin have written, Marx was pioneering an approach that "takes technological culture as a metaphor," and *The Machine in the Garden* thus emphasized a certain "sense of the machine as a sudden, shocking intruder upon a fantasy of idyllic satisfaction" (Divall and Shin 2012, 4; Marx [1964] 2000, 23; see also Marx 1988; Velez 2012, 220). Marx's book did not focus either exclusively or exhaustively on the locomotive, but rather envisioned it simultaneously as both "a cosmos as well as an industrial tool" (Marx [1964] 2000, 205). The whistle of the train announces a social transformation, and perhaps more pointedly, "The sensory attributes of the engine—iron, fire, steam, smoke, noise, speed—evoke the essence of industrial power and wealth" (204).

The depth of Leo Marx's interest in literature is complemented by other twentieth-century studies carried out in a national key—not just of American poetry by James Bodenstedt (1992), but moreover French literature by Marc Baroli (1964) and German poetry by Johannes Mahr (1982).[6] In the twenty-first century, scholars continue to delve into North American literature's fascination with the railroad—there is an annotated bibliography by Grant Burns (2005) to consider, as well an important study of the railway in African American literature by Darcy Zabel (2004; connected to the interest displayed in an earlier dissertation, Zabel 2001). Kevin G. Flynn (2002) expands critical interest in the North American railway to Canadian literature, and Michael Matthews (2013) has crafted a cultural history of the iron horse in Mexico. Indebted, in many respects, to the books by Schivelbusch and Marx, the contemporary study of train representations continues to accelerate in the twenty-first century. Single-authored books covering the national contexts of Uruguay/Argentina, Japan, India, and Brazil—Sarah M. Misemer's *Moving Forward, Looking Back: Trains, Literature, and the Arts in the River Plate* (2010), Alisa Freedman's *Tokyo in Transit: Japanese Culture on the Rails and Road* (2010), Marian Aguiar's *Tracking Modernity: India's Railway and the Culture of Mobility* (2011), and Martin Cooper's *Brazilian Railway Culture* (2011)—have the additional advantage of paying close attention to humanities representations of trains in theater, prose literature, film and visual art. While this survey of the English-language studies of railway cultures is necessarily incomplete, particularly when one takes into account article-length publications, it is safe to assume that scholarship in other languages has been delving into the study of trains at an equally frenetic pace. What is not as easy to find, however—given the undeniable tendency for train scholarship to reaffirm national boundaries—is a transnational vision of railway cultures. It is to this situation that our book responds.

Compared with its increased visibility in the twenty-first century, the notion of transnational studies was neither as popular nor as entrenched in the discipline of History when Schivelbusch originally published his book in German in 1977. One notes today a great number of books that adopt a transnational perspective on social science topics. This perspective is frequently used in order to shake up somewhat limiting understandings of the way in which individuals and groups negotiate scales of social experience that are themselves culturally constructed.[7] For example, *Transnational Lives: Biographies of Global Modernity, 1700–present* very lucidly asserts, "Human lives elude official classifications," explaining, "The transnationalism—the mobility, confusion and sheer messiness—of ordinary lives threatens the stability of national identity and unsettles the framework of national histories" (Deacon, Russell, and Woollacott 2010, 1–2). As *Transnational Ruptures: Gender and Forced Migration* (Nolin 2006) and *Transnational Families: Ethnicities, Identities and Social Capital* (Goulbourne et al. 2010) both emphasize, the nation-state cannot be ignored, but must be seen as one of many constellations of power that impact the movement and migration of people across the globe.[8] The author of *Transnational Urbanism: Locating Globalization* strikes this balance well when he writes, "In contrast [to the discourse of globalization], the transnationalist discourse insists on the continuing significance of borders, state policies, and national identities even as these are often transgressed by transnational communication circuits and social practices" (Smith 2001, 3).[9] In bringing increased attention to the way in which human relationships cannot be fully explained through national paradigms, these and other works in effect actualize a number of discourses that historically gain greater visibility with the irruption of train travel.

Looking backward, the railway's connection with transnationality is patently obvious. From its beginnings, many in Europe asserted the power of trains to bring people, and by extension, all of humanity, closer together.[10] The global expansion of the railroad effected unprecedented levels of geographic interconnection, such that "by 1910 the railroad was established on every continent" (Osterhammel 2014, 911).[11] Most often, railway construction involved transnational dynamics at the interconnected levels of design, financing, direction, and labor.[12] These dynamics were far from egalitarian, of course. Monetary gains sourced from the railway business were disproportionately enjoyed by social actors and private companies from industrialized nations. Capitalist accumulation strategies ensured that the wealth created by workers who were local or, in some cases, actively recruited from other countries, was absorbed into persisting (post)colonial networks.[13]

There was, in a sense, a contradiction in the way nation-states became involved in what was inherently the transnational project of railroad construction. Irene Anastasiadou mentions "the role of railways in building nation states" but also underscores that the "Internationalisation of European railways started early in the nineteenth century" (2007, 172, 173). While "transport networks, and more specifically railways, were placed in the service of the political goals of nation states and empires," it was nonetheless true that, "politically, the redefinition of borders posed problems of ownership of lines in many parts of Europe" (172, 173). Moreover, this contradiction between national interests and the transnational scope of the railway is just as palpable today as it has been throughout the railroad's history. The scholar remarks on the 1918 plan for a "large-scale railway artery that would connect Paris with Dakar through Spain" using the vocabulary of transnational trade.[14] "Coupled with the construction of a railway tunnel under the Channel," she writes, "the projected railway line and the tunnel under the straits of Gibraltar would provide a direct railway link from European capitals such as Brussels, London, Paris and Madrid to their African colonies, while it would also intensify exchange between them" (176–77). As can be seen in the 2017 announcement of Chinese financial backing for a planned Ethiopian railway,[15] the train continues to be a way of rethinking an expansive global transportation network tied to the interests of individual nations but exceeding the scope of the national.

At the most general level, analyzing the transnational character of the railway involves paying attention to many distinguishable but overlapping spheres. The outline provided in the collection titled *The Transnational Studies Reader: Intersections and Innovations* (Khagram and Levitt 2008b) is helpful in thinking through analytically distinct categories that nonetheless overlap in the social realities of the railway experience and its history.[16] In their introduction to the volume, editors Sanjeev Khagram and Peggy Levitt sketch out what they refer to as the three primary varieties of transnationalism: empirical transnationalism, methodological transnationalism, and theoretical transnationalism (2008a, 2).[17]

There may not yet be a book-length text that approaches railway history from an explicitly transnational framework, but we would argue that existing approaches have necessarily had to deal with what should be seen as the inherently transnational character of the railroad. In line with empirical transnationalism, Schivelbusch's original text itself arguably contributes to the comparative-historical study of similarities and differences in railway travel.[18] While not specifically addressing transnationalism, the edited volumes *Trains, Literature, and Culture: Reading/ Writing the Rails* (Spalding and Fraser 2012) and *Trains, Culture, and Mobility: Riding the Rails* (Fraser and Spalding 2012), as well as a special section of the journal *Transfers* on "Railways and Urban Cultures" (Spalding 2014) implicitly engage the framework of methodological transnationalism to reveal the transnational form of the railway experience across specific social contexts. Even more compelling, a masterful book like Todd Presner's *Mobile Modernity: Germans, Jews, Trains* (2007) illustrates the power of theoretical transnationalism—by moving beyond national history to forge what the author calls a "complicated cultural geography of German/Jewish modernity."[19]

Individual chapters in this book may be transnational in one or more of the three primary senses identified by Khagram and Levitt (2008b) in *The Transnational Studies Reader*. Nonetheless, as a whole, *Transnational Railway Cultures* shows a preference for a nontraditional variant of transnational studies that the editors call philosophical transnationalism.[20] This approach "starts from the metaphysical assumption that social words and lives are inherently transnational. In other words, transnational phenomena and dynamics are the rule rather than the exception, the underlying reality rather than a derivative by-product" (2008a, 2). In truth, the acceptance and strength of philosophical transnationalism is quite evident in certain areas of contemporary interdisciplinary research. In order to demonstrate this concisely in a way that contributes to the study of railway cultures, specifically, it is important to acknowledge the intersection of transport history and studies of culture that is part and parcel of mobility studies.

In truth, the notion of mobility has already proven to be a powerful theoretical tool in refashioning the interdisciplinary field of transport history in transnational terms. Key landmarks of mobility studies include Tim Cresswell's *On the Move: Mobility in the Western World* (2006), John Urry's *Mobilities* (2007), and the creation of the peer-reviewed journals *Mobilities* (founded in 2006) and *Transfers: Interdisciplinary Journal of Mobility Studies* (founded in 2011). Significantly, mobility studies affirm philosophical transnationalism by taking transnationalism to be the rule of contemporary society rather than the exception. In their editorial to the inaugural journal issue of *Mobilities*, Kevin Hannam, Mimi Sheller, and John Urry defined the field broadly as "encompassing studies of corporeal movement, transportation and communications infrastructures, capitalist spatial restructuring, migration and immigration, citizenship and transnationalism, and tourism and travel" (2006, 9–10; see also Sheller and Urry 2006). Material culture and national culture are specifically mentioned in that editorial, and railway culture in general—

in the sense we attribute to Schivelbusch—figures broadly into those arguments by John Urry in his book *Mobilities*, for example where he explores the railway compartment, the objectification of passengers, the railway station, train timetables, and the drastic social shifts prompted by train travel in everyday life (2007, 93, 94, 95–100, 104).[21]

Scholarship in this new articulation of transport and mobility studies generally speaking is clearly aware of and relevant to the humanities research. In "Mobilizing the History of Technology" (2010), published in the journal *Technology and Culture*, Colin Divall underscores the need for transport history to reach wider audiences: "The so-called cultural and spatial turns that have remodeled many other areas of the humanities and social sciences open up exciting possibilities, for transport is a deeply spatio-cultural act" (Divall 2010, 950). And yet it is not clear that cultural texts themselves, combined with humanities methods, are precisely what he has in mind. In an earlier publication, Divall and George Revill explicitly stated, "We need a conception of culture that does more than merely consider (although this is no simple matter) how and why transport technologies are represented in the arts and popular imagination" (2005, 109). Indeed, work in the social sciences often steers away from the specific nature of cultural texts under the guise of appealing to the broad cultural imaginary (101). This is not necessarily an error, as culture is a curious force that overflows specific texts and involves everyday social life. Yet in the present book we continue to believe that the textual humanities are crucial to the future directions of mobility studies. It is true that broader cultural understandings create and give social and not merely technological meaning to transport. Humanities methods informed and enriched by insights from transport and mobility studies are nimble enough to engage with these broader understandings of culture through analysis of specific texts themselves. Such an approach, we believe, furthers the call by Divall and Revill to pay attention to "transport technologies as mediation between the imaginable and the material" and "transport technologies as a creative producer of spaces" (105, 106).[22]

Transfers: Interdisciplinary Journal of Mobility Studies has perhaps done the most to further connections between transport and mobility history and humanities research methods. As recounted in its inaugural editorial in 2011, its editorial team and referees were recruited with a specific intent to include "literary scholars, artists, cultural critics," and its stated goal was to "combine the empiricism of history with more recent methodological approaches that have reshaped the social sciences and the humanities" (Mom et al. 2011, 7, 3, respectively). Subsequent editorials have consistently underscored the need "to bring critical mobilities frameworks into closer conversation with the humanities by encouraging empirical collaborations and conceptual transfers across diverse disciplinary fields" (Clarsen 2015a, 41).[23] Just as important, the journal has been strongly "committed to trans-disciplinary and transnational research that opens up global perspectives" (Mom and Kim 2013, 1; Merriman et al. 2013). Its vision resonates productively with Khagram and Levitt's notion of philosophical transnationalism. One editorial declares that "transnational approaches denaturalize the nation, thus rendering our historical imaginings less parochial by tracking the networked relationships and global circulation of entities and relationships across borders"; another encourages authors to move beyond "the North Atlantic sphere" in their analyses and think more capaciously about "imaginary travel, imaginary worlds of connection and imaginary geographies" (Clarsen 2015a, 41; 2015b, 115). The intersection between transport mobilities research and the humanities remains a vibrant, if sometimes overlooked, component of the broader railway imagination.

Whether in *Transfers* or in other venues from the humanities, an increasing number of article-length studies have been published that prioritize humanities methods in exploring the cultures of train travel.[24] Just as the railway covers a vast distance so too does the literature on railway culture constitute a vast terrain. Yet in terms of book-length publications, there is a need for further study.[25] Substantial analyses such as Gijs Mom's *Atlantic Automobilism: Emergence and Persistence of the Car, 1895–1940* (2015), as well as Peter Merriman's *Driving Spaces: A Cultural-Historical Geography of England's M1 Motorway* (2007) and *Mobility, Space and Culture* (2012), have pushed transport history farther into cultural terrain than previous work. Nevertheless, there is still more to be done in order to understand railway cultures through the textual humanities. Reflecting on one of the most-studied national traditions of railroad study in his book *Railways and Culture in Britain: The Epitome of Modernity*, Ian Carter was able to remark that accounts of the British railways have tended to be "lopsided"—in other words, "they pay little attention to social issues and less to culture" (2001, 3).[26]

Twenty years later we believe that there is still a need for a book such as this one—a book that takes on multiple humanities representations of railway travel in a specifically transnational framework.[27] Methodologically speaking, *Transnational Railway Cultures* certainly deals in the "mobility, confusion and sheer messiness" (Deacon, Russell, and Woollacott 2010, 1–2) of transnationalism as noted above. Motivated by the basic premise of philosophical transnationalism, the contributions to this volume collectively acknowledge the shifting transnational ground of contemporary transport and mobility studies. Individual authors each define and approach the transnational aspects of railway transport in their own way. It is important to understand, however, that transnationalism is also important to the study of humanities representations and not just railway cultures themselves. Intriguingly, as Nataša Ďurovičová (2010) writes in her preface to World Cinemas, Transnational Perspectives, a book coedited with Kathleen Newman (Ďurovičová and Newman 2010), "the prefix 'trans-' implies relations of unevenness and mobility" (Ďurovičová 2010, x). Cinema in particular is increasingly transnational, not only in terms of its depiction of contemporary mobile lives, but also in terms of flexible models of production that frequently involve multiple nations.[28] Selected chapters in this book cover films whose characters' mobile lives suggest extended and overlapping boundaries of national identities and cultures. Others treat cinematic coproductions. Cultural production on the whole has in a sense always been transnational in scope. The cultures in which literary movements, traditions of painting and visual art, and the creation of musical compositions have been immersed have very rarely, if at all, been hermetically developed in isolation from the transnational flow of ideas.[29] As chapters in this volume suggest, the representation of the train in cultural texts—not only cinema but also prose, poetry, painting, and musical composition—makes it quite difficult to sustain hermetic notions of nationhood. Each functions as a window into shifting conditions, messiness, unevenness, and mobility as lived in social spaces and as represented in artistic practices across the globe.

Whether speaking of cinema specifically, or more broadly of literature and visual art, the railway is now an icon deeply rooted in representational practices. While it "belongs to a collective, transnational cultural consciousness that has long cast the railway as the scene or agent in nightmarish scenarios," the train is at times also a more positive symbol of "freedom, adventure and new possibilities" (Aguiar 2011, 153; see also Klein 1994, 20–21). If it is tempting to see the train as an icon with a singular identity, one must be reminded of its connection with a range of competing and overlapping concerns. As Amy G. Richter writes in her book Home on the Rails: Women, the Railroad, and the Rise of Public Domesticity, "nineteenth-century journalists, travelers and poets used it [the train] as shorthand for social diversity, national integration, technological innovation, and corporate organization" (2005, 4).[30] Whether a symbol of routine mobilities, ruin, or redemption, as George Revill remarks in Railway (2012), the icon of the train has left its stamp in the realm of high art, in popular culture and in the wider imagination.[31] In the main, these chapters privilege "the railway as a set of cultural symbols, meanings, images, artefacts and activities" precisely by giving priority to textual humanities representations (14). In doing so, they frequently deal with Wolfgang Schivelbusch explicitly, and implicitly they reinvigorate Leo Marx's fascination regarding the value, impact, and insights of artistic discourse.

Chapter Summaries

In chapter 1, "The Railway Arts: Sound and Space beyond Borders," Aimée Boutin argues that train travel holds a privileged position among the new means of transportation developed during the nineteenth century because of its effect on the senses. Wolfgang Schivelbusch and others have concentrated on the new ways of seeing enabled by the railway; from the train window, the landscape appears as panoramic and proto-cinematic. The railway, however, affected the other senses as well. Rather than focus on the relation between vision and speed, this chapter explores the sounds of the railway to consider how the railway affected perceptions of sound and space. How did travelers experience railway travel with their eyes and ears when they traversed distances at high speed? Did this new sensory experience change the conception of the landscape? Furthermore, did the spatialization of sound transform awareness of space-time and if so, how did this new attentiveness translate into writing? Transposing Schivelbusch's original inspiration to an artistic key, Boutin adapts the framework of empirical transnational to in a comparative analysis of Charles-Valentin Alkan's *Le chemin de fer, étude* (*The Railway*), op. 27, the first musical representation of the railway composed in 1844, and poems on the railway, notably Louisa Siefert's pantoum "En Passant en chemin de fer" and Robert Louis Stevenson's "From a Railway Carriage." These analyses show how variations in intensities and in rhythm used to represent the journey through space, sound out new transnational conceptions of space as multi-perspectival and permeated/permeating.

Chapter 2, Benjamin Fraser's "The Sonic Force of the Machine Ensemble: Transnational Objectification in Steve Reich's *Different Trains* (1988)," combines transportation and mobility studies with work on avant-garde music, semiotics, and transnational imaginaries in a cultural studies approach to Steve Reich's *Different Trains* (1988). In *The Railway Journey*, train theorist Wolfgang Schivelbusch famously emphasized the dehumanizing effects of train travel noting both what he called the "machine ensemble," which interjected itself between the traveler and the landscape, noting also the traveler's conversion into "the object of an industrial process" ([1977] 1986, 24, 73, respectively). A transportation and mobility studies approach to Reich's piece reveals how the avant-garde composer's three-movement recording—commissioned by Betty Freeman for Kronos Quartet—reproduces this machine ensemble, representing it through multiple levels of aural signification. Blending tones of recorded speech, train sounds and sirens with multitracked musical notes, Reich's composition uses sonic variants of iconic, indexical, and symbolic signification. The composition's content bridges two very distinct forms of dehumanization: the evils of the Holocaust and the alienations routinely experienced under globalized industrial capitalism. Following Raymond Williams, the cultural studies approach to music used here gives equal weight to both musical content/form and also the extra-musical American-European referents that inspire and structure what is undeniably a transnational representation of railway travel.

John D. Schwetman's "A Genealogy of Apocalyptic Trains: *Snowpiercer* and Its Precursors in the Transnational Literature of Transport," chapter 3, focuses on South Korean director Bong Joon-ho's 2013 film *Snowpiercer,* which quickly developed a devoted following as a result of its mixture of cagey political satire and stunning visual effects. While its deviations from the conventions of science fiction indicate that it derives more from the aesthetics of railroad travel and the symbolic power of railroads than it does from the science-fiction objectives of projecting future scenarios logically from present-day trends, *Snowpiercer* succeeds as a satirical dramatization of the apocalypse. Through close readings of the images of apocalyptic trains culled from media with transnational appeal, Schwetman argues it is possible to stitch together the structural elements of the Snowpiercer itself. Trains that appear in the opening montage of Nicholas Meyer's made-for-television film *The Day After* (1983), China Miéville's novel *The Iron Council* (2004), Steven Spielberg's remake of *The War of the Worlds* (2005), and Cormac McCarthy's *The Road* (2006), all come together to form a complex transnational meditation on collapsing rail infrastructure and the end of civilization. As a symbol of a globalized, hierarchical economic system in a state of collapse built on elements of its literary and cinematic precursors, the Snowpiercer of Jacques Lob's graphic novel series and of Bong Joon-ho and Kelly Masterson's screenplay satisfies the expectations of its viewers. In the end it provides a concrete, visual emblem of a more abstract potential decline and collapse that has been observed more generally in transnational representations of the railway.

Chapter 4, "Dangerous Borders: Modernization and the Gothic Mode in *Pánico en el Transiberiano* (1972) and *Howl* (2015)" by Fernando Gabriel Pagnoni Berns and Juan Juvé, explores the way in which fantastic films illustrate the inability of modern thinking and advancements in technology to erase the old, uncanny imagination of a global world filled with monsters, fears about the human condition, and obscurantism. Transnational films always speak about anxieties about borders, citizenship, and national belonging, and in the filmic fantastic fears about mechanization, modernization, and social class are turned into a dark fantasy about uncanny trains and the fear about obsolescence, both human and mechanical. *Pánico en el transiberiano* (*Howl,* Eugenio Martín, 1972) takes place in 1906, in China, when a British anthropologist (Christopher Lee) discovers a frozen prehistoric creature and decides to transport it to Europe aboard the trans-Siberian express, but during the trip the monster thaws out and starts to kill the passengers one by one. As a transnational coproduction between Spain and the United Kingdom, the film highlights the many fantastic scientific progresses of humanity (forensic sciences, anthropology, the train itself) against a backdrop of blind obscurantism (specially illustrated in the communist countries and passengers), and the supernatural within a context of Eurohorror. If the nineteenth-century steam railway epitomized modernity's relentlessly onrushing advance in the United Kingdom, the film illustrates the futility of battling the atavistic mind, while the train is just a space for oppression (including social oppression) and darkness.

In chapter 5, "Anachronism, Ambivalence, and (Trans)National Self-Reference: Tracking the English Literary Chunnel from 1986 On," Heather Joyce embraces the Chunnel as a touchstone for cultural critics in the twenty-first century. At the same time that it is insistently territorial, encompassing contending and contradictory claims of extension and abrogation of sovereignty by the nations it connects, it presages what Emily Apter calls a "state of postnational borderlessness" (2002, 287) and connects with key insights from transnational studies. The cultural inflection of representations of the Chunnel on the British side reflects the role the Channel has played in enabling the nation to imagine itself politically and culturally in relation to France and the rest of Europe. Though representations of the Chunnel echo and extend this existing narrative of historic self-reference, they also draw on the symbolic value that railways have accrued since their inception. The "new, reduced geography" that Wolfgang Schivelbusch associates with railway travel ([1977] 1986, 35) means that the Chunnel predictably promises to bridge nations, as Patience Agbabi's poem "Chunnel/Le Tunnel sous la Manche" makes clear; it also engenders the defensive territoriality that we see in Nicola Barker's novel *Darkmans*—a defensiveness provoked by what the inception of the Chunnel means not only for transnational relations but transregional ones, as well. These contending formulations converge in depictions of the mode of transport itself. The Eurostar brings together the contrapuntal histories of the national rail system and localized rail travel in London; in doing so, it calls into question the extent to which convivial groupings such as those envisioned by Paul Gilroy can move beyond being political expediencies that continue to facilitate the nation's self-understanding of itself as modern.

Chapter 6, "Crossing Borders on and beyond the Train in *Joan of Arc of Mongolia* (1989)," by Steven Spalding, explores an obscure but important filmic representation of the Trans-Siberian Railway connecting Russia and Asia. The exotic scenery of the great train journey has intervened in this film to break the linear, masculine teleology of the train in order to set its protagonists on a detour out of time. The film's two-part structure allows the film to accomplish a number of deliberate and fascinating symbolic movements—all with a wry satirical sensibility—from portraying and parodying stereotypical European and international train travelers, Russian peasants, military officers, and train service personnel, and the interactions among these heterogeneous groups, to debunking the legendary mythos around the Trans-Siberian as tsarist (i.e., masculine) legacy and accomplishment. In the second part, the train—along with its attendant symbolism—has been defeated by the least likely of antagonists, a peaceful band of nomadic Mongolian women on horseback and their brightly decorated leader. This chapter examines the film's feminist project of intercultural exchange through its use of the train as locus of symbolic and narrative creation, and through the positive feminist transnationalism underlying the film's playfulness and irony. The characters' whimsical abduction by the Mongolian princess transforms their journey in fundamental ways, as they are challenged to shed cultural familiarity and all the reassuring effects of the train (à la Schivelbusch) and confront cultural difference head on.

In chapter 7, "'The Cosmopolitan Writer: Exploring Representations on the Underground Railways of Buenos Aires and Paris through Julio Cortázar," Dhan Zunino Singh investigates a peculiarity of railway travel pertinent to the work of subway scholars. Specifically, he explores the experience of descending within an explicitly transnational frame. Cross-culturally, to ride under the city has triggered specific representations associated with death, hell, the underworld, and so on. These atavistic representations are more related to the space in which travel takes place (the tunnel) than to the notions of movement that guide analyses of above-ground travel. The practices and relations that have emerged from consideration of the subway's subterranean paths have been the subjects of a wide range of cultural representations (films, literature, comics, music, and so on), many of which are tied to the peculiarities of specific urban environments across the globe. This chapter analyzes the representations of the Buenos Aires subway through the work of Argentinean writer Julio Cortázar, linking his texts to other cultural products in order to establish the impact the subway has had on its surrounding culture since its implementation in 1913. More broadly, it engages the metropolitan railway (metro) as a transnational space and reflects on shared cultural meanings expressed also in the Paris Metro and London Underground. Cortázar's significant fascination with the underground enables scholarship to explore a variety of considerations related to traveling with crowds, anonymity, visual and embodied effects of the subway, bodily proximity and social distance, sociability, speed, love stories, and the underworld.

Chapter 8, Abhishek Chatterjee's "Literary Railway Bazaars: Transnational Discourses of Difference and Nostalgia in Contemporary India," takes on the commonplace that there is no better symbol of national integration than the railway network in India. All of the country's railway stations tend to look and feel the same, irrespective of differences in culture, cuisine, or people—not in some postmodern discourse of sameness but in timescapes of colonial nostalgia. The Indian railway network, sometimes described as the British Empire's most enduring legacy to the jewel in its crown, retains a colonial flavor and an old-world charm. There is a transnational aspect to this legacy, as it has stoked the Orientalist imagination of writers like Paul Theroux in *The Great Railway Bazaar* (1975) and *Ghost Train to the Eastern Star* (2008) as well as filmmakers like Wes Anderson in *The Darjeeling Limited* (2007). While Theroux saw token images of poverty, starvation, and filth through the windows of his first-class compartment, Anderson's film looks at India as a fantasy of spiritual mystique and self-discovery. With air travel becoming more accessible to the Indian middle class, train journeys in contemporary India have become the mainstay of travel for millions of huddled masses, and a far cry from the romance of the journey motif. This chapter thus builds on existing humanities analysis of railway cultures in India (Aguiar 2011), examining these aspects of train journeys and the travelogue in light of accounts by contemporary Indian writers.

In chapter 9, "Memories of Trains and Trains of Memory: Journeys from Past-Futures to Present-Pasts in *El tren de la memoria* (2005)," Araceli Masterson-Algar analyzes the representation of train travel in a fiction film directed by Marta Arribas and Ana Pérez. The film revisits the history of transnational migration from Spain to northern Europe, specifically to Nuremberg, Germany, during the mid-1960s. The train in this film narrates a journey that is deeply marked in the bodies of those who left as immigrants half a century ago, and who now remember through the physical act of returning to Nuremberg in the present. The rails of nostalgia bridge pasts, presents and futures through the sensorial experiences of the journey, articulating the Madrid of the 1960s and Nuremberg's past as an industrial center to both cities' present as tourist destinations. By doing so, *El tren de la memoria* works as the vehicle to tighten the loose stitches of Spain's memory of emigration while accounting for the lived experiences of the country's new residents in the global city.

Chapter 10, Scott D. Juall's "Nord-Sud: The Paris Metro and Transnational Avant-Garde Artistic Mobilities and Movements in Early Twentieth-Century Paris," explores the way in which the modern metro influenced the trajectory of visual art from a transnational perspective. In 1900, the Compagnie du chemin de fer métropolitain de Paris (metropolitan railway company of Paris) opened its first line, and within ten years eight metro lines were in service. Between 1910 and 1916 the Société du chemin de fer électrique souterrain Nord-Sud de Paris (North-South society of electric underground trains of Paris), a competing private company, constructed the Parisian Nord-Sud subway Line A, which played an integral role in developing early twentieth-century and visual and literary arts in Paris. Facilitating exchanges among avant-garde writers, painters, art theorists, and art dealers between the two regions of the French capital, it prompted the development of a close relationship between modern public transportation in twentieth-century Paris, transnational art circuits, and transnational art criticism. Part of a major network of physical and artistic movements guiding and orienting some of the most dynamic transformations in modernist art and literature between 1910 and 1918, the Nord-Sud works of art brought attention to the intimate links between the metro line and artistic movements in modernist Paris, as seen in several works of the period: Italian futurist Gino Severini's paintings and illustrations, all titled *Nord-Sud* (numerous artworks, 1911–17); Catalan proto-surrealist Joan Miró's painting *Nord-Sud* (1917); and French cubist Georges Braque's ink drawing *Nord-Sud* (1918). *Nord-Sud, Revue littéraire* (16 issues, March 1917–October 1918), was an ephemeral Parisian literary review edited by poet Pierre Reverdy.

Benjamin Fraser is professor in the College of Humanities at the University of Arizona. He is the founding editor of the *Journal of Urban Cultural Studies* and coeditor, with Steven Spalding, of *Trains, Culture, and Mobility* (2012) and *Trains, Literature, and Culture* (2012). He is the author of ninety articles and book chapters and ten single-authored books, including *The Art of Pere Joan* (2019), *Visible Cities, Global Comics* (2019), *Toward an Urban Cultural Studies: Henri Lefebvre and the Humanities* (2015), and *Digital Cities: The Interdisciplinary Future of the*

Urban Geo-Humanities (2015). His publications have appeared in *Catalan Review, Transfers: Interdisciplinary Journal of Mobility Studies, Cultural Studies, Social and Cultural Geography, Environment and Planning D: Society and Space,* and *Emotion, Space and Society.*

Steven Spalding holds a PhD from the University of Michigan and a DEA from the Université de Paris VIII. He is editor of the special section on "Railways and Urban Cultures" (2014) in *Transfers: Interdisciplinary Journal of Mobility Studies* and coeditor, with Benjamin Fraser, of the books *Trains, Culture, and Mobility* (2012) and *Trains, Literature, and Culture* (2012). After more than twenty-five years of teaching at colleges and universities in the United States, France, and Switzerland, he is an independent scholar who writes about French cultural studies, mobility studies, and urban studies. His interests involve twentieth- and twenty-first-century French and francophone novels, films, and comics.

Notes

1. Schivelbusch ([1977] 1986) covers this ground extensively. See also Osterhammel: "'Twas the new calamity of the train crash: Charles Dickens barely survived one in 1865 on a journey from the south coast to London; in Russia, where Tsar Alexander III suffered the same experience in 1888; as well as in India and Canada" (2014 75). General fears about the railroad were, as Paul Youngman notes, somewhat paradoxical: "Freud and Schivelbusch emphasized the paradox inherent in rail technology: the world becomes both smaller and larger, frightening and tame at the same time" (2005, 11).
2. For example, "the nineteenth century became the age of the speed revolution" (Osterhammel 2014, 74; see also Divall and Shin 2012; Spalding 2014; Studeny 1995; Virilio 1977).
3. Importantly, Schivelbusch's work was very soon complemented by studies carried out by cultural historians such as Hermann Glaser (1981) and Dirk Hoeges (1985) in Germany, and Jeffrey Richards and John M. MacKenzie (1986) in England. The work of Remo Ceserani (1993, 1995) is also notable in this regard for its transnational approach.
4. The present account differs from arguments that the railway had solely a homogenizing effect on local cultures, one that can be seen, for example, in the statement, "However different the cultural reactions and modes of employment, the effects of rail travel were in principle the same all over the world" (Osterhammel 2014, 74).
5. Freedman makes this case in her book, noting, "Partly because of the spatial design of the city, Tokyo vehicles are social and cultural spaces different from the New York subway, London Tube, Paris Metro, Mumbai railway, and other metropolitan commuter networks. . . . Behaviors and interactions not possible elsewhere occur inside passenger cars and in stations. These small gestures and encounters greatly influence the ways that individuals experience national history and describe the events of their own lives" (2010, 5).

6. Along these lines, see also Marshall (1991).
7. Scale as a socially constructed tool and discourse is best treated from a geographical perspective by Marston (2000). See also Brenner (2004), Howitt (2003), and Taylor (1982).
8. "The subject or problematic of transnational families, therefore, raises intriguing or provocative questions about such matters as migration, identities, communities, resources and relationships in the contemporary world" (Goulbourne et al. 2010, 3); "Though mobility is identified as a key feature of transnationalism, it must be recognized that the agency and life choices of the world's refugees are quite different from those of (im)migrants and the social processes that bind the two contexts when physical presence is impossible in the home country. As with all people on the move, refugees undoubtedly maintain a 'double consciousness,' but the transnational social fields they forge and maintain are decidedly different from those created by labour migrants, international entrepreneurs, and transnational political activists. For refugees, physical mobility is often short-term, one-way, and violence-induced" (Nolin 2006, 183).
9. The notion of *Transnational Urbanism* is quite relevant to a number of chapters in this book where individual cities are explored.
10. One prominent example is given in the article "Europe's System Builders": "In 1833 the Saint-Simonean and future French minister Michel Chevalier had singled out railways as the ultimate tool to tie peoples and countries into interdependency, co-operation, and peace" (Van der Vleuten et al. 2007, 322).
11. Also, by the same author, "However different the cultural reactions and modes of employment, the effects of rail travel were in principle the same all over the world" (Osterhammel 2014, 74).
12. "The great railroads of the world took shape along construction sites that were transnational in character. British and French capital were dominant before 1860, but afterward national sources of finance made increasingly important contributions. The materials, craft labor, and technical know-how were seldom only local; European and North American planners and engineers everywhere monopolized the higher rungs of the job ladder. Skilled workers with experience were also in great demand. Only few of the countries engaged in railroad construction had the heavy industry and machinery sector necessary to organize it by themselves" (Osterhammel 2014, 692). The transnational character of the railroad, of course, has not always been emphasized in the literature. A recent special section introduced by Sjöblom works to correct for the fact that even in policy studies, "The literature consists mainly of single-nation studies—international comparisons, regional perspectives and transnational narratives are badly needed" (Sjöblom 2011, 55). That section takes on "three case studies from the interwar period in Belgium, the Netherlands, and California" (51). Sjöblom asserts four significant commonalities across the group explaining that this is the time when "transport coordination first became a major issue" (51).
13. In the case of the construction of the transcontinental railroad in the United States (from Chicago via Omaha to Sacramento), "The Transcontinental also hired approximately 100,000 Chinese workers" (Osterhammel 2014, 692).
14. In 1918 (the date given in her 2011 book *Constructing Iron Europe*), "Henri Bressler, a member of the French Society of Civil Engineers, proposed to the French Minister of Public Works and Foreign Affairs the construction of a large-scale railway artery that would connect Paris with Dakar through Spain" (Anastasiadou 2007, 176; see also 2011).

15. For more on this, see Hladik (2017).
16. We regard the basic premise of the reader, as conveyed in two concise quotations, as very crucial for a transnational study of the railway: "Social life crosses, transcends and sometimes transforms borders and boundaries in many different ways." "Even contemporary nation-states and the nation-state system have been transnationally constituted and shaped over time and space in powerful ways" (Khagram and Levitt 2008a, 1). Other views of transnationalism are of interest. Though he is primarily interested in viewing the social relationships implicated in migration studies through the notion of transnationalism, Boccagni notes, "Transnationalism continues to be, in one and the same expression, both a theoretical lens (or a research programme) and a set of empirical phenomena (Morawska, 2003)" (Boccagni 2012, 119). Boccagni notes that transnationalism is sometimes "controversial" and "not without contention" (118, citing Waldinger 2011). In "Toward a Transnational History of Technology," Van der Vleuten distinguishes three uses of the term transnational: first "cross-border flows" (2008, 978); second, "the historical role of international *nongovernmental* organizations (and the relations and flows that they represent) in shaping the modern world." (979; my emphasis); and third "decentering the nation-state from its position as the principal organizing category for scholarly inquiry" (982).
17. Empirical transnationalism "focuses on describing, mapping, classifying, and quantifying novel and/or potentially important transnational phenomena and dynamics." Methodological transnationalism "involves, at a minimum, reclassifying existing data, evidence and historical and ethnographic accounts that are based on bounded or bordered units so that transnational forms and processes are revealed." And theoretical transnationalism "formulates explanations and crafts interpretations that either parallel, complement, supplement, or are integrated into existing theoretical frameworks and accounts" (Khagram and Levitt 2008a, 2).
18. Under the definition of empirical transnationalism, the editors write, "TS [transnational studies] uses comparative-historical and ethnographic strategies to identify and explain similarities, differences, linkages and interactions among different transnational phenomena" (Khagram and Levitt 2008a, 2).
19. Compelling, in this sense, is Presner's statement: "I do not restrict myself to Germany as a preexisting territorial unit of reference because the argument that I am presenting is not based on nationality. The deterritorialized Germany that I am examining begins in Berlin and Delos and moves to Sicily, New York City, the North Sea, Nuremburg-Fürth, Palestine, Auschwitz, Vienna, Prague, Antwerp, and Paris. What emerges—through the multiplicity of places of contact, mobility, and contention—is a complicated cultural geography of German/Jewish modernity, not a national literary history" (2007, 13). Note, too, John Urry's remark, "The railway system is central to modernity's appearance" (2007, 95–96); and Tony Judt's statement: "More than any other technical design or social institution, the railway stands for modernity" (2010, 60).
20. This variant is one of a pair of nontraditional approaches that "challenge conventional paradigms and praxis more fundamentally, moving beyond dominant forms of scholarship, philosophical assumptions and prescriptive orientations" (Khagram and Levitt 2008a, 3).
21. One is reminded of the empirical transnationalist argument regarding the similarities of railway culture in a comparative-historical sense: "An incredibly powerful, speeding mechanical apparatus is foregrounded as a relatively fa-

miliar feature of everyday life even within places otherwise made up of green and pleasant land. This is a nineteenth-century phenomenon in Europe, a late nineteenth-century phenomenon in North America and an early twentieth-century phenomenon in much of India, Africa and Latin America (Vaughan 1997; Richards, Mackenzie 1986: ch 9)" (Urry 2007, 93). Martha Thorne puts this somewhat differently when she writes, "The creation of the modern railway occurred almost simultaneously in the U.S.A. and Great Britain" (2001, 11).

22. The larger intent of analyses that reconcile transport history with humanities representations, we believe, lies in the potential reconciliation of what C. P. Snow, in a speech from 1959, famously called "The Two Cultures" (of Science and of Poetry. Remarking on Snow, specifically, Youngman writes, "As explanatory narratives, both science and poetry are culturally determined systems that represent reality in a specific historical and cultural context" (2005, 152). On C. P. Snow and his controversy with F. R. Leavis over the compatibility of a literary culture and a scientific culture see Fraser (2015a, 5–11); see also Leavis (1972) and Snow ([1959] 1993). We note that there are numerous academic railway centers whose faculty and students might be interested in reconciling the literary and scientific cultures of railway transport in a way complementary to what we do here. These include the Transport Research Institute at Edinburgh Napier University, the Centre for Mobilities Research at Lancaster University, the Centre for Mobilities and Urban Studies at Aalborg University, the Center for Mobilities Research and Policy at Drexel University, the Cultural Mobilities Research center at Leuven University, and the Institute of Railway Studies at the University of York. In addition, Texas A&M has the Center for Railway Research and ambitions to be the premier academic railway center in the United States, but none of these centers seems yet to be connected with a publishing program that moves beyond the science and economics of rail transportation.

23. See also "But we have also been interested in areas that have been less often framed in terms of mobilities, like media and communication studies, cultural studies, film studies, literary studies, museology, critical legal studies, and the creative arts." (Clarsen 2015b, 116).

24. In addition to many if not most all of the essays in the collections by Beaumont and Freeman (2007), Fraser and Spalding (2012), Spalding and Fraser (2012), and Spalding (2014), see Fraser (2015a, 2015b), Masterson-Algar (2014), and Thornbury (2014).

25. We note, for example, that this book has no direct counterpart or competition (other than our own volumes and special section: Fraser and Spalding 2012; Spalding and Fraser 2012; Spalding 2014). That said, there has been a significant increase of interest in the cultural imaginaries of global transportation among publishers over the past decade. The existing three books in the series "Explorations in Mobility" with Berghahn Books (https://www.berghahnbooks.com/series/explorations-in-mobility), edited by Mom, Sheller, and Clarsen, deal in part, but not substantially, with cultural artifacts in their exploration of transportation themes. Further supporting the remarks of Ian Carter (2001, mentioned in the body text), the significant number of book titles (more than fifty) in the Railroads and Transportation line with Indiana University Press focus overwhelmingly on historical approaches—not artistic representations—and almost exclusively on trains in Anglophone contexts (http://www.iupress.indiana.edu/index.php?cPath=1037_1272). The Transport and Society book series (now with Taylor and Francis Group, formerly with Ashgate—https://www.routledge.com/

Transport-and-Society/book-series/TSOC) does, however, include selected titles incorporating cultural approaches.

26. Carter's book (2001) treads through print literature with some comment on the
    visual arts and cinema.

27. There is a transnational component to the scholarship by Bannerjee 2004, Nina
    Lee Bond 2011, as well as the examination Leah Garrett (2001) provides of the
    train in modern Yiddish literature.

28. "Cinema has developed from national cinemas to transnational cinematic prac-
    tices as a result of globalization, which has reduced the power of the nation
    state. Increasingly filmmakers are trained abroad, receive multi-national fund-
    ing, and make films for a world market, and increasingly narratives involve char-
    acters that travel across borders" (Mennel 2008, 10). See also Ezra and Rowden
    (2006), *Transnational Cinema: The Film Reader*. Interestingly, of course, the train
    is virtually unavoidable in early film; see Lynne Kirby's *Parallel Tracks: The Rail-
    road and Silent Cinema* (1997).

29. Of course, this has not stopped culture from being shaped or harnessed by the
    interests of national ideology. Consider the history of the novel as a literary form
    that develops in tandem with a specifically modern nationhood formation in
    the nineteenth century. But to accept this as a totalizing explanation of what
    the novel form is and what individual novels mean is a naturally reductive view
    in the sense that this perspective tends to reaffirm rather than question or chal-
    lenge the project of national identity.

30. On the same page, the author also mentions the appearance of the train in the
    writings of Foucault (1986), De Certeau (1988), and Berman (1988). Freedman
    (2010), Richter (2005), and Thornbury (2014) all make significant contributions
    to the productive entanglement of the discourse of gender with that of train
    travel.

31. "Evidence for the social and political as well as economic importance of rail-
    ways in an industrializing world is manifest in the huge range of cultural ma-
    terials, from painting to music and ceramics to film, that mediate its role in
    both popular and elite imaginations. It is certainly true that railways have left a
    firm imprint in the canons of high art. . . . Yet the railway is an equally powerful
    symbol in popular culture" (Revill 2012, 9); "It is clear that the cultural imprint
    of the railway on popular and elite cultures has far transcended the realms of
    art, however this is defined, and etched itself on the ways we think and behave.
    Railways continue to play a role in the popular imagination" (12).

References

Aguiar, Marian. 2011. *Tracking Modernity: India's Railway and the Culture of Mobility*.
    Minneapolis: University of Minnesota Press.
Anastasiadou, Irene. 2007. "Networks of Powers: Railway Visions in Inter-War Eu-
    rope." *Journal of Transport History* 28, no. 2: 172–91.
Anastasiadou, Irene. 2011. *Constructing Iron Europe: Transnationalism and Railways
    in the Interbellum*. Amsterdam: Amsterdam University Press.
Anderson, Wes, dir. 2007. *The Darjeeling Limited*. DVD. Beverly Hills, CA: 20th Century
    Fox Home Entertainment.
Apter, Emily. 2002. "Afterword: From Literary Channel to Narrative Chunnel." In *The
    Literary Channel: The International Invention of the Novel*, edited by M. Cohen
    and C. Dever 286–93. Princeton, NJ: Princeton University Press.

Bannerjee, Anindita. 2004. "The Trans-Siberian Railroad and Russia's Asia: Literature, Geopolitics, Philosophy of History." *Clio* 34, no. 1–2: 19–40.

Baroli, Marc. 1964. *Le train dans la littérature française*. Paris: Éditions N. M.

Beaumont, Matthew, and Michael J. Freeman, eds. 2007. *The Railway and Modernity: Time, Space, and the Machine Ensemble*. Oxford, UK: Peter Lang.

Berman, Marshall. 1988. *All That Is Solid Melts into Air: The Experience of Modernity*. New York: Penguin.

Boccagni, Paolo. 2012. "Rethinking Transnational Studies: Transnational Ties and the Transnationalism of Everyday Life." *European Journal of Social Theory* 15, no. 1: 117–32.

Bodenstedt, James C. 1992. "The Railroad in American Poetry." Master's thesis, The College at Brockport, State University of New York. https://digitalcommons .brockport.edu/cgi/viewcontent.cgi?article=1119&context=eng_theses.

Bond, Nina Lee. 2011. "Tolstoy and Zola: Trains and Missed Connections." PhD Diss. Columbia University, New York. https://academiccommons.columbia.edu/doi/ 10.7916/D82Z1CGH.

Brenner, Neil. 2004. *New State Spaces: Urban Governance and the Rescaling of State-hood*. Oxford: Oxford University Press.

Burns, Grant. 2005. *The Railroad in American Fiction: An Annotated Bibliography*. Jackson, NC: McFarland & Co.

Carter, Ian. 2001. *Railways and Culture in Britain: The Epitome of Modernity*. Manchester, UK: Manchester University Press.

Ceserani, Remo. 1993. *Treni di carta: L'immaginario in ferrovia: l'irruzione del treno nella letteratura moderna*. Genova: Marietti.

Ceserani, Remo. 1995. "Introduzione." In *Strade ferrate: La tematica del treno e della ferrovia nei testi di Jules Verne, Gabriele D'Annunzio, Gabriel García Márquez e parecchi altri scrittori* by Pierluigi Pellini, Marina Polacco, and Paolo Zanotti, 7–34. Pisa: Nistri Lischi.

Clarsen, Georgine. 2015a. "Special Section on Settler-Colonial Mobilities." *Transfers* 5, no. 3: 41–48.

Clarsen, Georgine. 2015b. "Ideas in Motion: Frontiers of Mobility Studies." *Transfers* 5, no. 1: 114–21.

Cooper, Martin. 2011. *Brazilian Railway Culture*. Newcastle upon Tyne, UK: Cambridge Scholars.

Cresswell, Tim. 2006. *On the Move: Mobility in the Modern Western World*. New York; London: Routledge.

De Certeau, Michel. 1988. *The Practice of Everyday Life*. Translated by Steven Rendall. Berkeley: University of California Press.

Deacon, Desley, Penny Russell, and Angela Woollacott, eds. 2010. *Transnational Lives: Biographies of Global Modernity, 1700–present*. New York: Palgrave Macmillan.

Divall, Colin. 2010. "Mobilizing the History of Technology." *Technology and Culture* 51, no. 4: 938–60.

Divall, Colin, and George Revill. 2005. "Cultures of Transport: Representation, Practice and Technology." *Journal of Transport History* 26, no. 1: 99–111.

Divall, Colin, and Hiroki Shin. 2012. "Cultures of Speed and Conservative Modernity: Representations of Speed in Britain's Railway Marketing." In Fraser and Spalding, *Trains, Culture, and Mobility*, 3–26.

Ďurovičová, Nataša. 2010. "Preface." In Ďurovičová and Newman, *World Cinemas*, ix–xv.

Ďurovičová, Nataša, and Kathleen E. Newman, eds. 2010. *World Cinemas, Transnational Perspectives*. New York and London: Routledge.

Ezra, Elizabeth, and Terry Rowden, eds. 2006. *Transnational Cinema: The Film Reader.* London: Routledge.

Flynn, Kevin G. 2002. "Destination Nation: Writing the Railway in Canada." PhD Diss., McGill University. ProQuest Dissertations Publishing, 2002. NQ78686.

Foucault, Michel. 1986. "Of Other Spaces." *Diacritics* 16, no. 1: 22–27.

Fraser, Benjamin. 2015a. *Toward an Urban Cultural Studies: Henri Lefebvre and the Humanities.* Bakingstoke, UK: Palgrave Macmillan.

Fraser, Benjamin. 2015b. "Urban Railways in Buenos Aires: Spatial and Social Alienation in the Documentary Film *El tren blanco.*" *Transfers: Interdisciplinary Journal of Mobility Studies* 5, no. 2: 5–22.

Fraser, Benjamin, and Steven Spalding, eds. 2012. *Trains, Culture, and Mobility: Riding the Rails.* Lanham, MD: Lexington.

Freedman, Alisa. 2010. *Tokyo in Transit: Japanese Culture on the Rails and Road.* Stanford, CA: Stanford University Press.

Garrett, Leah. 2001. "Trains and Train Travel in Modern Yiddish Literature." *Jewish Social Studies* 7, no. 2 (Winter): 67–88.

Glaser, Hermann. 1981. *Maschinenwelt und Alltagsleben: Industriekultur in Deutschland vom Biedermeier bis zur Weimarer Republik.* Frankfurt: Krüger.

Goulbourne, Harry, Tracey Reynolds, John Solomos, and Elisabetta Zontini, eds. 2010. *Transnational Families: Ethnicities, Identities and Social Capital.* New York: Routledge.

Hannam, Kevin, Mimi Sheller, and John Urry. 2006. "Editorial: Mobilities, Immobilities and Moorings." *Mobilities* 1, no. 1: 1–22.

Hladik, L. (2017, Feb 16). "First Transnational Railroad Built in Africa through Chinese Backing." Proquest. University Wire Retrieved from http://search.proquest.com .jproxy.lib.ecu.edu/docview/1868834454?accountid=10639.

Hoeges, Dirk. 1985. *Alles veloziferisch: Die Eisenbahn—vom schönen Ungeheure zur Ästhetik der Geschwindigkeit.* Rheinbach-Merzbach: CMZ-Verlag.

Howitt, Richard. 2003. "Scale." In *A Companion to Political Geography*, edited by J. Agnew, K. Mitchell, and G. Toal, 138–57. Oxford, UK: Blackwell.

Judt, Tony. 2010. "The Glory of the Rails." *New York Review of Books* (23 Dec.): 60.

Khagram, Sanjeev, and Peggy Levitt. 2008a. "Constructing Transnational Studies." In Khagram and Levitt, *The Transnational Studies Reader*, 1–22.

Khagram, Sanjeev, and Peggy Levitt, eds. 2008b. *The Transnational Studies Reader: Intersections and Innovations.* New York and London: Routledge.

Kirby, Lynne. 1997. *Parallel Tracks: The Railroad and Silent Cinema.* Durham, NC: Duke University Press.

Klein, Maury. 1994. *Unfinished Business: The Railroad in American Life.* Hanover, NH: University Press of New England.

Leavis, F. R. 1972. *Nor Shall My Sword: Discourses on Pluralism, Compassion and Social Hope.* New York: Barnes and Noble.

Mahr, Johannes. 1982. *Eisenbahnen in der deutschen Dichtung: der Wandel eines literarischen Motivs im 19. und im beginnenden 20. Jahrhundert.* Munich: Fink.

Marshall, Ian. 1991. "Steel Wheels on Paper: The Railroad in American Literature." *Railroad History* 165 (Autumn): 37–62.

Marston, Sallie. 2000. "The Social Construction of Scale." *Progress in Human Geography* 24, no. 2: 219–42.

Marx, Leo. (1964) 2000. *The Machine in the Garden: Technology and the Pastoral Ideal in America.* New York: Oxford University Press.

Marx, Leo. 1988. "The Machine in the Garden." In *The Pilot and the Passenger: Essays on Literature, Technology, and Culture in the United States*, 113–26. New York: Oxford University Press.

Masterson-Algar, Araceli. 2014. "The *Subte* as Looking Machine into the City: *Moebius's* Trajectory through Buenos Aires." *Transfers* 4, no. 2: 68–85.

Matthews, Michael. 2013. *The Civilizing Machine: A Cultural History of Mexican Railroads, 1876–1910*. Lincoln: University of Nebraska Press.

McCarthy, Cormac. 2006. *The Road*. New York: Vintage Press.

Meikle, Jeffrey L. 2003. "Leo Marx's *The Machine in the Garden*." *Technology and Culture* 44, no. 1: 147–59.

Mennel, Barbara. 2008. *Cities and Cinema*. London: Routledge.

Merriman, Peter. 2007. *Driving Spaces: A Cultural-Historical Geography of England's M1 Motorway*. Oxford, UK: Blackwell.

Merriman, Peter. 2012. *Mobility, Space and Culture*. London: Routledge.

Merriman, Peter, Rhys Jones, Tim Cresswell, Colin Divall, Gijs Mom, Mimi Sheller, and John Urry. 2013. "Mobility: Geographies, Histories, Sociologies." *Transfers* 3, no. 1: 147–65.

Meyer, Nicholas, dir. 1983. *The Day After*. New York: ABC Circle Films.

Miéville, China. 2004. *The Iron Council*. New York: Del Rey Press.

Misemer, Sarah M. 2010. *Moving Forward, Looking Back: Trains, Literature, and the Arts in the River Plate*. Lewisburg, PA: Bucknell University Press.

Mom, Gijs. 2015. *Atlantic Automobilism: Emergence and Persistence of the Car, 1895–1940*. New York: Berghahn.

Mom, Gijs, et al. 2011. "Hop on the Bus, Gus." *Transfers* 1, no. 1: 1–13.

Mom, Gijs, and Nanny Kim. 2013. "Editorial." *Transfers* 3, no. 3: 1–5.

Nolin, Catherine. 2006. *Transnational Ruptures: Gender and Forced Migration*. Aldershot, UK: Ashgate.

Osterhammel, Jürgen. 2014. *The Transformation of the World: A Global History of the Nineteenth Century*. Translated by Patrick Camiller. Princeton, NJ: Princeton University Press.

Presner, Todd. 2007. *Mobile Modernity: Germans, Jews, Trains*. New York: Columbia University Press.

Reich, Steve. 1988. *Different Trains: Electric Counterpoint*. CD. New York: Nonesuch Records.

Revill, George. 2012. *Railway*. London: Reaktion Books.

Richards, Jeffrey, and John M. MacKenzie. 1986. *The Railway Station: A Social History*. Oxford: Oxford University Press.

Richter, Amy G. 2005. *Home on the Rails: Women, the Railroad, and the Rise of Public Domsticity*. Chapel Hill: University of North Carolina Press.

Schivelbusch, Wolfgang. (1977) 1986. *The Railway Journey: The Industrialization of Time and Space in the 19th Century*. Berkeley: University of California Press.

Sheller, Mimi, and John Urry. 2006. "The New Mobilities Paradigm." *Environment and Planning A* 38, no. 2: 207–26.

Sjöblom, Gustav. 2011. "Introduction: The Return of Transport Coordination." *Transfers* 1, no. 2: 50–60.

Smith, Michael Peter. 2001. *Transnational Urbanism: Locating Globalization*. Malden, MA; Oxford, UK: Blackwell.

Snow, C. P. (1959) 1993. *The Two Cultures*. Cambridge: Cambridge University Press.

Spalding, Steven, ed. 2014. "Railways and Urban Cultures." Special section of *Transfers* 4, no. 2: 42–130.

Spalding, Steven, and Benjamin Fraser, eds. 2012. *Trains, Literature, and Culture: Reading/Writing the Rails*. Lanham, MD: Lexington Books.

Spielberg, Steven, dir. 2005. *The War of the Worlds*. Hollywood, CA: Paramount Pictures.

Studeny, Christophe. 1995. *L'Invention de la vitesse: France, XVIIIe–XXe siècle*. Paris: Gallimard.

Taylor, P. J. 1982. "A Materialist Framework for Political Geography." *Transactions of the Institute of British Geographers* 7: 15–34.

Theroux, Paul. 1975. *The Great Railway Bazaar*. Harmondsworth, Middlesex, UK: Penguin.

Theroux, Paul. 2008. *Ghost Train to the Eastern Star: On the Tracks of the Great Railway Bazaar*. Boston: Houghton Mifflin.

Thornbury, Barbara. 2014. "Tokyo, Gender and Mobility: Tracking Fictional Characters on Real Monorails, Trains, Subways and Trams." *Journal of Urban Cultural Studies* 1, no. 1: 43–64.

Thorne, Martha. 2001. "Renaissance of the Train Station." In *Modern Trains and Splendid Stations: Architecture, Design and Rail Travel for the Twenty-First Century*, edited by Martha Thorne, 11–23. Chicago: Merrill/The Art Institute of Chicago.

Urry, John. 2007. *Mobilities*. New York: Polity.

Van der Vleuten, Erik. 2008. "Towards a Transnational History of Technology: Meanings, Promises, Pitfalls." *Technology and Culture* 49: 974–94.

Van der Vleuten, Erik, Irene Anastasiadou, Vincent Lagendijk, and Frank Schipper. 2007. "Europe's System Builders: The Contested Shaping of Transnational Road, Electricity and Rail Networks." *Contemporary European History* 16, no. 3: 321–47.

Velez, Michael. 2012. "Train, Trestle, Ticker: Railroad and Region in Frank Norris's *The Octopus* and María Amparo Ruiz de Burton's *The Squatter and the Don*." In Fraser and Spalding, *Trains, Culture, and Mobility*, 219–35.

Virilio, Paul. 1977. *Speed and Politics: An Essay on Dromology*. New York: Columbia University Press.

Youngman, Paul A. 2005. *Black Devil and Iron Angel: The Railway in Nineteenth-Century German Realism*. Washington, DC: Catholic University of America Press.

Zabel, Darcy Ann. 2001. "'Two Trains Running': The Train as Symbol in Twentieth-century African American Literature." PhD Diss., University of Connecticut. https://opencommons.uconn.edu/dissertations/AAI3025046.

Zabel, Darcy. 2004. *The (Underground) Railroad in African American Literature*. New York: Peter Lang.

CHAPTER 1

The Railway Arts
Sound and Space beyond Borders
Aimée Boutin

> Dévorant un espace de quinze lieues à l'heure, la vapeur, puissant machiniste, . . . change à chaque instant les points de vue, apporte coup sur coup au voyageur ébouriffé scènes gaies, scènes tristes, intermèdes burlesques, fleurs brillantes d'un feu d'artifice, visions qui s'évanouissent à peine apparues.
>
> (Devouring the distance at the rate of fifteen leagues an hour, the steam engine, that powerful stage manager, . . . shifts the point of view every moment; in quick succession it presents the astonished traveler with happy scenes, sad scenes, burlesques interludes, brilliant fireworks, all visions that disappear as soon as they are seen.)
>
> —Benjamin Gastineau, *La Vie en chemin de fer*

In this description of looking out the compartment window of a speeding train, nineteenth-century French journalist Benjamin Gastineau accounts for a new sensory experience enabled by railway travel, what Wolfgang Schivelbusch qualified in *The Railway Journey* as "panoramic travel": "it was the ability to perceive the discrete, as it rolls past the window, indiscriminately" (1986, 61). Thus, railway culture brought into being a distinctly new form of panoramic perception that was shared across nineteenth-century industrialized European nations and later extended to a transnational scale. Rather than focus on the relation between vision and speed as Gastineau and Schivelbusch do, this chapter explores the sounds of the railway to consider how the railway affected perceptions of rhythm and space. How did pan-European travelers experience railway travel with their eyes and ears when they traversed distances at high speed? The journalist Gastineau identified as distinct in his experience the compression of distances, the shrinking of timeframes, and "shifts [in] the point of view" (1861, 31), all of which suggest a broader impact on the experience of space-time than on sight alone.

Railway space is frequently associated with visual metaphors including maps, grids, and lines, but when we think of its broader impact on sensory perception—the regular rhythmic beat of the wheels on the track, the shriek of the steam whistle, the jerky clamor of moving carriages— we more easily understand how rhythm and sound reflect and create the modern, transnational experience of mobility.

Railway culture produced novel, shared sensory experiences that were not contained by national borders. Schivelbusch's pioneering book *The Railway Journey* (1986) tracks the transformations that rendered mechanized movement distinct from travel on foot, by horse-drawn coach, or by steamer during the Industrial Revolution. Schivelbusch drew from German (Heinrich Heine, Karl Marx, Sigmund Freud), British (William Wordsworth, Thomas De Quincey, John Ruskin), and French (Victor Hugo, Constantin Pecqueur, Paul Verlaine) observers (among others), documenting a transnational phenomenon central to the rise of western European modernity in the nineteenth century and to the acceleration of modern industrialization on other continents in the twentieth century. Even though individual nations organized public railway networks and timetables differently, the impact of technology on lived experience shared a common pattern across borders. Rail passengers experienced a new sociality in train compartments or stations, but also were subjected to recently developed forms of regimentation and commodification that made them feel more like nameless parcels than human travelers. Unprecedented levels of speed introduced unfamiliar types of traumatic neurosis and shock experience, but also created new mental states of reverie or reading. And more central to the argument of this chapter, the railway heralded a new perception of landscape, time, and space. Schivelbusch argues that the railway reduced the journey to points of departure and arrival, with no distinct sense of place in between these destinations; thus, localized places along the railroad were annihilated or erased as space was telescoped and time compressed. Building on Schivelbusch's analysis, John Urry in *Mobilities* reflects further on what he terms the shift from land to landscape. Where land is a tangible and functional resource, landscape is "an intangible resource whose key feature is its appearance or look." He adds, "It was 'landscape' that came to be viewed as swiftly passing framed panorama, involving a 'panoramic perception' rather than something lingered over, sketched or painted" (Urry 2007, 102). According to Schivelbusch and Urry, the circulation of travelers, goods, and ideas through mechanical locomotion changed people's relationship with their environment. These changes raised newfound questions about the ontological basis for knowing what the future holds and where humanity is headed.

Schivelbusch's attention to the development of an industrialized consciousness crossing geographic or national borders suggests that the railway played a significant role in what Sanjeev Khagram and Peggy Levitt have broadly defined as "philosophical transnationalism," namely the investigation of "ontological and epistemological assumptions about the nature of the world and what knowledge consists of" (2008, 8), with particular emphasis on interactions among forms and social worlds. Understood in these terms, railway culture brought to the fore questions about the relationship between travel and the senses, notably the mobile perception of space and time. In effect, the railway impacted the whole human sensorium (contra a statement such as Urry's on the look of landscape quoted above); although railway space has typically been conceived in relation to vision and the visual arts, musical and poetic examples tune in to the rhythm of the railway and the way sound shapes proximity and distance. To quote sound theorist and cultural critic Steven Connor, "The most important distinguishing feature of auditory experience . . . [is] its capacity to . . . reconfigure space" (1997, 206). He contrasts "the rationalized 'Cartesian grid' of the visualist imagination" with acoustic space, adding, "Where auditory experience is dominant, we might say, singular, perspectival gives way to plural, permeated space. The self defined in terms of hearing rather than sight is a self imagined not as a point, but as a membrane . . . a channel through which voices, noises and musics travel" (206). Connor's conception of sonic space challenges conventional paradigms that elevate vision above the other senses rather than seeking to break down the boundaries between the senses. It follows that the fluidity of sonic space would test the borders that in practice too often keep textual, visual, and musical fields distinct and bounded. The connections between visual, sonic, and tactile representations of space break down divisions between discrete types of perception in the same way that railways bridged city and countryside or crossed national frontiers.

The shared sensory experiences of panoramic travel were variously expressed in different but interrelated artistic forms. Indeed, music and poetry inspired by the railway proliferated across Europe and America in the nineteenth century, and can be said to be part of a common transnational modernist tradition. Charles-Valentin Alkan's *Le Chemin de fer, étude* (*The Railway*), op. 27 (1844), among the first musical representations of the railway, most obviously appeals to the ear rather than the eye. Through music, we are moved through space as we experience the railway journey as an event that unfolds in time and space. A similar shared experience was expressed in transnational railway poetry. Because of the two poems' quasi-musical patterning, Louisa Siefert's "En passant en chemin de fer" ("While Passing by on the Railway") (1868) and Robert Louis Stevenson's "From a Railway Carriage" ([1885] 2003) also privilege the rhythm over the spectacle of the railway. These three texts take as their inspiration the way the railway journey spatializes sound as the speeding train is heard moving through the landscape. Alkan's piano piece makes clear how sound can define a "fluid, mobile and voluminous conception of space" as described by Connor (1997, 207). Alkan experimented with rhythmic variations and with new, multi-perspectival conceptions of space that will be more clearly developed in Siefert's and Stevenson's poems. Moreover, the two poems use rhythm to heighten the sense of permeability of the passenger in the train compartment. By artfully representing spatiotemporal shifts in perspective, the poems use rhythm to contradictory ends, both suggesting a certain ambivalence toward where progress is headed and assuaging that anxiety through regular poetic patterns.

This chapter is primarily concerned with early aesthetic responses to the railway in nineteenth-century France, and suggests that they anticipate the philosophical and aesthetic experimentation with sound, time, and space that are usually associated with early twentieth-century modernisms.[1] Alkan and Siefert are representative of their era's reaction to industrialization, but since both are marginal figures in their respective canons, and are omitted from scholarly accounts of railway music or literature, their prescient engagements with modernity have not retained scholars' attention. The addition of the Scottish poet's 1885 poem—which in contrast is well known and used here as a foil to draw out similarities and contrasts with the earlier French works—also suggests the transnational nature of railway perception. The analysis is focused on the railway journey and on panoramic travel, rather than on social interactions in the train compartment or the railway station. By insisting on sound and rhythm, I seek to nuance the visual framework generally used to discuss panoramic travel and to cast the railway journey as an embodied and immersive experience. For what remains striking about these works today is their ability to evoke in our minds and in our bodies the simultaneously perilous and exhilarating sensation of riding the rails.

Charles-Valentin Alkan's *Le Chemin de fer, étude,* op. 27 is considered the first realistic musical representation of the railway (Beck 1969, viii; Rimm 2002, 28). As such, it stands out among transnational railway-inspired music. A contemporary of Hector Berlioz and Frédéric Chopin, Alkan composed the étude in 1844, the same year that Joseph Mallord William Turner painted *Rain, Steam and Speed—The Great Western Railway.* The étude is pioneering in that its composition coincides with the very beginnings of the French railway. Despite a sluggish start in the late 1830s—after the railway was successfully implemented in England and Belgium—the French rail network began its pervasive expansion in earnest after 1842 when the "Loi relative à l'établissement des grandes lignes de chemins de fer" (law relating to the establishment of the main railway lines) was passed. Alkan's virtuoso extremely fast tempo piano piece mimics the train speeding along, the journey of the passengers, and the train's arrival in the station (Alkan 1844).[2] Alkan was both a composer and a virtuoso pianist; he was also an eccentric and a recluse whose programmatic music led him to be marginalized by a canon that valued absolute over descriptive music. Alkan's sonic realism contrasts with his contemporaries' musical compositions inspired by the railway. Johann Strauss's *Eisenbahn-Lust-Walzer* (*Railway Pleasure Waltz*, op. 89, 1837) and his *Souvenir de Carneval, quadrille* (*Carnival Souvenir, Quadrille*, 1847), op. 200, Hans Christian Lumbye's *Kobenhavns Jernbane-damp Galop* (Copenhagen railway steam galop, 1847), and Berlioz's *Le Chant des chemins de fer* (Song of the railways, 1846) are not descriptive (metaphoric), but are instead meant to accompany inaugurations, balls, and banquets (metonymic) (*Locomotiv-Musik 1* n.d.). Alkan's étude (1844), like Gioachino Rossini's *Un Petit Train de plaisir comico-imitatif* (A little pleasure train comico-imitative, a piece for piano collected in the sixth album of *Péchés de vieillesse* [Sins of old age], vol. 6, *Album pour les enfants dégourdis* [The album for lively children], 1857–68), captures every sonic detail of a railway excursion—ostensibly any excursion, given the emphasis the term "étude" in the piece's title places on form over context. Unlike Alkan's joyful composition, though, Rossini's parodies the genre (as his ironic title intimates), and ends in a tragicomic derailment. It is notable that in Alkan's étude the train safely slows down and glides into the station.

In his study entitled *Charles Valentin Alkan,* William Alexander Eddie describes the 509-bar piece as follows[3]:

> Op. 27 in fact operates as a referential tone poem with the opening scalic figuration continuously varied over a "choo choo" train bass ostinato which functions as a pedal with only one harmonic change during the first 52 bars. The first episode is more abstract in patterning before the opening figuration returning followed by a train whistle motive and braking motive vividly portrayed. There are repetitions and variations of previous material to provide a coherent structure. Alkan diminutes motives to produce an exciting coda. (Eddie 2007, 99)

This musical representation of the railway conveys the sound of the locomotive's acceleration and deceleration, as well as the lightness of being that speed evokes in the passengers. Given the contrast with Alkan's other more philosophical pieces such as *La Grande Sonate: Les quatres âges,* op. 33 (The four ages, 1847), some critics such as Nicolas Bell in *The Encyclopedia of the Romantic Era 1760–1850* consider that the piece "descends to the banality of direct representation" (2004, 12). In an article in *Romantisme,* Britta Schilling writes, "Ses antagonistes critiquèrent de telles compositions [*Le Chemin de Fer*] parce que trop rudes et superficielles et manquant de profondeur" (1987, 39) (Alkan's antagonists criticized *The Railway* because they felt it was too rough and superficial, and lacked depth). In an era of absolute music, some judged the imitative nature of *Le Chemin de Fer* prejudicially. The *vivacissimamente* tempo was also viewed negatively, highlighting Alkan's own virtuosity at a time when self-promotion went against the prevailing aesthetic.[4] Others regard this program music as an important early precursor to Arthur Honegger's *Pacific 231* (1923), which famously represents the locomotive.[5] Composer-pianist Kaikhosru Shapurji Sorabji went so far as to claim it as "an amazingly powerful piece of evocative suggestion which makes the feeble fatuities of Arthur Honegger . . . appear all the more feeble and ineffective" (quoted in Rimm 2002, 28). To Alkan's credit, he explores the railway both as a theme (program music) as well as a form, exploiting the genre of musical composition known as the *perpetuum mobile* and the form of *ostinato* (the persistent repetition of a rhythmic pattern).

Alkan's railway music narrates phases of a journey that successfully concludes at its unnamed destination, thereby emphasizing description and formal arrangement over the kind of sentiment one might expect from romantic music.[6] In fact we might say that the pounding beat in Alkan's étude is poised between Romanticism and modernism. He incorporates the train whistle, even though whistling sounds are not part of the traditional repertoire of musical sounds in the mid-nineteenth century—though it will be one of the categories of sounds that Luigi Russolo argues in *L'arte dei rumori* (*The Art of Noises*, 1913) should be added to the range of orchestral sounds. It is worth noting, however, that the music does not capitalize on the affective power of the train whistle—it does not sound lonesome, longing, or foreboding; it does not arouse yearning, regret, or fear—but neither does Alkan use the whistle mockingly, as Rossini does in *Un Petit Train de plaisir.* By reproducing the rhythm of the locomotive and the toot of the whistle, moreover, Alkan could be placed in line with Pierre Schaeffer, whose first piece of *musique concrète* (a term coined by Schaeffer referring to music prepared from recorded sounds) was a composition of field recordings of train noises titled *Étude aux chemins de fer* (Railway study;

1948). By focusing the listener's attention on the sounds of the railway in the absence of their source, Schaeffer aimed to reduce listening to the act of attending to the sonic object itself, rather than to the specific dramatic context in which the sounds occurred or to states of mind that they evoke.[7] To some extent (and in full awareness of the anachronism), interpreting Alkan in light of Shaeffer helps bring into focus the importance of form in Alkan's *Le Chemin de fer, étude* (1844), while also acknowledging how much the music narrates the railway journey.

In terms of its form, Alkan's piece is fast, perhaps too much so. Music critics Toni Geraci and Georges Beck disagree as to whether or not the metronomic notation is accurate.[8] Whether prescriptive or merely indicative, Geraci's argument that the notation suggests machines pushing people to their limits seems convincing: "Il *perpetuum mobile* di Alkan si spinga verso il limite estremo della velocità" (The perpetuum mobile of Alkan pushes against the extreme limits of speed) (1999, 160; my translation). Geraci goes on to compare the virtuosity of Alkan's perpetuum mobile, or perpetual and rapid motion, to that achieved by industrial machinery in Karl Marx's reflections on the prolongation of the work day in *Capital* (1867).[9] We might wonder whether the excessively fast tempo is meant to connote the possibility of reckless speed leading to an accident. Given the smooth coda depicting the train's safe arrival at the station, however, it seems that the music does not evoke such foreboding and that Alkan is confident that the route forward toward modernity is unobstructed.

Imitating the sound of the speeding train leads Alkan to innovate not only in terms of form and rhythm, but also in terms of translating speed from a visual and aural experience into a musical one. As Geraci remarks, *Le Chemin de fer, étude,* recreates through rhythm the blurring optical effects produced by velocity that Turner captures in *Rain, Steam, and Speed: The Great Western Railway* (1999, 155). To characterize this distorted, technology-enhanced, proto-cinematic perception, Schivelbusch (1986) coined the term "panoramic travel": the railway sets the landscape in motion, shrinks depth perception, and synthesizes the succession of fragmented scenes of separate spaces seen from the compartment window into a panorama.[10] Alkan's piano étude is remarkable for the way it represents the spatialization of sound as the music conveys a sense of panoramic travel through the landscape. The spatial dimension of sound is achieved by the sweeping movement across the keyboard and contrasts between high and low keys and tones; furthermore, different rhythms recreate a virtual journey in time and space from departure to arrival, with moments of acceleration and deceleration, and perception of movement over hills and valleys. When the train ploughs through stations or towns without stopping, we hear the train whistle, and then, at journey's end the whistle motif returns to signal the train's arrival. We are immersed in the railway experience.

Where is the listener positioned in relation to the movement: as an observer or participant? My impression is that the listener is placed in the paradoxical position of being both observer of the train passing by and passenger inside the carriage of the speeding train. Logically one could not take in the whole journey if one were not a passenger on the train looking at the panoramic landscape from the compartment window. However, the music also seems to spread the changing landscape out before our eyes and ears with an expansion of space that could also be perceived from the point of view of someone immobile (as listeners typically are) watching and hearing the train go by.

Thus, Alkan announces a multi-perspectival conception of space that will be more clearly developed in Siefert's poem. Alkan's precocious musical representation of the sounds of the railway at different moments in the journey suggests that musicians were able to hear and to capture the effect of movement on the new landscape and soundscape earlier than French poets, novelists and painters were. Benjamin Gastineau's newspaper essays collected in *La Vie en chemin de fer* (Life on the railway) (1861) are frequently cited as prescient evidence of this new sensibility; indeed, Schivelbusch bases his definition of panoramic travel on Gastineau's "synthetic philosophy of the glance" (1986, 60). The best-known example of railway poetry in French, Paul Verlaine's "Le paysage dans le cadre des portières" ("The Landscape Revealed from the Train Carriage Windows") from *La Bonne Chanson* (*The Good Song*), dates from 1869–70, around the same year as Claude Monet painted *Train dans la campagne* (*Train in the Countryside*). As Marc Baroli has stated about the realization that the railway offered new artistic resources and sensibilities to writers, "Il semble que les poètes en aient pris conscience avant les prosateurs et se soient les premiers engagés dans cette voie" (It seems that poets were conscious of it before prose writers and that they were the first to pursue this track) (1964, 145; my translation).

A contemporary of Paul Verlaine, Louisa Siefert's "En passant en chemin de fer. Pantoum" (1868) was published in *Rayons perdus* (Lost rays) a year and a half prior to the better-known "Le paysage dans le cadre des portières" (Verlaine 1870). Both poems evoke the landscape in motion as seen from the train compartment window. We know the context mainly from the poem's title "En passant en chemin de fer" because, unlike Verlaine, Siefert does not mention the window frame that scholars often equate with a camera. Siefert's frameless view is more immersive; the omission of specific place markers, as in Alkan, enhances readers' ability to be absorbed. As befits panoramic travel, the passenger in Siefert's poem has the illusion of standing still while immersed in a landscape set in motion.

Siefert was affiliated with the French Parnassian school, whose prominent members included Théodore de Banville, Charles-Marie Leconte de Lisle, José de Hérédia, and the early Paul Verlaine, and she was included among them in *Le Parnasse contemporain*, the periodical that served as a platform for their aesthetic program. The focus on technology that is more readily associated with French modernists such as Blaise Cendrars (*La Prose du Transsibérien et de la Petite Jehanne de France* [*Prose on the Trans-Siberian Railway and of Little Jehanne of France*], 1913), is not initially what we expect from the aestheticism of the Parnassian school of the 1860s and 70s. For example, Leconte de Lisle, known for drawing poetic inspiration from antiquity and ancient Oriental civilizations, referred to "l'alliance monstrueuse de la poésie et de l'industrie" (the monstrous alliance of poetry and industry) in his preface to *Poèmes et Poésies* (Poems and poesy) of 1855 (1895, 224).[11] Recent scholarship has however interrogated the Parnassians's ambiguous relationship to modernity and to industrialization. In her reading of English Parnassian poetry of the 1880s through the lens of Walter Benjamin's theories on the temporality of lyric and technological reproducibility, Marion Thain, for instance, argues that the Parnassian poetic form constituted a "challenge to the experience of time as linear progression" through the use of repetition that "puts poetry in tune with the culture of commodity abundance," "deracination," "reification," and "mass production" of the age of mechanical reproduction (2016, 104). Thain in fact cites a villanelle by William Ernest Henley titled "In the clatter of the train" (1887) that uses "the tune of the machine" to cast the age-old theme of love in a modern context (96–97).

Siefert uses the form of the pantoum to represent the railway journey and to render the landscape in motion. The pantoum was introduced in nineteenth-century France by Victor Hugo[12] and popularized by Charles Asselineau, Théodore de Banville, and Charles-Marie Leconte de Lisle. Among the most well-known pantoum we find Charles Baudelaire's "Harmonie du soir" ("Evening Harmony") from *Les Fleurs du mal* (*Flowers of Evil*), which twists together a meditation on love and images of dusk (1857). The Parnassians, and Banville especially, revived interest in traditional fixed forms such as the rondeau, villanelle, and the terza rima; though not early-modern European in origin, the pantoum shared a similar circular structure. The pantoum's Malay origins connect it to magical incantation (Ward 2012)—a suitable connotation for a poem on panoramic travel. One of several pantoums written by Siefert, "En passant en chemin de fer" comprises a series of twelve quatrains of octosyllables in which the second and fourth lines of each quatrain become the first and third lines of the next stanza. As per the strictures of the regular pantoum, the first and last lines of the poem are identical. In his discussion of the pantoum in *Petit Traité de poésie française* (Little treatise on French poetry), Banville referenced Siefert's poem, but in his opinion (one that I do not share) she did not sufficiently exploit the alteration of meaning through context.[13] On the other hand, the writer and architect Clair Tisseur thought that Siefert's pantoum was "le plus charmant pantoum que je connaisse" and stated specifically that "l'émotion de l'âme y dispute à l'harmonie des mots" (the most charming pantoum that I know of. . . . The emotions of the soul compete with the harmony of the words) (1893, 324; my translation). The poem conveys the rhythmic movement of the steam engine through the cyclical patterning of the pantoum and the alternating rhyme scheme. The repeating pattern generates a very dynamic form, well suited to the expansiveness of the railway. In effect, Siefert places poetic rhythm at the forefront of her treatment of panoramic travel, in contrast to the visual politics of platitude and straight, leveling lines associated with railway construction.

Siefert's pantoum is not about speed, acceleration, and linear time; instead, its use of repetition slows down the pace and invites reflection on the cyclical relationship between past and present or the multilayered nature of time. "En passant en chemin de fer" follows two alternating lines of argument—one metaphysical following the movement of thought, and one more lyrical in which the perception of nature in motion serves as objective correlative. The form therefore gives concrete expression to anxieties about progress, even as it asks if the rails can open up possibilities for a sick and suffering heart and whether there is a point of no return ahead:

> Peut-être ouvririez-vous l'espace
> À son cœur malade & souffrant?
>
> Emporté plus loin dans la vie,
> Le voyageur reviendra-t-il?
>   (Siefert 1868, 31, ll. 24–25, 32–33)
>
> (Would you open space perhaps
> For his sick & suffering heart?

Carried farther in life,
Will the traveler return?)

Will we indeed arrive at the planned destination as the listener se-
curely did in Alkan's piano étude? As Paliyenko reminds us, this type of
philosophical probing is typical of Siefert's poetry, as in the poem titled
"Vivere memento" from the Latin "remember to live":

Que sont les jours de l'homme & qu'est sa destinée
        Devant l'éternité?
Ce qu'est l'herbe jetée au gouffre formidable,
Ce qu'est ce monde-ci perdu dans l'insondable
        Et dans l'immensité!
    (Siefert 1868, 58)[14]

(What are man's days & what is his destiny
        Before eternity?
What is grass thrown into a formidable abyss,
What is this world lost within the fathomless
        And within immenseness!)

The pantoum's duality manifests "the mixture of introspection and
philosophical inquiry into the human condition" developed further in
her aptly titled collection *Les Stoïques* (The Stoics) from 1870 (Paliyenko
2016, 191).

The pantoum moreover impacts the representation of panoramic
travel: the poem evokes a succession of images of paths, shadows,
flowers, and sheep indiscriminately, but yet also "choreographs the
landscape" (Schivelbusch [1986, 60]) by imposing order and rhythm on
these alternating scenes. By recreating the rhythm of the steam locomotive through the regular beat of octosyllabic meter combined with
the repetition of phrases, the poem also heightens the hapticity of train
travel. Through voicing the poem, we reexperience in our bodies the
movement of the railway journey. At the same time, however, the poem
harnesses the railway, and harmonizes what must have been the violent jerky motion of the compartment, so that the overwhelming sense
here is of gentle and regular rhythm.[15] Siefert's poem makes technology
natural.

The poem plays with multiple viewpoints, so that it is hard to say
definitively whether one is inside the compartment looking out at the
petits chemins (small paths), or outside of the compartment watching
the train pass by. This interplay between exterior and interior is a req-
uisite property of the pantoum that, according to Banville, is supposed
to interweave two distinct meanings—one descriptive, one sentimen-

tal—in each stanza. In keeping with Siefert's frequent shifts in personal voice in her poetic craft (Paliyenko 2016), there are similarly three subjects in the poem: "vous les petits chemins," "le voyageur," and "moi" (you, little paths; the traveler; me). The repetition of lines in different contexts, which is a requirement of the pantoum, also plays into the intersection of multiple viewpoints. Siefert's pantoum uses the figure of hypallage, or the reversal of the syntactic relations between two words to heighten the play of multiple viewpoints. For instance, in the first stanza, the passage "discrets, furtifs & solitaires" (discrete, furtive, & solitary) would logically apply to "regards humains" (human gaze) but syntactically relates to "petits chemins." Similarly, "abrités du froid & du vent" (sheltered from cold & wind) syntactically relates to "petits chemins" but logically could describe the traveler sheltered in the compartment. Are "petits chemins" the paths seen through the window or are they the rails? I cannot help but conclude that the equivocation seems deliberate given how the poem scrupulously avoids the compound word "chemin de fer" [ʃəmɛ̃ də fɜr], while simultaneously disseminating the sounds [f], [ɜr], and [mɛ̃] in the alliteration *furtifs* and *frais* and rhymes *solitaires/mystères* and *chemins/humains* in the first and last stanzas.[16]

By playing with multiple viewpoints and dissimulating the mechanical source of wonderment, Siefert practices what Michel de Certeau refers to as trompe l'oeil in a passage worth quoting in full: "Le train généralise la *Mélencolia* de Dürer, expérience spéculative du monde: être hors de ces choses qui restent là, détachés, absolues, et qui nous quittent sans qu'elles y soient pour rien; être privé d'elles, surpris de leur éphémère et tranquille étrangeté. Émerveillement dans l'abandonnement. Pourtant elles ne bougent pas. Elles n'ont de mouvement que celui que provoquent entre leurs masses les modifications de perspective moment après moment; mutations en trompe l'œil" ([1980] 1990, 166). ("The train generalizes Dürer's *Melancholia*, a speculative experience of the world: being outside of these things that stay there, detached and absolute, that leave us without having anything to do with this departure themselves: being deprived of them, surprised by their ephemeral and quiet strangeness. Astonishment in abandonment. However, these things do not move. They have only the movement that is brought about from moment to moment by changes in perspective among their bulky figures. They have only trompe l'oeil movements" [Certeau, trans. Rendall, 1984, 111–12].)

Siefert's pantoum indeed evokes the distance that separates the train passenger from the landscape and speculates about the strangeness or estrangement of panoramic travel.

Siefert's poem speaks of spatiotemporal displacement or, in other words, the heightened sense of being transported to another time and place. The immersive view creating the impression of being at once here and there is a feature of the panorama. The annihilation of space as the speaker—"emporté plus loin dans la vie" (carried farther in life)— moves about in time creates an existential malaise in the traveler that transforms the railway journey into a quest for knowledge. Here Siefert's poem connects to a familiar trope in nineteenth-century treatments of the railway—that of the traveler who seeks an ideal journey "anywhere out of the world."[17] Siefert's railway journey turns inward, as the loco- motive becomes a time machine, or a dream induction machine. The image of the landscape rushing by becomes a metaphor of time pass- ing. That is the meaning I would attribute to the evocation of the pas- toral scenes in stanzas 8, 9, 10, and 11, of lambs grazing on the grass, of peacefulness, of "la fraîcheur sauvage & champêtre" (the cool & savage wilderness) and of the elusive "bonheur" (happiness). These scenes fig- ure what is out of reach, or past experiences that are irrecoverable, as the bucolic landscape that preexisted the construction of the railway and cannot be retrieved. In Siefert's poem there is a profound medita- tion on loss that betrays an anxiety about the promise of modernity that is kept in check by the regular rhythm of the chosen form. The pantoum ends how it began—but with a slight difference—as the speaker com- pares her dreams to the mysterious railway.

Some of the complexities of Siefert's treatment of sound, space, and time are best illuminated by comparisons with Robert Louis Stevenson's poem "From a Railway Carriage." Although Stevenson's poem from *A Child's Garden of Verses* (1885) was written for children, it aptly con- veys a decisively modern experience of "panoramic travel." The author of *Treasure Island* (1883) and *The Strange Case of Dr Jekyll and Mr Hyde* (1886) claimed not to be a poet, but his verses on the railway beautifully make use of poetic resources to recreate in our imagination the exhila- rating feel of the railway journey.

The short sixteen-line poem foregrounds the impact of train travel on sensory experience with a focus on the visual and the haptic. The smells and sounds that used to be part of the experience of travel by coach or on foot are not evoked. Speed blurs vision, creating a phantasmagoria as the references to fairies and witches in the first line of the poem im- mediately suggest. The accumulation of indistinct "bridges and houses, hedges and ditches" point to architectural features spotted too quickly to distinguish in detail. As in Siefert, the train compartment window as framing device, or as technological apparatus enabling movement, is not mentioned; in fact, we would not immediately know the poem was about train travel if the title did not give it away. As the technological means remains implicit, the supernatural experience of moving fast is naturalized through a comparison to flying in Line 6. No other locomotives or tracks can be seen from the carriage window. Instead, horses and cattle, as well as cart, mill, and river evoke the old economy based on horsepower, grain, and river transport that the railway and other forms of mechanization are replacing. Like Siefert, Stevenson implicitly counterposes or intertwines the bucolic and the technological, raising unanswered questions about which route would deliver elusive happiness, or as Siefert expresses it: "Le bonheur était là, peut-être, / Dans un de ces petits chemins" (Happiness was there, perhaps,/ In one of those little paths).

The panoramic effect is rendered more successfully through rhythm, alliteration, and syntax than through the poem's visual imagery. Essentially vision is a blur: an agrarian landscape of hill and plain unfolds quickly as a panorama devoid of depth ("thick as driving rain" [Line 6]) because perceived "in the wink of an eye" (Line 7), "each a glimpse and gone forever" (Line 16). Rhythm supplements vision's deficiencies. Rocking lineation (counterpointed lines caesura to caesura) and sound repetition (than, and) in lines 1–4 give the impression of the rhythm of locomotion, while alliteration ([f], [dg], [ch], [l]) implicitly conveys the sounds of the pistons and steam engine. These devices, like those used in Siefert's pantoum, effectively create haptic perception that invites the readers' somatic responses.[18] Enjambment in lines 5–6 and 7–8 suggests the train is speeding up and whizzing past a station. Hypallage, a device also used by Siefert, is used in Line 8 to attribute the whistling of the steam engine to the station it passes by. Shifting perspectives—used to such great effect in Siefert's poem—are used sparingly by Stevenson.

Anaphora and parataxis in Stevenson's second stanza, much like the syntactic parallelism in lines 1–4, also contribute to the panoramic effect. The succession of glimpses in lines 9, 11, 12, 13 and 15 introduced by "here is" use place deixis to convey a sense of presence and simultaneity. The result is a montage of scenes strung together. "From a Railway Carriage" thus represents how the train can be an instrument for alternative perception, that sets nature in motion and synthesizes a succession of disparate scenes.

Through reference to the outmoded horse-powered economy, the poem subtly suggests that movement through space might also be a shift in time; but the end of the poem ambiguously evacuates time ("gone for ever!") so that the phantasmagorical journey in the railway carriage might consist of travel out of time. The child, the tramp, the person who would be stringing daisies are all suspended in time in a manner that invites comparison with the occupant of the railway carriage. Since the poem emphasizes feeling (excitement) or musicality rather than the subjective voice of an "I" who perceives or evolves, the poem effects a here-and-now that connects movement through space with the suspension of time so as to preserve the illusion of moving "faster than fairies" indefinitely.

In conclusion, the works of Alkan, Siefert, and Stevenson use a range of forms that accentuate variations in intensities and in rhythm to represent the railway journey as a transnational shared experience of technoogy's impact on industrialized consciousness. Although all three works represent the proto-cinematic visual distortion that Schivelbusch highlights as the modern feature of panoramic travel, a fuller account of these works shows the extent to which they draw on aurality and hapticity rather than mere visuality. The perpetuum mobile and the pantoum are especially apt forms that use sound and rhythm to immerse the reader/listener in the journey through space and time, and across borders. Perhaps more than the other two works, Siefert's poem creates a multi-perspectival, mobile, and voluminous space that permeates the boundaries between interior and exterior as we move inside and outside the train compartment, and in and out of present time. By representing the rhythmic shifts in space-time, Siefert's poem evokes anxieties about where the future is headed while simultaneously allaying these fears and rendering technology harmonious.

Aimée Boutin is professor of French in the Department of Modern Languages and Linguistics at Florida State University. Having worked extensively on the surge of women's writing in the first half of the nineteenth century, her interests have extended to nineteenth-century cultural history, studying how the sounds of the past are incorporated in literary and cultural texts. In that light, she edited a special issue on "The Flâneur and the Senses" (2012) in the online journal *Dix-Neuf*; published *City of Noise: Sound and Nineteenth-Century Paris* (University of Illinois Press, 2015); and contributed to the *Bloomsbury Handbook of Sonic Methodologies* (2020). Her articles on French poetry, women writers, sound, and urban studies appear in *Nineteenth-Century French Studies, Women in French, French Review, L'Esprit créateur,* and *Nineteenth-Century Contexts.* Her new project is on French women writers and the railway. She spent Spring and Summer 2021 in residence at the Collegium de Lyon (Institute of Advanced Studies) in Lyon, France.

Appendix: Poems

Louisa Siefert, "En passant en chemin de fer. Pantoum" (*Rayons perdus,* 1868)

Louisa Siefert, "While Passing by on the Railway"

Discrets, furtifs & solitaires,
Où menez-vous, petits chemins?
Vous qu'on voit, pleins de frais
    mystères,
Vous cachant aux regards humains.

Où menez-vous, petits chemins
Tapissés de fleurs & de mousse?
Vous cachant aux regards humains,
Que votre ombre doit être douce!

Tapissés de fleurs & de mousse,
Abrités de froid & du vent,
Que votre ombre doit être douce
A celui qui s'en va rêvant!

Abrités du froid & du vent,
Le voyageur vous voit & passe.
A celui qui s'en va rêvant,
Peut-être ouvririez-vous l'espace?

Le voyageur vous voit & passe,
Il se retourne en soupirant :
Peut-être ouvririez-vous l'espace
A son cœur malade & souffrant?

Il se retourne en soupirant,
Emporté plus loin dans la vie.
A son cœur malade & souffrant
Votre silence fait envie.

Emporté plus loin dans la vie,
Le voyageur reviendra-t-il?
Votre silence fait envie,
chers petits chemins d'avril!

Discreet, furtive & solitary,
Where do you lead, little paths?
You whom we see, full of fresh
    mystery
Hiding from the human gaze.

Where do you lead, little paths
Shrouded in flowers & moss?
Hiding from the human gaze,
How your shadow must be soft!

Shrouded in flowers & moss,
Sheltered from cold & wind,
How your shadow must be soft
To he who goes forth dreaming!

Sheltered from cold & wind,
The traveler sees you & sweeps past.
To he who goes forth dreaming,
Would you open space perhaps?

The traveler sees you & sweeps past,
He turns back with a sigh:
Would you open space perhaps
For his sick & suffering heart?

He turns back with a sigh,
Carried farther in life.
For his sick & suffering heart
Your silence stirs up envy.

Carried farther in life,
Will the traveler return?
Your silence stirs up envy,
O dear little April paths!

Le voyageur reviendra-t-il	Will the traveler return
Fouler l'herbe que l'agneau broute?	Trampling grass that sheep graze?
chers petits chemins d'avril!	O dear little April paths!
Qui l'attend au bout de sa route?	Who awaits him at the journey's end?
Fouler l'herbe que l'agneau broute,	Trampling grass that sheep graze,
Au moins, ç'aurait été la paix.	At least, it would've been peace.
Qui l'attend au bout de sa route?	Who awaits him at the journey's end?
Pourquoi fuit-il l'ombrage épais?	Why does he flee the thick shades?
Au moins ç'aurait été la paix,	At least it would've been peace,
La fraîcheur sauvage & champêtre.	The cool & savage wilderness.
Pourquoi fuit-il l'ombrage épais?	Why does he flee the thick shades?
Le bonheur était là, peut-être.	Happiness was there, perhaps.
La fraîcheur sauvage & champêtre,	The cool & savage wilderness,
Loin de tous les regards humains,	Far from all human gazes,
Le bonheur était là, peut-être,	Happiness was there, perhaps,
Dans un de ces petits chemins.	In one of those little paths.
Loin de tous les regards humains,	Far from all human gazes,
Mes rêves cachent leurs mystères,	My dreams hide their mysteries,
Dans un de ces petits chemins	In one of those little paths
Discrets, furtifs & solitaires!	Discreet, furtive & solitary!
	(Translation by Aimée Boutin
	and Jena Whitaker)

Robert Louis Stevenson, "From a Railway Carriage" ([1885] 2003)

1   Faster than fairies, faster than witches,
2   Bridges and houses, hedges and ditches;
3   And charging along like troops in a battle,
4   All through the meadows the horses and cattle:
5   All of the sights of the hill and the plain
6   Fly as thick as driving rain;
7   And ever again, in the wink of an eye,
8   Painted stations whistle by.

9   Here is a child who clambers and scrambles,
10 All by himself and gathering brambles;
11 Here is a tramp who stands and gazes;
12 And here is the green for stringing the daisies!
13 Here is a cart runaway in the road
14 Lumping along with man and load;
15 And here is a mill, and there is a river:
16 Each a glimpse and gone forever!

Notes

1. For an interpretation of modernist engagement with the railway, see Papalas (2015).
2. The Wikipedia site provides an easy-access recording http://en.wikipedia.org/wiki/Le_chemin_de_fer_(Alkan), accessed 11 March 2015. Additional recordings are listed in the chapter references. It is noteworthy that Alkan composed at least one other piece inspired by vehicles, *Les Omnibus variations* op. 2 (1829). He also composed a piece inspired by rockets, *Les Fusées* op. 55 (1859).
3. The score can be viewed online at http://20031987.free.fr//027.pdf, accessed 4 March 2015.
4. I thank Denise Von Glahn for these comments.
5. For more on music inspired by the railway see Braun 2000; Carter 1993. Surprisingly both omit Alkan from their historical treatment of this theme.
6. Paraphrasing critic Maurizio Biondi, Geraci comments that Alkan's étude reflects the death of the Romantic mode and the elimination of subjectivity as interior voice (Geraci 1999, 156n36). Several musicologists including Biondi comment on the lack of melodious form in the piece and offer a range of interpretations of this quality.
7. Schaeffer defines reduced listening or écoute réduite in *Traité des objets musicaux* (1966, 270–71). Implicitly acknowledging that it is hard not to make associations or refer to preconceived ideas when hearing a piece such as *Étude aux chemins de fer* that cites the sound source in the title, Brian Kane sums up some of the contradictions in Schaeffer's intended use of the railway for *musique concrète*: "The 'trainness' of the sounds, when heard in the way Schaeffer intends, is separated from their purely musical values. In other words, the étude studies rhythms, not trains" (2014, 28). Many listeners though still strain to hear trains.
8. Georges Beck writes, "Remarquons, en passant et une fois pour toutes, que les mouvements métronomiques d'Alkan sont presque tous trop rapides, et ne sauraient être pris au pied de la lettre" (Let me remark in passing and once and for all, that the metronomic movements in Alkan are almost all too fast, and cannot be taken literally) (1969, v; my translation).
9. Marx uses the term "perpetuum mobile" in *Capital* (1867, vol. 1, chap. 15, sec. 3B).
10. The panorama refers to a type of trompe l'oeil painting developed by Robert Barker in the late eighteenth century. Its 360-degree view gave spectators the illusion of being immersed in the scene.
11. Leconte de Lisle's statement occurred in the context of an extensive debate about poetry and industry in France after the publication of Maxime Du Camp's *Les chants modernes* (1855); see Caraion 2008 for an overview and compilation of primary sources including Leconte de Lisle.
12. Hugo includes a French translation of a *pantoun* by Ernest Fouinet in an extensive note (no. 11) in *Les Orientales* (1829).
13. For more on the reception of Siefert's poetry, see Paliyenko's *Genius Envy* (2016, 185, 195–96, 288n9; Banville 1872, 219). Banville may have been prejudiced against female poets; in contrast, Tisseur's favorable opinion of Siefert may be influenced by their both being natives of Lyon. I would like to thank Adrianna Paliyenko for introducing me to this pantoum.
14. Siefert's philosophical inquiry is explored in depth in chapter 6 of *Genius Envy* (Paliyenko 2016, 164–96; for a discussion of "Vivere memento," see 2016, 182–85). Paliyenko explains that Siefert suffered from chronic illness so it is noteworthy that she wrote about the body in pain in her railway poem.

15. I thank Seth Whidden for this observation.
16. I thank Jena Whitaker and Kathryn Haklin for these observations on rhyme patterning.
17. "Anywhere Out of the World" is a poem by Charles Baudelaire (*Le Spleen de Paris. Petits poèmes en prose* XLVIII, 1869).
18. The various musical settings of the poem capitalize on the rhythm. For a list of settings, see RLS Website (n.d.).

References

Alkan, Charles-Valentin. 1844. *Le Chemin de fer, étude* (*The Railway*), op. 27.

Banville, Théodore de. 1872. *Petit traité de poésie française.* Paris: A. Le Clère. Gallica ark:/12148/bpt6k50423r. Accessed 11 March 2015.

Baroli, Marc. 1964. *Le train dans la littérature française.* Paris: Editions N. M.

Baudelaire, Charles. 1857. "Harmonie du soir." In *Les Fleurs du mal* XLIII.

Baudelaire, Charles. 1869. "Anywhere Out of the World." In *Le Spleen de Paris. Petits poèmes en prose* XLVIII. *Œuvres complètes de Baudelaire.* Paris: Michel Lévy.

Beck, Georges, ed. 1969. *Charles Valentin Alkan: Oeuvres choisies pour piano.* Paris: Heugel and Cie.

Bell, Nicolas. 2004. "Alkan." In *Encyclopedia of the Romantic Era 1760–1850,* vol. 1, edited by Christopher John Murray, 11–12. London: Taylor and Francis.

Braun, Hans-Joachim. 2000. "'Movin' on': Trains and Planes as a Theme in Music." In *"I Sing the Body Electric": Music and Technology in the 20th Century,* edited by Hans-Joachim Braun, 106–20. Hofheim, Germany: Wolke Verlag.

Caraion, Marta. 2008. *Les philosophes de la vapeur et des allumettes chimiques: littérature, sciences et industrie en 1855,* Histoire des idées et critique littéraire, v. 444. Geneva: Droz.

Carter, Ian. 1993. "Train Music." *The Music Review* 54, no. 3–4: 279–90.

Cendrars, Blaise. 1913. *La Prose du Transsibérien et de la Petite Jehanne de France.* Paris: Les Hommes Nouveaux.

Certeau, Michel de. 1984. *The Practice of Everyday Life.* Translated by Steven Rendall. Berkeley: University of California Press.

Certeau, Michel de. (1980) 1990. *L'Invention du quotidien 1. Arts de faire.* Paris: Gallimard, Folio essais. First published 1980 by Union générale d'édition, Paris.

Connor, Steven. 1997. "The Modern Auditory I." In *Rewriting the Self: Histories from the Middle Ages to the Present,* edited by Roy Porter, 203–23. New York: Routledge.

Du Camp, Maxime. 1855. *Les chants modernes.* Paris: Michel Lévy.

Eddie, William Alexander. 2007. *Charles Valentin Alkan.* Burlington, VT: Ashgate.

Gastineau, Benjamin. 1861. *La Vie en chemin de fer.* Paris: Dentu.

Geraci, Toni. 1999. "Note sui treni. Incontri tra musica e ferrovia in Russia e Francia nel secolo della rivoluzione industriale," *Il Saggiatore Musicale* 6, no. 1–2: 145–81.

Hugo, Victor. 1829. *Les Orientales.* Paris: Ch. Gosselin et Hector Bossange.

Kane, Brian. 2014. *Sound Unseen. Acousmatic Sound in Theory and Practice.* Oxford: Oxford University Press.

Khagram, Sanjeev, and Peggy Levitt. 2008. "Constructing Transnational Studies." In *The Transnational Studies Reader: Intersections and Innovations,* edited by S. Khagram and P. Levitt, 1–22. New York: Routledge.

Leconte de Lisle, Charles-Marie. 1895. "Preface à *Poèmes et Poésies.*" In *Derniers poèmes. L'Apollonide. La Passion. Préfaces des Poèmes antiques et des Poèmes et poésies. Poètes contemporains. Discours sur Victor Hugo (discours de récep-*

tion à l'Académie française, le 31 mars 1887), edited by José Maria de Here-
dia and André de Guerne, 222–30. Paris: A. Lemerre. Gallica, BNF, ark:/12148/
btv1b86183930. Accessed 30 April 2017.

Marx, Karl. 1867. *Capital.* Marx Engels Archive. https://www.marxists.org/archive/
marx/works/1867-c1/index.htm. Accessed 9 March 2015.

Monet, Claude. 1870. *Train dans la campagne.* Oil on canvas, 50 × 65 cm. Musée
d'Orsay, Paris.

Paliyenko, Adrianna M. 2016. *Genius Envy: Women Shaping French Poetic History,
1801–1900.* University Park: Pennsylvania State University Press.

Papalas, Marylaura. 2015. "Speed and Convulsive Beauty: Trains and the Historic
Avant-Garde." *Studies in 20th and 21st Century Literature* 39, no. 1: 1–23.

Rimm, Robert. 2002. *The Composer-pianists: Hamelin and The Eight.* Portland, OR:
Amadeus Press.

RLS Website. n.d. "Robert Louis Stevenson Archive." http://www.robert-louis-steven
son.org/richard-dury-archive/music.htm. Accessed 10 March 2015.

Russolo, Luigi. 1913. *L'arte dei rumori: manifesto futurista.* Milan: Direzione del Mov-
imento Futurista (A. Taveggia).

Schaeffer, Pierre. 1948. *Étude aux chemins de fer. Cinq Études de bruits, étude no. 2.
Concert de bruits.* Radio broadcast, 5 October 1948. Paris: Office de radiodiffusion-
télévision française (ORTF).

Schaeffer, Pierre. 1966. *Traité des objets musicaux.* Paris: Seuil.

Schilling, Britta. 1987. "Charles Valentin Alkan: Un solitaire dans le romantisme fran-
çais." *Romantisme* 17, no 57: 33–44. http://www.persee.fr/web/revues/home/
prescript/article/roman_0048–8593_1987_num_17_57_4879. Accessed 4 March
2015.

Schivelbusch, Wolfgang. (1977) 1986. *The Railway Journey: The Industrialization of
Time and Space in the 19th Century.* Berkeley: University of California Press.

Siefert, Louisa. 1868. "En passant en chemin de fer." In *Rayons perdus.* Paris: Lemerre.

Stevenson, Robert Louis. 1883. *Treasure Island.* London: Cassell.

Stevenson, Robert Louis. 1885. *A Child's Garden of Verses.* London: Longmans,
Green/ Scribner's.

Stevenson, Robert Louis. 1886. *The Strange Case of Dr Jekyll and Mr Hyde.* London:
Longmans, Green.

Stevenson, Robert Louis. 2003. *The Collected Poems of Robert Louis Stevenson,* edited by Roger C. Lewis. Edinburgh: Edinburgh University Press.

Thain, Marion. 2016. *The Lyric Poem and Aestheticism: Forms of Modernity.* Edinburgh: Edinburgh University Press.

Tisseur, Clair. 1893. *Modestes Observations sur l'art de versifier.* Lyon: Bernoux et
Cumin.

Turner, J. M. W. 1844. *Rain, Steam, and Speed: The Great Western Railway.* Oil on
canvas, 91 × 121.8 cm. National Gallery, London.

Urry, John. 2007. *Mobilities.* Cambridge, UK: Polity.

Verlaine, Paul. 1870. "Le paysage dans le cadre des portières." In *La Bonne Chanson*
VII. Paris: Lemerre.

Ward, Geoff. 2012. "On the Pantoum and the Pantunite Element in Poetry." In *A Companion to Poetic Genre,* edited by Erik Martiny. Oxford, UK: Wiley-Blackwell.

Recordings of Alkan's Le Chemin de fer, étude

Biret, Idil. 2011. Perf. *Piano Concerto No. 1 / 12 Preludes / Francaix, J.: Piano Sonata / Alkan, C.V.: Le chemin de fer.* Saygun, A. A., cond. Biret Archive Edition, Vol. 11. Naxos Music Library Catalogue No. 8.571288. CD.

Laurent, Martin. 1995. Perf. *Alkan, Charles. Railway (The) / Preludes / Etudes / Esquisses.* Martin, Laurent; Ringeissen, Bernard. Naxos Music Library Catalogue No.: 8.553434. CD.

Locomotiv-Musik 1: A Musical Train Ride. Slovak State Philharmonic Orchestra. Marco Polo 8.223470. https://www.naxos.com/catalogue/item.asp?item_code= 8.223470.

CHAPTER 2

The Sonic Force of the Machine Ensemble

Transnational Objectification in Steve Reich's Different Trains (1988)

Benjamin Fraser

Introduction

Different Trains (1988), composed by Steve Reich (1936–) and commissioned by Betty Freeman for Kronos Quartet (Reich 2002a, 158), is structured by three movements tying together the United States and Europe: the first movement, titled "The United States before the War," is followed by "Europe during the War," and the final movement, "After the War." This transnational suture is made through reference to two divergent experiences of train travel contemporary to World War II. Regarding the premise of the piece, Reich has explained that, "As I grew older, I often reflected on my good fortune to be born in America since, as a Jew, if I had been in Europe in those years I would have been on quite *different trains*" (1996, 20; emphasis added). Here the personal details of the composer's early childhood, which had never before been featured in his music, are linked via musical composition with the contemporaneous personal stories of others. That is, between 1939 and 1942, Reich in his early childhood traveled from New York to Los Angeles and back again by train to visit each of his divorced parents. At the same time, of course, trains in Europe carried Jews to their incarceration and death in concentration camps. Through Reich's rich musical contrast, the train becomes an important vehicle for much more than mere historical reflection in the simple sense. Incorporating recordings of train whistles, as well as interviews with Holocaust survivors, a railway porter, and the composer's own governess, and mimicking the variable speed and acceleration of train transport, Reich in effect creates a musical essay asking listeners to hold in the mind simultaneously two distinct images of the train experience. In this way, *Different Trains* captures both the ordinariness and the exceptional horrors of mobile modernity in a unique transnational structure.

This approach is not incompatible with existing work on mobility studies and the Holocaust, in particular Todd S. Presner's monograph *Mobile Modernity: Germans, Jews, Trains*. Setting up his wider argument, which ties the Holocaust to mobile modernity in the form of what he asserts as a cultural geography, Presner writes that, from the nineteenth to the twentieth century, "the railway emerged as an embodied, transnational space emblematic of both the emancipatory hopes and the destructive nightmares of an epoch. Not unlike the latent mythology of the arcade, the rapid expansion of the railway was driven by its unprecedented capacity to produce capital and facilitate transnational material support" (2007, 3).[1] We must be careful not to instrumentalize the railway as an inherently problematic technology, nor attribute an elevated agency to the train by severing it from its social use and human context. As Presner reminds us, the train is merely a vehicle in a much wider social production of death, one that does not rely on a specific form of technology to be carried out (211). But as Reich's piece pushes us to consider, train travel is significant in both the historical reality of the Holocaust and the wider social imaginary contemporary to it. In the sections of this essay that follow, I continue the push of scholarship that blends humanities methods with cultural studies and train/transport mobilities (e.g., Fraser 2015; Fraser and Spalding 2012; Misemer 2010; Spalding 2014; Spalding and Fraser 2012). Appealing to the general premise of the cultural studies method outlined by Raymond Williams (2007), I give equal weight to the historical context and social imaginary of train travel on one hand—the cultural geography contemporary to the Holocaust in both the US and European contexts—and to Steve Reich's musical text itself on the other—its formal properties and nuances of sonic signification.

Composed as a concise review of existing criticism, the first section, "*Different Trains* (1988) and Reich's Musical Evolution," situates the musical nuances of this particular composition within Reich's oeuvre more generally, remarking on the notion of its documentary value as well as its connection with the Holocaust theme. As evident in the terms contained in its subtitle, the second section, "Sonic Semiotics: Icon, Index, and Symbol," uses a basic Peircean semiotic language to move beyond the limitations of the notion of mere documentarism that has dominated existing scholarship on Reich's musical references to extramusical reality. The third section, "Wolfgang Schivelbusch and the Machine Ensemble," builds on previous sections, drawing parallels between the pioneering train theorist's perspective on *The Railway Journey* (1979) and a transportation and mobility studies perspective on Reich's composition. In the end, *Different Trains* reproduces the machine ensemble, representing it through a layered referential process of aural signification anchored in the interplay of iconic and indexical signification.

Different Trains (1988) and Reich's Musical Evolution

Undoubtedly, *Different Trains* must be seen in context of the evolution of Reich's record of musical composition, as well as in the general context of Holocaust studies. The composer's ingenious use of tape recording in 1960s work such as *It's Gonna Rain* (1965) and *Come Out* (1966) created music from the speech of, respectively, "a black preacher, Brother Walter, preaching about the Flood" in San Francisco and "Daniel Hamm, now acquitted and then 19 years old, describing a beating he took in Harlem's 28th Precinct police station," both recorded in 1964 (Reich 1996, 15, 16).[2] These early works have been somewhat broadly criticized for using "speech samples in such a way that they lose their original linguistic connotation" (Puca 1997, 537). More recently, scholars such as Sumanth Gopinath (2009) and Maarten Beirens (2014) have gone farther, explaining these works as not merely as stripping away the context underlying the recorded speech, but moreover as doing violence to the speech that drives the music. Siarhei Biareishyk goes farther, citing evidence of a "functional equivalence" established between "Reich's composition and contemporary whiteness" (2012, 76).[3] Nonetheless, the continuing evolution of Reich's music since the 1960s can be described as a movement away from the pursuit of "pure sound" (Beirens 2014, 217) that characterized his earlier compositions and toward retaining, and thus prioritizing, the context of original speech recordings.

Providing a viewpoint consistent with a holistic understanding of Reich's patterns of artistic creation over time, Antonella Puca (1997) notes that, in *Different Trains*, "Reich is careful to preserve the semantic content of the words in his musical manipulation of the recorded material" (549). Beirens concurs, writing,

> In the later sampler-based pieces from *Different Trains* onwards, Reich generally includes the speech samples in such a way that both the semantic and musical, speech melody-like qualities, are clearly perceptible, drawing the music from the speech samples while at the same time introducing the speaker (with his or her individual memories and opinions) as a privileged witness, included for its documentary value. This documentary approach allows the composer to tackle complicated political and historical narratives through the voices of the people from whom he

borrows their words as well as the basic musical material embedded in those words. (Beirens 2014, 217)

This much-debated notion of the documentary value of Reich's later works—and the relationship established therein between speech and music—deserves closer attention before moving onward.

Regarding his method of musical composition, Reich (2002) has explained, "The basic idea is that speech recordings generate the musical material for musical instruments" (158); "Sampled speech and other sounds generate melodic lines for strings" (261). The composer has written that the recordings figuring prominently in *Different Trains* specifically are those of "my governess Virginia, now in her seventies, reminiscing about our train trips together," "a retired Pullman porter, Lawrence Davis, now in his eighties, who used to ride lines between New York and Los Angeles, reminiscing about his life," "recordings of Holocaust survivors Rachella, Paul, and Rachel—all about my age and now living in America—speaking of their experiences," and "recorded American and European train sounds of the 1930s" (151–52). Throughout the piece, the "melodic lines for strings" that mimic sampled speech are present in this pattern: women's speech is doubled by the viola, men's speech is doubled by the cello, and train whistles are always doubled by fiddles (Kim 1999, 355; see also Weiss 2001). As musicians familiar with the piece will recognize, "the strings then literally imitate the speech melody taking into account its pitch profile, its timbre and its inherent rhythm" (Puca 1997, 550). For example, when Mr. Davis says "nineteen forty," the cello echoes the pitch of his speech, now converted into musical notes progressing at the same interval present in the original recording. The "other sounds" mentioned by Reich (261) are incorporated in a manner faithful to the titles of the individual movements: thus American train whistles are used in the first movement, "The United States before the War," and European train whistles are used in the second movement, "Europe during the War" (182), establishing a connection in the music between these distant but contemporary sound spaces. The question is whether these musical elements should be seen as contributing to the documentary nature of the piece.

As already seen in the extended quotation by Beirens above, which uses the term "documentary value," recorded speech in *Different Trains* in particular has been received by critics as evidence of what Reich himself has called its "documentary aspect."[4] The composer's implicit use of a political theme in *Come Out* (1965)—which functions as a musical index to an incident of police brutality (Reich 1996, 16)—can be seen as leading him eventually toward the more explicit use of historical and

technological themes that connect with sociopolitical and ethical questions: the content of *Three Tales* (a 2002 video opera by Reich and Beryl
Korot), for example, which is divided into "Hindenburg, on the crash of
the German zeppelin in New Jersey in 1937; Bikini, on the Atom bomb
tests at Bikini atoll in 1946–1954; and Dolly, the sheep cloned in 1997, on
the issues of genetic engineering and robotics" (Reich n.d.). The speech
incorporated into *Different Trains* can also be seen as part of a sustained
pattern of introspective reflection by Reich on his Jewish identity carried out through the 1970s, which led also to his use of Hebrew cantillation in *Tehillim* (1981) (see Puca 1997).

   In line with assessments by Puca (1997) and Beirens (2014), scholar
Amy Lynn Wlodarski also admits that the speech works differently in
Different Trains than in Reich's early works from the 1960s (Wlodarski
2010, 113n63; see also 2015), but she goes farther in questioning the
notions of documentarism and objectivity as they apply to *Different
Trains* (see in particular 103; see also Miklaszewska 2013). This questioning leads Wlodarski to identify a productive correspondence between
Reich's work and scholarship theorizing Holocaust testimonial more
generally, in that she finds that the work under study is best seen as a
"problematic secondary witness." She writes,

> *Different Trains* is itself a problematic secondary witness, one susceptible
> to the same fracture of subjectivity endemic to the accounts of primary
> witnesses, in which survivors struggle not only with the ruptures of mem-
> ory caused by trauma, but also with the impossibility of translating those
> memories into language and narrative. As a result, *Different Trains* is itself
> shaped by the aesthetics and inaccurate nature of testimony: ultimately,
> it is Reich's own Holocaust testimony, one crafted from the voices of wit-
> nesses other than himself. (Wlodarski 2010, 104)

   As evident in this extract and the article as a whole, the ambivalence
of Wlodarski's perspective comes from the way in which she sees *Different Trains* to preserve the fractures and ruptures associated with Holocaust trauma while reminding that its creator has no direct experience of
this trauma. The scholar successfully unravels the triumphant narrative
sustaining the moral value of *Different Trains* and justifying its canonical presence in music history surveys and Jewish Studies courses—in
other words, that it was, in critic Richard Taruskin's words, "the only ade-
quate musical response . . . to the Holocaust" (quoted in Wlodarski 2015,
128). In order to accomplish this, she demonstrates convincingly that
claims of documentarism belie the work's evident dramatic, theatrical,
emotional, and subjective qualities. This is a pertinent argument and in
addition one that squares with the push of the humanities scholarship

regarding the construction, functioning and reception of artistic works much more generally, which privileges these very qualities in artistic production.

As Wlodarski points out, following advances in Holocaust studies, the use of survivor stories as historical fact, which arguably strips them of emotional context, deserves to be taken as suspect.[5] I do not seek to engage this point within the discourse of Holocaust studies, but instead to point out that Reich's claims of his work's documentary value may themselves be of questionable import.[6] That is, scholarship echoing the composer's claims risks illustrating the intentional fallacy of artistic criticism, which explains the value of a work of art in terms of its creator's intentions. In this sense, then—to the degree that musical criticism of *Different Trains,* prompted by Reich's statements or not, has itself treated the piece as evidence of documentarism—it has failed to explain the piece itself as a work of art. The significance of Wlodarski's article thus stems from the need for criticism to more intentionally define the relationship between signification in musical composition and extra-artistic reality; in short, for scholars themselves to treat *Different Trains* as a work of art and not as a historical document.[7] A cultural studies approach attentive to musical form can accomplish this by noting the connections Reich establishes between iconic, indexical, and symbolic forms of signification in the piece. These layers of signification create an ensemble structure within *Different Trains* that problematize and bring productive nuance to the relationship the work establishes between artistic appropriations of sound, musical composition, and the extra-artistic social world.

Sonic Semiotics: Icon, Index, and Symbol

The present cultural studies reading of *Different Trains* is grounded in a respect for the work of art itself as a certain kind of product. That is, the discourse of art is irreducible to a message, though it may contain or operate as one or more messages, and it is moreover qualitatively and singularly distinct from historical and social discourse, even as it articulates a relationship with historical and social forms of meaning beyond its borders. In this sense, previous scholarship affirming the documentary nature of Reich's composition (some of which is mentioned above) could be just as suspect as the composer's own claim to documentarism. Similarly suspect are Reich's claims—and the wider claims of minimalist movements—that art created under certain conditions remains autonomous from personal, subjective, or emotional considerations (e.g., see Wlodarski 2010, 106, 134). Also, implicit in my approach are studies by cultural geographers that have pioneered work on emotional geographies and sound geographies, demonstrating that understandings of place are constructed and negotiated through aural practices, and that there are important links between emotion and sound.[8] And finally—as a complement to the way in which the linguistic context of recorded speech has been prioritized in some previous studies on more recent Reich, and understanding that they are not lyrics in a conventional sense—I assert that paying attention to how speech and other recordings function as signs in *Different Trains* can help displace the hegemony through which lyrics have historically been privileged in studies of music.[9] Moving beyond the historical discourse implied in the term "document," a semiotic approach focused on the sonic force of *Different Trains* illustrates how Reich's composition plays with the false border between music as representation and extra-artistic reality by marshaling iconic, and indexical, signification.

Iconic and indexical forms of signification are crucial to the effect that Reich's composition has on listeners, and are the basis for the more symbolic forms of signification that blend the metaphorical power of sound and speech in his music. To begin with the iconic, there can be no doubt that Reich's composition stages the experience of train travel through carefully constructed and arranged aural cues that operate through iconic relationships—those that might be described as being characterized by patterns of formal resemblance or imitation. Naomi Cumming has pointed out, "Listening to the opening of *Different Trains* there is no mystery to the fact that the repetitive patterns played by the string quartet—recorded over itself four times—are supposed to represent the motion of a train" (1997, 130). When the tempo speeds up to 194 beats per minute or slows down to 64 beats per minute (Miklaszewska 2013, 135), listeners may justifiably feel that the train may be accelerating or slowing down.[10] In this way, "the mechanization of movement in *Different Trains* is able both to elicit a response of empathetic bodily motion, and a resistance born of the feeling of being driven" (Cumming 1997, 137). In semiotic terms, the variable tempo of the musical composition is functioning as an iconic sign, mimicking in form or shape the variable tempo of its referent the train. The result is that this auditory sign induces the listener to adopt the subject position of a train passenger. Joanna Miklaszewska uses the idea of imitation (2013, 135) to discuss the rendering of recorded speech segments into musical notes by the viola, cello, and fiddles, but "iconic signification" would be a better term. Here it is the formal resemblance between sign and referent established through these forms of iconic signification that creates an important distinction between the signifying power of speech and the signifying power of musical sound in *Different Trains*. It is important to note that both the sign and the referent in these cases of iconic signification are situated within the musical composition itself. Musical instruments in the piece refer listeners to samples of recorded speech, which are themselves part of the musical composition. Thus, at this iconic layer of signification, Reich's piece introduces a semiotic split internal to the music.

This iconic layer of signification, of course—while analytically distinct—is not in practice autonomous from the layer of indexical signification that coexists in *Different Trains*. This relatively autonomous indexical layer of signification involves the piece's artistic appropriation of recorded speech samples, and requires a few introductory remarks if we are to understand how the latter function in this context. To explain, critics of Reich's music have focused more often on what might be called the subtractive power, implied in the way that recording, editing, suturing, and reintroducing speech in another context and separation of speech from a speaker than they have on the additive power of this process. Both the subtractive and the additive perspectives are complementary to one another, and neither deserves to be pursued at the other's expense; however, acknowledgment of the additive power of speech recording has not been sufficiently explored in existing Reich criticism—this perhaps due to Reich's own discourse on his purported compositional objectivity regarding their use. That is, the process of sampling certainly implies artistic creators who—despite Reich's seeming insistence to the contrary, I would add—necessarily introduce their perspectives through every musical decision they make. But recorded speech will still function with some degree of relative autonomy to a creator's perspective, since these words now act as references to a time and place embodied in the speech acts of the recorded speakers. In truth, however edited, processed, and changed these speech recordings may be (Wlodarski [2015] sheds light on this complex dynamic) and arguably even more so the more that an editing process functions to draw attention to the presence of an artistic creator who might otherwise go unobserved—they are not solely a historical or documentary record but they are rather simultaneously an aesthetic element or artistic sign. The speech recordings sampled in Reich's musical essay function as indexical signs in the discourse of art; they are part of a rich sonic connective tissue whose operation the listeners may be likely to question and perhaps even investigate. Because they are now artistic signs, these speech recordings function as aural indexes pointing directly to an embodied time and place, to an individual emotional geography whose full context lies elsewhere. The specificity of the whistle recordings from Europe included in the composition's second movement, for example, are also important instances of indexical signs—as direct recordings of actual European trains of the period, they constitute a link to a sonic geography existing outside of the music, what Joanna Miklaszewska has called the "audiosphere of occupied Europe" (2013, 132).

The relationship between the forms of iconic and indexical signification discussed above is particularly important in *Different Trains*, since they create an ensemble structure comprising both an internally focused iconic energy and an externally focused referential/indexical energy. The piece's aural indexes refer to an extra-musical space and time through speech and whistles, which become links to the emotional soundscapes of historical memory (one that listeners in the twenty-first century increasingly do not share with some earlier listeners of Reich's composition). But the distances introduced into the music through these indexes—again, these are distances through which the musical piece is connected with referents external to the piece—are themselves replicated through the music's emphasis on iconic signification. That is, the imitation of speech by musical instruments becomes a way of introducing, in musical terms internal to the piece, the distance between sign and referent. It is significant that this distinction is internal to the work of art itself. That is, the indexical link between musical form and the embodied place and time of extra-musical 1939–42 is mirrored, complemented, and reproduced internally to the music in the link between the indexes and their iconic resemblance or imitation. Musical iconicity here recapitulates musical indexicality. In a layered process, then, the recurring instances of aural forms of iconic signification and indexical signification throughout Reich's composition make listeners aware of the distancing implied in semiotic practices and artistic representation. The mechanism of resemblance Reich establishes between iconic signs and their referents, both internal to the piece, works productively with the deictic operation implied in indexical signification, in which sampled sounds functioning as musical signs pointing directly and outward toward a referenced and extra-artistic reality. One can think of these two semiotic operations as part of the piece's doubled motor: energy is created through iconic signification internal to the piece, and then transformed into movement through embodied space-time external to the piece by indexical signification.

In this way a motor structure emerges in *Different Trains* and carries listeners forward through the composition. This structure is at once a musical structure and a semiotic structure; it is this structure on which all symbolic and metaphorical meaning in the piece is based. Basic human emotions—sadness, fear, tension, relief—come to be infused into the musical composition through specific choices Reich makes in terms of pacing, minor/major intervals, rhythm, harmony and so on. That is, on the basic building blocks of these iconic and indexical musical references to extra-musical reality listeners may actively construct more-symbolic, more-metaphorical, and even more-imaginative interpretations about what is happening during the musical narrative, what is going on inside the train, or outside of the train, in the life of a Jewish child in America, or in the lives of Jews in Europe at the time. The iconic and indexical forms of signification in *Different Trains*—the instrumental imitation of samples and the speech recordings and the recorded whistles themselves—thus have a particular potential to act on sympathetic listeners in tandem.[11] As Blum points out, sympathetic listeners may even participate, in their mind's eye, in movements toward a concentration camp: "With regard to Reich's *Different Trains,* what is evoked for the listener is not simply the beauty of the piece's form, but the very lives of the persons whose speech is embodied in the piece. In this way, the movement of the trains toward the camps might be one in which the listener participates. Though the body of the listener is far removed from the experiences narrated, modern listening can tug at my inwardness and challenge the comfort that I enjoy in the site marked by that distance" (1996, 127; see also Cumming 1997, 130).[12]

These connections between sound and emotional geography that are implicit in Blum's remark can also be summed up through reference what geographer Deborah Thien calls "the motion of emotion" (2005, 451) and the power of music to "reorient consciousness" identified by music scholar Tia DeNora (2003, 62; see also Fraser 2011). The richly textured semiotic structure of *Different Trains* thus forcefully inserts itself between the listener and the musical composition and becomes a mediation of aural experience, a productive link between art and life and a movement driving the listener to reconcile two divergent experiences of train travel. In this way, it carries out a function complementary to that which Wolfgang Schivelbusch identified in the experience of train travel as the machine ensemble.

Wolfgang Schivelbusch and the Machine Ensemble

As is evident in Wolfgang Schivelbusch's *The Railway Journey: The Industrialization of Time and Space in the 19th Century* (1979), the history of train travel and its social use is one driven by the systematization of transportation elements previously taken to be relatively autonomous.

While previously "route and means of transportation existed independently from one another," under railway transport, road and vehicle became one (16; see also 19).[13] Understanding the nature and the effects of this systematization can also inform the present transport and mobility reading of Reich's *Different Trains* (1990). First, understanding the layered role of the mechanical as experienced within the train's machine ensemble reveals a parallel construction to the semiotic structure of Reich's musical composition. And second, on the basis of these ties between layered mechanism in train travel and layered semiotics in Reich, one can assert a number of other functional equivalencies between theories of train travel and *Different Trains.*

Most significantly, the systematization of the railway in its broadest social context[14] began with a primary and layered pattern of mechanization. As chapter 2 ("The Machine Ensemble") of Schivelbusch's book (1979) asserts, "The machine character of the railroad was dual: first, the steam engine (locomotive) generated uniform mechanical motion; secondly, that motion was transformed into movement through space by the combined machinery of wheel and rail" (20). Together, these two layers of mechanization completed a "detachment from nature initiated by the discovery of steam power" (20). But in the doubled mechanical structure of the train's detachment from nature there was also, perhaps paradoxically, a built-in awareness of this detachment. In this final section of the chapter I explore first the detachment and second the passenger's awareness of it, each with reference to Reich's composition.

The railway passenger was separated from the landscape by a speed and velocity that contrasted greatly with earlier forms of horse-drawn carriage travel. This separation constituted a qualitative shift in the travel experience and resonated with other alienations that arose in the specific context of train travel: that is, regarding interpersonal relationships, the class character of segregated train travel from its origins (Schivelbusch 1979, 71–72); and regarding the relationship of human to machine—in other words, the way in which all passengers, in their passivity, became "the object of an industrial process" (73).[15] As Alan Trachtenberg explains, "Mechanized by seating arrangements and by new perceptual coercions (including new kinds of shock), routinized by schedules, by undeviating pathways, the railroad traveler underwent experiences analogous to military regimentation—not to say 'nature' transformed into 'commodity'" (1986, xiv).[16] In brief, the key qualities of train transport's mechanical motion—"regularity, uniformity, unlimited duration and acceleration" (Schivelbusch 1979, 9)—functioned to alienate passengers from the textures of natural rhythms. Reich's piece introduces but also plays with regularity and uniformity through the acceleration of the musical tempo of *Different Trains*, in fact. If—as in Blum's compelling assertion (1996, 127)—listeners of Reich's piece imagine themselves as train passengers, they will tend to experience the military regimentation and the objectification experienced by European Jews moving toward the camps, or, for that matter, the more routine traveler objectification experienced by a child as a passive train passenger in the contemporary United States. In each case, the sonic force of the composition's steady beat, the onslaught of perceiving multiple tracks of sound, and the pre-sentation of human elements refracted through mechanical means are overwhelming.

Moreover, it is important that the alienation of the train passenger from the landscape contained the potential for disalienation, or at the very least an awareness of the state of alienation. The speed and ve-locity of travel were evident to travelers in the fleeting image of the passing landscape, which thus rendered the machine ensemble of train travel visible. In Schivelbusch's account, the passenger of modern train travel was alienated from the landscape outside of the train car, a lay-ered alienation of which the visible elements of the machine ensem-ble—such as telegraph poles and wires—served as a reminder.

> The empirical reality that made the landscape seen from the train window appear to be "another world" was the railroad itself, with its excavations, tunnels, etc. Yet the railroad was merely an expression of the rail's techno-logical requirements, and the rail itself was a constituent part of the ma-chine ensemble that was the system. It was, in other words, that machine ensemble that interjected itself between the traveler and the landscape. The traveler perceived the landscape as it was filtered through the ma-chine ensemble. . . . The rail traveler's perceptions were changed by the intervention of the machine ensemble between him and the landscape; there was a material demonstration of that intervention in those [tele-graph] poles and wires, which were a part of the machine ensemble. They interposed themselves, both physically and metaphorically, between the traveler and the landscape. (Schivelbusch 1979, 24, 31)

Put concisely, the machine ensemble "interjected itself between the traveler and the landscape" (Schivelbusch 1979, 24), but at once also foregrounded its own alienating function. In a similar way, Reich's piece operates based on a layered semiotic approach where strategies of iconic representation and duplication, complemented by the use of speech and whistle recordings as indexes, draw the listener's attention to the constructed-ness of the piece and thus also to the social land-scape beyond the borders of the music.

The train theorist writes of the way in which "pre-industrial traf-fic is mimetic of natural phenomena" and how, in train travel, "steam power dissolved that mimetic relationship" (Schivelbusch 1979, 9). Seen as working in tandem, iconic and indexical representations in Reich's musical essay work to complement Schivelbusch's analysis of the passenger's travel experience in sonic terms. In *Different Trains,* the use of iconic resemblance—the imitation of speech by musical instruments—operates as a musical parallel to the gap previously filled by mimeticism in pre-train travel. The notes repeating the cadence and pitch of sampled speech—Mr. Davis's voicing of "1940," for example—illustrate musically the opening of just such a parallel gap. In *Different Trains,* this gap is one of representation between sign and referent, and in this transport and mobility reading, its parallel in the train experience is the technologically rendered detachment of the train passenger from the landscape. But while the mimeticism of iconic signification restages for us the human detachment from nature entailed in train travel, the specificity of indexical signification reaffirms the embodied space and time of human cultural geographies. The sampled speech recordings in *Different Trains* can thus be understood—like the sight of telegraph poles and wires within the machine ensemble—as concrete reminders of the process of artistic creation and of the transnational interplay between history and geography that drives Reich's piece. The two-layered motor driving the composer's artistic process—driven by iconic signification in the first pass (as a parallel to the steam engine) and by indexical signification in the second pass (as a parallel to the spatial extension of the railway)—echoes the production of a new spatiality implicit in train travel: "Motion was no longer dependent on the conditions of natural space, but on a mechanical power that created its own new spatiality" (10). In light of Schivelbusch's work, Reich's musical essay uses aural signification to produce a new transnational fusion of two distinct cultural geographies (Europe and the United States).

Reich's piece counteracts a key point made by Schivelbusch regarding train travel. The transportation scholar had documented how modern train travel effected "the loss of a communicative relationship between man and nature" (Schivelbusch 1979, 11). This loss is clearly reflected in *Different Trains,* in the mechanical nature of his artistic process, and in the sonic force of the machine ensemble, represented musically as documented above. But Reich's rich aural semiotics also work to restore a communicative relationship between humankind and nature. As with the train itself, this relationship is one mediated by, but not limited to, technology. The human voice in recorded sampling and its echoing in strings exemplify two complementary fusions of the human and the machine (understood broadly as technology/tool/instrument). What is foregrounded is the notion of distance: distance in representational terms, distance in geographical terms, distance in interpersonal terms. But part of the push in *Different Trains* is to recognize that, through movement, distance can be closed. Reich's composition illustrates the dual power of modern technology: it can be used to routinely alienate and objectify, or, in exceptional circumstances, it can even aid in mass killing. Yet it can also be used to connect, to bring together, and, musically, to unite through transnational juxtaposition.

Conclusion

Steve Reich's *Different Trains* reproduces the alienation, distance, and ambivalent potential that Wolfgang Schivelbusch theorized in the machine ensemble, representing it through multiple levels of aural signification. The distinction between iconic signification and recorded speech internal to *Different Trains,* and on top of that the correspondence between distinct forms of iconic, indexical, and symbolic signification within the music, creates a layered semiotic experience. The larger question that may emerge for readers and listeners interested in Reich's work is this: Is it ultimately an aestheticization of politics or is it a politicization of music? I would place *Different Trains* in particular in the latter category. Part of the effect of the machine ensemble was arguably that "the perception of spatial distance" was lost (Schivelbusch 1979, 12). But in bringing together US train travel and European train travel during a single period, *Different Trains* brings us to perceive distance again: spatial distance, temporal distance, cultural distance, historical distance, and perhaps also moral/ethical distance, as well. This is no small feat.

Benjamin Fraser is professor in the College of Humanities at the University of Arizona. He is the founding editor of the *Journal of Urban Cultural Studies* and coeditor, with Steven Spalding, of *Trains, Culture, and Mobility* (2012) and *Trains, Literature, and Culture* (2012). He is the author of ninety articles and book chapters and ten single-authored books, including *The Art of Pere Joan* (2019), *Visible Cities, Global Comics* (2019), *Toward an Urban Cultural Studies: Henri Lefebvre and the Humanities* (2015), and *Digital Cities: The Interdisciplinary Future of the Urban Geo-Humanities* (2015). His publications have appeared in *Catalan Review, Transfers: Interdisciplinary Journal of Mobility Studies, Cultural Studies, Social and Cultural Geography, Environment and Planning D: Society and Space,* and *Emotion, Space and Society.*

Notes

1. See also, "Connections are not made according to the necessity of succession but rather according to the contingency of geography and the possibility of mobility. This means that a cultural geography is radically fractured and discontinuous; it resembles a pile of snapshots of a dialectic. At the same time that succession is given up, it also becomes impossible to assign modality or direction to historical events. Geographies of simultaneity or constellations of possibility are the result" (Presner 2007, 12).

2. Reich notes, "*Come Out* was composed as part of a benefit presented at Town Hall in New York for the re-trial, with lawyers of their own choosing, of the six boys arrested for murder during the Harlem riots of 1964" (1996, 16).

3. A lengthy but helpful quotation on this subject is the following: "But intensification alone does not account for the sense of violence attributed to Reich's early pieces. The gradual and inevitable progression from the semantic to the sonic in Come Out, from discrete meaning to non-articulated sound, is very powerful in the manner in which it strips away what is being said as well as many of the idiomatic characteristics of who is speaking. One has to ask, therefore, what can be achieved by removing the very elements that are supposed to lie at the centre of the work? Why would a composer choose to treat recorded speech in such a way that it obscures the qualities which were actually identified as the motivation behind the selection of the speech in the first place? What happens to the persona of the speaker when his or her voice is rendered beyond the point of being recognisable or even identifiable as a human voice? And how should we understand this move towards the 'coming apart' of the speech/speaker, if not through the notion of violence, as Gopinath has suggested? (Gopinath, 2009, p. 136)" (Beirens 2014, 216).

4. "What particularly interests me in using spoken language, as opposed to setting a text to music for voices to sing, is what could be called the 'documentary aspect' of recorded voices. The particular voices of my governess, the porter, and the Holocaust survivors in *Different Trains* tell the actual story of a period in history from just before to just after World War II. There is no singer's 'interpretation' but, rather, this: people bearing witness to their own lives. Their speech melody is the unpremeditated organic expression of the events they lived through" (Reich 2002b, 198).

5. Wlodarski writes, "The kind of authority attributed to these sources has come under scrutiny in the field of Holocaust studies, with scholars debating the consequences of transforming highly subjective survivor testimonies into a historical discourse in which their witness is lifted out of its emotional context and made to serve as fact rather than memory" (2010, 103). It is crucial, in my reading, that Reich's work is not reducible to a secondary representation of Holocaust trauma alone. Instead, it is a composition whose meaning comes from the collision of two narratives or sets of experiences. As Peter Blum put it concisely, "Steve Reich's recent work, *Different Trains,* is a powerful juxtaposition of American romanticism regarding railroads with the terrible finality of a rail journey for the Jews in Nazi Germany" (1996, 126).

6. Interested readers can consult the two chapters from Reich's *Writings on Music* cited in this chapter (Riech 2002a, 2002b) as well as the other writings collected in that volume.

7. There is a parallel in the push in Holocaust studies noted by Wlodarski to approach both primary and secondary witness "as an aesthetic act rather than as a historical one" (2010, 135). Another interesting aspect of Wlodarski's article is its careful exploration of the correspondences between the formal and narrative structure of Reich's work and the formal and narrative structure of the Fortunoff interviews with Holocaust survivors that figure in his piece (109–16).

8. On emotional geographies see Anderson and Smith (2001); Bondi (2002a, 2002b); Davidson and Milligan (2004); Wood and Smith (2004); on sound geographies see Smith (1997, 2000, 2001) and Wood, Duffy, and Smith (2007); regarding the latter point, see also Levitin (2006) and Sacks (2007).

9. See work by Frith (1988, 105–6, 120–21); Frith (1996, 158–82).

10. Note that Cumming (1997) asserts the significance of several specific changes in tempo in her article.

11. Cumming (1997) and Schwarz (1993) tend to subordinate the indexical/iconic to the symbolic/psychoanalytic (and exclude considerations from transportation and mobility studies in this respect), but similarly point to the importance of external references in *Different Trains*: "The trains of *Different Trains* are not 'merely' a mask for psychological drives, because their historical identity as vehicles of mass transport is ensured by the external cues of the hoots, sirens, and warning bells. Without this external reference, the importance of linking internal, psychological states, experienced as present, with remembered events in the recent past would be lost" (Cumming 1997, 138). Schwarz mentions "iconic representation" (e.g., 1993, 40) but not indexical signification; Cumming mentions the word "index" (1997, 147) but does not tie the word to aural signification.

12. The present study regards use of the term "very lives" in the quotation by Blum not from a documentary perspective, but rather from one that acknowledges their function as indexical artistic signs.

13. Schivelbusch writes, "The machine ensemble, consisting of wheel and rail, railroad and carriage, expanded into a unified railway system, which appeared as one great machine covering the land" (1979, 29).

14. As Alan Trachtenberg notes, train transport was not merely a technology in the simple sense, but also entailed "a new system of behavior: not only of travel and communication but of thought, of feeling, of expectation" (1986, xiii).

15. Elsewhere I cite from Schivelbusch (1979, 72, 73), noting, "The form of the train-carriage itself also evolved differentially according to the class experience of its travelers so that first-class travelers were relatively sheltered from their awareness of the "industrial origin and nature of the railroad", while lower-class travelers felt more clearly the experience of being "the object of an industrial process" (2015, 11).

16. This quotation starts, "Personal travel by railroad inevitably (if unconsciously) assimilated the personal traveller into a physical system for moving goods. ... It was a decisive mode of integration of people into their new status within the system of commodity production" (Trachtenberg 1986, xiv).

References

Anderson, K., and S. Smith. 2001. "Editorial: Emotional Geographies." *Transactions of the Institute of British Geographers* 26, no. 1: 7–10.

Beirens, Maarten. 2014. "Voices, Violence and Meaning: Transformations of Speech Samples in Works by David Byrne, Brian Eno and Steve Reich." *Contemporary Music Review* 33, no. 2: 210–222.

Biareishyk, Siarhei. 2012. "Come Out to Show the Split Subject: Steve Reich, Whiteness and the Avant-Garde." *Current Musicology* 93 (Spring): 73–93.

Blum, Peter C. 1996. "Typification, Transcendence and Critique: On the Social Construction of New Age Music." In *All Music: Essays on the Hermeneutics of Music*, edited by Fabio B. Dasilva and David L. Brunsma, 117–32. Brookfield, VT: Ashgate.

Bondi, Liz. 2002a. "Introduction." In Bondi, *Subjectivities, Knowledges and Feminist Geographies*, 1–11.

Bondi, Liz, ed. 2002b. *Subjectivities, Knowledges and Feminist Geographies*. Lanham, MD: Rowman and Littlefield.

Cumming, Naomi. 1997. "The Horrors of Identification: Reich's 'Different Trains.'" *Perspectives of New Music* 35, no. 1: 129–52.

Davidson, J., and C. Milligan. 2004. "Editorial: Embodying Emotion Sensing Space: Introducing Emotional Geographies." *Social and Cultural Geography* 5, no. 4: 523–32.

DeNora, Tia. 2003. *After Adorno. Rethinking Music Sociology*. Cambridge: Cambridge University Press.

Fraser, Benjamin. 2011. "Re–Scaling Emotional Approaches to Music: Basque Band Lisabö & the Soundscapes of Urban Alienation." *Emotion, Space and Society* 4: 8–16.

Fraser, Benjamin. 2015. "Urban Railways in Buenos Aires: Spatial and Social Alienation in the Documentary Film *El tren blanco*." *Transfers: Interdisciplinary Journal of Mobility Studies* 5, no. 2: 5–22.

Fraser, Benjamin, and Steven Spalding, eds. 2012. *Trains, Culture, and Mobility: Riding the Rails*. Lanham, MD: Lexington Books.

Frith, Simon. 1988. *Music for Pleasure*. Routledge: New York.

Frith, Simon. 1996. *Performing Rites. On the Value of Popular Music*. Oxford: Oxford University Press.

Gopinath, Sumanth. 2009. "The Problem of the Political in Steve Reich's *Come Out*." In *Sound Commitments: Avant-garde Music and the Sixties*, edited by Robert Adlington, 121–44. Oxford: Oxford University Press.

Kim, Rebecca Y. 1999. "From New York to Vermont: Conversation with Steve Reich." *Current Musicology* 67/68: 345–66.

Levitin, Daniel J. 2006. *This is Your Brain on Music: The Science of a Human Obsession*. New York: Plume.

Miklaszewska, Joanna. 2013. "Contemporary Music Documenting the Nazi Terror: Steve Reich's *Different Trains*." *Polish Journal of the Arts and Culture* 8, no. 5: 125–37.

Misemer, Sarah M. 2010. *Moving Forward, Looking Back: Trains, Literature and the Arts in the River Plate*. Lewisburg, PA: Bucknell University Press.

Presner, Todd S. 2007. *Mobile Modernity: Germans, Jews, Trains*. New York: Columbia University Press.

Puca, Antonella. 1997. "Steve Reich and Hebrew Cantillation." *Musical Quarterly* 81, no. 4: 537–55.

Reich, Steve. 1990. *Different Trains, Electric Counterpoint*. CD. New York: Nonesuch Records.

Reich, Steve. 1996. "My Life with Technology." *Contemporary Music Review* 13, no. 2: 13–21.

Reich, Steve. 2002a. "Chamber Music: An Expanded View." In *Writings on Music 1965–2000*, edited by Paul Hillier, 156–58. Oxford: Oxford University Press.

Reich, Steve. 2002b. "Music and Language." In *Writings on Music 1965–2000*, edited by Paul Hillier, 193–201. Oxford: Oxford University Press.

Reich, Steve. n.d. "Biography." http://www.stevereich.com/bio.html. Accessed 16 January 2015.

Reich, Steve, and Beryl Korot. 2002. *Three Tales*. Video documentary opera, premiere at Vienna Festival.

Sacks, Oliver. 2007. *Musicophilia: Tales of Music and the Brain*. New York: Knopf.

Schivelbusch, Wolfgang. 1979. *The Railway Journey: The Industrialization of Time and Space in the 19th Century*. Berkeley: University of California Press.

Schwarz, David. 1993. "Listening Subjects: Semiotics, Psychoanalysis, and the Music of John Adams and Steve Reich." *Perspectives of New Music* 31, no. 2 (Summer): 24–56.

Smith, Susan J. 1997. "Beyond Geography's Visible Worlds: A Cultural Politics of Music." *Progress in Human Geography* 21, no. 4: 502–29.

Smith, Susan J. 2000. "Performing the (Sound)world." *Environment and Planning D: Society and Space* 18, no. 5: 615–37.

Smith, Susan J. 2001. "Editorial: Emotional Geographies." *Transactions of the Institute of British Geographers* 26, no. 1: 7–10.

Spalding, Steven. 2014. "Railways and Urban Cultures." Special section of *Transfers: Interdisciplinary Journal of Mobility Studies* 4, no. 2: 42–130.

Spalding, Steven, and Benjamin Fraser, eds. 2012. *Trains, Literature, and Culture: Reading/Writing the Rails*. Lanham, MD: Lexington Books.

Thien, Deborah. 2005. "After or Beyond Feeling? A Consideration of Affect and Emotion in Geography." *Area* 37, no. 4: 450–56.

Trachtenberg, Alan. 1986. "Foreword." *The Railway Journey: The Industrialization of Time and Space in the 19th Century* by Wolfgang Schivelbusch, xiii–xvi. Berkeley: University of California Press.

Weiss, Rachel E. 2001. "Musical Persona: The Use of Human Speech in the Music of Steve Reich." MM Thesis in Music History, West Virginia University.

Williams, Raymond. 2007. "The Future of Cultural Studies." In *Politics of Modernism: Against the New Conformists*. 151–62. London; New York: Verso.

Wlodarski, Amy Lynn. 2010. "The Testimonial Aesthetics of *Different Trains*." *Journal of the American Musicological Society* 63, no. 1 (Spring): 99–141.

Wlodarski, Amy Lynn. 2015. *Musical Witness and Holocaust Representation*. Cambridge, UK: Cambridge University Press.

Wood, Nicola, Michelle Duffy, and Susan J. Smith. 2007. "The Art of Doing (Geographies of) Music. *Environment and Planning D: Society and Space* 25, no. 5: 867–89.

Wood, Nicola, and Susan J. Smith. 2004. "Instrumental Routes to Emotional Geographies." *Social and Cultural Geography* 5, no. 4: 533–48.

CHAPTER 3

A Genealogy of Apocalyptic Trains

Snowpiercer *(2013) and Its Precursors in the Transnational Literature of Transport*

John D. Schwetman

Bong Joon-ho's film *Snowpiercer* (2013) appeared on theater screens around the world in 2013 and received numerous glowing reviews from critics.[1] Loosely based on the 1982 French graphic novel *Transperceneige* by Jacques Lob and Jean-Marc Rochette ([1982] 2014), the Korean-French-US film takes place almost exclusively on board a massive train powered by a perpetual-motion engine in the year 2031. The premise of both the film and the graphic novel is peculiar for a science fiction story insofar as it hinges on an overtly implausible set of presumptions about mobility and small-scale ecosystems. The background for the story is that of a dystopian future in which a desperate effort to combat global warming by deploying a fictitious substance called CW-7 into the atmosphere works too well and dramatically lowers the Earth's temperature. Reminiscent of ice-nine in Kurt Vonnegut's novel *Cat's Cradle* ([1963] 1991), CW-7 makes global temperatures dangerously cold for all life. Current science supports the possibility of anthropogenic global freezing, at least in some regions, as a possible outcome of climate change, but the story's scientific basis becomes less plausible when we consider the desperate retreat of the last remaining survivors of this worldwide catastrophe to the refuge of a luxury train that hurtles around the Earth at high speeds over specially constructed rails. Despite its implausibility, the film successfully challenges traditional theories of mobility as movement between places by making the train into a perpetually moving dystopian community. The Snowpiercer fictionally literalizes Hannam, Sheller, and Urry's claim: "In the emerging mobilities paradigm places themselves can be seen as becoming or traveling, slowly or quickly, through greater and shorter distances and within networks of both human and non-human agents" (2006, 13).

There is, of course, no scientific basis for the perpetual motion engine powering the train or for the protection that it offers its passengers.

More-stationary accommodations rooted to the Earth would make far more sense as a means of surviving a climate apocalypse. Whichever perpetual motion machine it is that powers the train, it would far more efficiently warm a fixed complex of communities under domes or underground, as one might encounter in the films *THX 1138* (Lucas 1971), *Logan's Run* (Anderson 1976), *The City of Ember* (Kenan 2008), *The Hunger Games: Catching Fire* (Lawrence 2013), or dozens of other dystopian narratives. And, of course, the failures of the Biosphere 2 experiment in Arizona in 1993 and 1994 demonstrated that even modest fixed-foundation apocalypse-survival refuges for small groups of people might be logistically unachievable. Putting an enclosed ecosystem on wheels and racing it down a globe-circumnavigating track would make such a strategy even more impractical. Lob and Rochette's graphic novel *Le Transperceneige* offers a few hints about the train's function when the protagonist Proloff comments on the peculiar historical circumstances of a sudden global cooling event and outlines a conspiracy revolving around the survivors: "But *somehow,* there was a *luxury super-train* with an extraordinary engine—just sitting in a station ready to go. A prototype with unheard of endurance . . . and on-board facilities that bordered on the *providential.* Everything designed to resist the rigors of winter, and drive on indefinitely, forever, through the snow that no-one had believed would ever fall" (Lob and Rochette [1982] 2014, 65; emphasis in original).

The implication in Proloff's monologue is that the descriptions of a luxury super-train are part of an elaborate deception, that this was always a cover story for a dastardly scheme of the wealthy and powerful to destroy the climate and endure the consequences in the safety of their machine. Proloff adds, "Yes, a train *miraculously* ready to welcome the big shots, the military and the upper classes—along with all their families and inherited wealth. . . . Let's be *fair,* though: they made the effort at the last-minute for the rest of us—hastily adding on extra carriages. Third-class carriages . . . suitable only for last-minute squatters. The ones who weren't part of the plan!" (Lob and Rochette [1982] 2014, 65; emphasis in original).

The notion that they could simply add a few third-class carriages to a luxury survival train at the last minute pushes way beyond the bounds of scientific credibility, but scientific discrepancies are not a problem if the authors' priorities are more aesthetic and politically allegorical. Lob and Rochette's end-of-the-world scenario artfully posits the train as the result of, but also a microcosm for, a dystopian social order, and as a pointed allegory for the expansion and excesses of transnational power structures. In this sense, Lob and Rochette's Snowpiercer instantiates

Divall and Revill's Foucauldian theory of "transport throughout history as a practice heavily informed by and informing power" (2005, 101). When directing the 2013 film version of the story, Bong Joon-ho seizes on this narrative concept and selectively builds on the graphic novel's potent social commentary on the transnational dimensions of industrialization and class difference.[2]

Transnationalism provides a key underpinning to my reading of Bong Joon-ho's film for a few reasons: (1) The film itself is a product of transnationalism within the current film industry. (2) The *Snowpiercer* presents a cinematic allegory of transnational spaces and interactions. And (3) the apocalyptic landscape through which the Snowpiercer travels has gotten that way because of the work of a transnational scientific project that was able to alter the climate on a global scale. Transnationalism, as defined in Sanjeev Khagram and Peggy Levitt's introduction to *The Transnational Studies Reader: Intersections and Innovations* (2008), rejects the naturalization of national boundaries as determinants of group identity and action and also rejects the other extreme of a monolithic regime of globalization. Instead, transnationalism emphasizes "human social formations and processes [that] have always been trans-border and trans-boundary" (Khagram and Levitt 2008, 1); in other words, it enables locally distinct interactions to transgress traditional national boundaries. Such transnational interactions have provided a necessary precondition to the filming of *Snowpiercer,* when internationally recognized Korean director Bong Joon-ho encountered the French graphic narrative on which he based this film. The transnational impulse continued through the film's production by bringing together a cast of performers from South Korea, the United Kingdom, and the United States, on a film set constructed in the Czech Republic, and then through its international distribution, requiring an especially contentious effort to release the film in the United States through an agreement with The Weinstein Company, which pressed for alterations to Bong's storyline that he did not wish to make.[3] Of course, nearly all present-day cinema exists within a transnational framework, "circulating," as Elizabeth Ezra and Terry Rowden write, "more or less freely across borders and utilizing international personnel" (2006, 2). *Snowpiercer* is also transnational in terms of its narrative content, which Ezra anticipates when she writes, "In such works, loss and deterritorialization are often represented not as transitional states on the transnational subject's path to either transcendence or tragedy, but instead as more or less permanent conditions" (7). Thus, in its ceaseless journey around the world the Snowpiercer is a rail-riding *Flying Dutchman* that, like its maritime counterpart, condemns its passengers to life in a permanent state of exile from nationally determined origins that have lost their meaning in a world constructed primarily around transnational networks.

What follows in this chapter is an elaboration on various component elements evident in literary works leading up to Bong Joon-ho's film that come together in his allegorical commentary on our present world, which is to say, a genealogy of aesthetic and scientific impulses that exist in prior literary works and that coalesce into the images and ideas in the film. By considering this genealogy of apocalyptic trains in literature, I will develop the train as a literary icon of the Industrial Revolution and trace its development through the Information Age and, into the dystopian future of the Snowpiercer. In *The Railway Journey,* Wolfgang Schivelbusch ([1977] 2014) has gathered together a wide array of historical and literary texts to produce a nuanced account of what railroads have come to represent, and, in this chapter, I follow in Schivelbusch's footsteps to assemble more recent sources and elaborate on the significance of the apocalyptic railway journey. Schivelbusch has argued persuasively for the railroad's distinctive status as a symbol of a human-constructed environment, "the central character—a kind of technological Napoleon—in the epic of early industrialization" (xix). In considering the railroad as an icon of literature and film, one might regard any material degradation of the railroad as a symptom of larger-scale civic breakdown, but the railroad is also arguably a cause of such breakdowns. This contestable claim becomes more persuasive when one traces the genealogy of apocalyptic trains leading up to *Snowpiercer,* suggesting that the expansion of global capitalism across national boundaries will eventually violently undo itself.

One may categorize the various components of the apocalyptic railroad that come together in *Snowpiercer* as the Industrial Revolution and the logically resulting globalization of markets for manufactured goods, the class conflict that intensifies because of industry's facility for concentrating power in very few hands, the Biblical motif of Noah's ark, the destructive climax when the system finally collapses, and the ruin left behind to remind others of what has elapsed. These strands in literature and culture converge in the film *Snowpiercer* to produce a radical depiction of the railroad as a tool of human development and progress that is simultaneously a harbinger of humanity's destruction through a series of transnational interactions that expand a bubble of global economic development outward to its breaking point. I will, thus, examine each of these elements in turn, with close readings of prior apocalyptic texts that have etched them into the literary tradition leading up to *Snowpiercer.*

The Industrial Revolution and Globalization

The made-for-television movie *The Day After* was broadcast in November 1983 to a massive viewing audience that was primed for its story of nuclear apocalypse by decades of Cold War tension (Meyer 1983). The film takes place squarely in the American heartland—Kansas City, Missouri, and the nearby college town of Lawrence, Kansas. Viewers all knew in advance that this film would provide them with a grim, uncompromising account of a nuclear missile exchange between the United States and the Soviet Union and its aftermath, and that its cast of representative characters—a resourceful farmer, a doctor, and a college student—would suffer the loss of everything they held dear. It was thus imperative for the film's director Nicholas Meyer to capture America's prosperity and civilization in the film's opening montage. One year later, Ronald Reagan's presidential campaign would win reelection on the basis of a similar montage that made up his famous "Morning in America" commercial. The montage that runs behind the opening credits of *The Day After* provides a series of iconic evocations of the American experience, beginning in the lush farmland outside of Kansas City, with silos of grain competing with silos of missiles, and then, in a series of aerial and close-up shots, the montage slowly makes its way into the metropolis itself with its skyscrapers, its monuments, and its athletic fields.

As the helicopter-borne camera floats over Missouri and Kansas farmland, it swoops over a freight train bearing grain, and the train's mournful horn interrupts John Baskin's lyrical instrumental opening music. It is only a brief glimpse of the train, but it takes on special significance over the course of the movie as a key emblem of everything that the happy Americans in the opening montage are about to lose. When they suddenly grind to a halt later in the film, the automobiles, not the trains, manifest the first signs of the electromagnetic pulse that disables much of the modern world in the instant before the missile-borne atomic bombs fall. And, as the survivors begin to put the pieces together, they scavenge and rehabilitate old horse-drawn carriages to move around in their much-diminished postapocalyptic world. The military somehow gets its jeeps moving again, but the reestablishment of America's continent-spanning rail network strikes the viewer as a distant pipe dream. Its destruction is the true marker of the world's end as portrayed in this iconic film, and this makes even the briefest glimpse of a freight train during the film's opening montage significant. To reinforce the impossibility of the rehabilitation of industry, one of the climactic scenes in the film dramatizes a meeting in a destroyed church between farmers and a government official who offers them advice about planting crops in the newly irradiated landscape. As the farmers ask questions about the proposal that they scrape the top layer of radioactive soil before planting, it becomes clear that they are many, many years away from reconstituting the large-scale agricultural system that has suffered so much damage during the nuclear attacks, and of which the freight train with its bulging grain hoppers during the opening credits was the most potent emblem. Like other apocalyptic works, *The Day After* uses its portrayal of the railroad as a central element of what James Berger calls "the post-apocalyptic representational impasse" (1999, 13) at the heart of a literary subgenre that struggles endlessly against the problem that, "if apocalypse in its most radical form were to actually occur, we would have no way even to recognize it, much less to record it" (13). In other words, the world portrayed within *The Day After* could never itself produce a film like *The Day After.* It could never tell the story of the land of plentiful food harvests falling apart beneath a barrage of missiles.

In addition, the freight train in the opening montage is arguably somewhat complicit in the subsequent nuclear exchange. Wolfgang Schivelbusch is eloquent on the topic of the train as a mobilization and concentration of previously dispersed energies. This concentration of energy produces benefits in the short term, but it also has the unintended consequence of increasing the destructive potential of human energy. Railroad travel stitches smaller communities together into more harmonious larger ones, sometimes through a promise of economic rewards and at others through violent coercion. All transportation technologies do this, of course, but the railroad represents a significant and sudden leap forward in this area of activity, and becomes fixed as an icon for all industrial progress in Europe and the United States. In his historical account of the railroad as a literary and representational motif of larger trends, Schivelbusch also links early accounts of the railroad to anxieties about the power of this technology to sow the seeds of destruction by subjecting its passengers to heretofore unheard-of stresses and to produce spectacular accidents: "The technical apparatuses destroyed themselves by means of their own power. The energies tamed by the steam engine and delivered by it as regulated mechanical performance destroyed that engine itself in the case of accident. The increasingly rapid vehicles of transportation tended to destroy themselves and each other totally, whenever they collided" (Schivelbusch [1977] 2014, 131). In his terms, the destructive force of the railroad is part and parcel of its creative potential. There would be no extricating the risk of destruction from the power of movement on such a large scale. As John Urry argues in *Mobilities*, "Complex machine systems create big accidents when systems malfunction, unlike the small accidents when a walker falls, a horse dies or a coach overturns" (2007, 94). In the context of *Snowpiercer,* it is significant that Urry addresses this possibility of destruction as he sets forth the railroad's role in emergent notions of mobility in his theoretical analysis of the subject.

Thus, *The Day After* provides evidence of this movement toward destructive violence in the post–World War II era as the "energies tamed" (Schivelbusch [1977] 2014, 131) by global trade likewise increased the likelihood of global conflict. The film conveys this internationalization of conflict quite clearly from an opening scene that precedes that of the montage of American prosperity in the opening credits. The first image that the viewer encounters is of a military aircraft on the tarmac of a US Air Force base, in which the crew goes through its preflight reports. While some warplanes might bristle with machine guns, bombs, or guided missiles, this plane contains banks of computers, and the conversations that the viewers overhear upon entering this plane consist of mundane, vaguely evocative status updates. The heated language of battlefield combat gives way to the bureaucratic imperative to keep track of vast volumes of information. Thus, the quiet confines of the logistics-support aircraft belie its status as one of the most potent and destructive pieces of military technology of the Cold War as it directs nuclear missiles across international boundaries. Built on the rail-transport networks, the air-travel networks facilitate global trade in peacetime and give military leaders valuable tactical information in wartime. The international conflict that produces the apocalypse of *The Day After* results from the internationalization of concerted human activity in peaceful competitions over resources and global power, and in violent military disputes involving the intercontinental ballistic missiles—a central visual element of *The Day After*—that eventually displace human-piloted aircraft as a means of delivering atomic payloads.

When considering the global dimensions of transnational rail travel, one encounters the problem that rail travel initially developed within a national framework and focused primarily on the reliable conveyance of goods and passengers within the borders of a cohesive nation-state. As railroads developed in Europe, variations in clearances, track gauges, and eventually electrical power standards all served to reinforce national boundaries separating rail networks. Even international trains traversing Europe until recently had to stop at border stations to change engines and symbolically mark the transfer of jurisdiction and power from one nation-state to the next. The story of the late-twentieth and early twenty-first centuries has been the story of efforts to displace the old nationalist rail networks of Old Europe with a newly international network of high-speed trains bursting across national borders and even beneath the English Channel, the work of a newly unified Europe-wide body politic under the auspices of the European Union. The Snowpiercer, too, is the product of this internationalist impulse, particularly in Bong Joon-ho's film version, which populates its train perversely with multilingual, international passengers. I describe this as "perverse" because the film claims that these passengers have been dwelling exclusively within the close confines of their train for eighteen years without learning how to speak a common tongue. When Deputy Minister Mason (Tilda Swinton) delivers her first speech to the subaltern passengers of the tail section, her assistants begin a synchronous interpretation of her speech into French, Spanish, and Mandarin Chinese before she cuts them off, claiming that they do not have time to interpret. This sudden curtailment of interpretation gestures toward the Korean-US-French film production's reluctance, perhaps, to complicate the film's own linguistic landscape. In a later scene, Anglophone characters resort to computerized synchronous interpretation devices to communicate with a Korean-speaking passenger named Namgoong Minsoo (played by Song Kang-ho). In our present-day reality, the passengers' eighteen years of living together in tight quarters would tend to erode linguistic peculiarities, but, as I have already mentioned, this film is more allegorical than realistic, and the filmmakers clearly wanted to comment on globalization through these scenes. This impulse to engage with a transnational film audience correlates with another implausible plot element, which is that the Snowpiercer circumnavigates the globe and traverses six continents. The undifferentiated winter landscape outside of the train windows visually contradicts this claim as the train rockets across a frozen Everywhere that is just as much a frozen Nowhere. In this sense, the Snowpiercer represents an extreme instantiation of the extension of power outward through the technologies of the Industrial Revolution, an extension outward that has made local, regional, and, eventually, national boundaries irrelevant as factors in the distribution and concentration of goods and political influence.

Class Conflict

Very much related to the problem of industrialization and its globalizing movement outward to ever-larger market shares is the problem of class difference. It is not a coincidence that the era of the most assertive internationalization of commerce and culture in human history occurs at the same time as the emergence of the most intractable and enormous chasms between different economic classes; indeed, it is on the topic of social class difference and revolution that the film version of *Snowpiercer* produces its most effective and politically pointed allegory. Examining the earlier works constituting the genealogy of this strand in the *Snowpiercer* narrative, one may turn away from railroad stories and instead to the maritime narratives that make up much of the literature of travel in the nineteenth century. After all, the most influential authors of maritime stories recognized that each ocean-going vessel was a microcosm. Aboard a ship, all of the complex problems of the wider world could manifest themselves within a more schematic, pared-down community of a few dozen men. In maritime narratives, a hierarchical shipboard microcosm emerges because of three factors: (1) transporting people inevitably isolates them from larger communities on land; (2) transporting people eliminates distance between them, forcing them into close proximity with each other and raising the stakes in any conflicts that might occur; and (3) the extreme dangers of ocean travel exacerbate the harm resulting from any community conflicts, especially those involving violations of the command structure. Among the most effective representations of the ship as microcosm occurs in Herman Melville's "Billy Budd, Sailor," and these three factors all play a role in the plot of Herman Melville's posthumously published maritime legal drama about a naïve young sailor's murder of a more senior officer and his consequent trial and execution. Melville makes the case for the ship as simplified version of life on land in "Billy Budd" when explaining the cultures of men who live primarily onboard ships: "The sailor is frankness, the landsman is finesse. Life is not a game with the sailor, demanding the long head—no intricate games of chess where few moves are made in straight-forwardness and ends are attained by indirection, an oblique, tedious, barren game hardly worth the poor candle burnt out in playing it" ([1924] 1986, 336–37). In his novella, Melville makes this point about the sailor's lack of the landsman's social subtleties in order to explain conflicts between the sailor, Billy Budd, and his foe, the master-at-arms Claggart, but the work also exploits this point more generally to position events on the warship HMS *Bellipotent* as allegories for more complicated land-based communities. The ship serves as a sort of Petri dish within which readers encounter pared-down interactions across a complex hierarchy without the distracting details that so often clutter equivalent dramas in more realistic land-based communities outside of the literary work.

This same gesture is evident in *Snowpiercer* in both graphic-narrative and cinematic forms, and it is an element of the story that inspired director Bong Joon-ho to make the film. In Jesús Castro-Ortega's (2014) documentary film on the adaption of the story for graphic novel to screen, Bong states that part of what drew him to Lob and Rochette's graphic novel set in a moving train is "the structure of the space is the structure of narrative."[4] Maritime narratives likewise exploit architectural elements of the ship to connote power relations within the crew, and Melville's "Billy Budd, Sailor" does so persuasively in its opposition between the angelic men in the masts, like Billy Budd, and the less scrupulous denizens of the below-decks like Budd's nemesis Sergeant-at-Arms Claggart. The architecture of the railroad train in *Snowpiercer* replaces the vertical heaven/hell opposition of Melville's *Bellipotent* with the horizontally directed structure of sequential narrative. Trains are, after all, linear, just like the plot of a film, as Bong Joon-ho notes in his reference above to the structure of narrative. Furthermore, movement through the train is distinctly episodic—it contains clear intervals marked by the gaps between carriages, and, in Bong Joon-ho's imaginative version of the train, many of these gaps are locked gateways that can open only through the lock-breaking skills of Namgoong Minsoo, the gateways' designer. Whereas there may be multiple paths between different decks of a ship, the extreme linearity of the train deprives passengers of such alternative routes: anyone moving from one car to another must pass through the intervening cars. In Lob's graphic novel *Snowpiercer* ([1982] 2014), the rear-most cars of the train house a subaltern class, and the foremost cars house the aristocracy. As Proloff travels forward in the graphic novel, he must travel through every intervening social class in the hierarchy, as well as through cars housing every single function that keeps the society within the train sheltered, fed, heated, and law-abiding. Bong Joon-ho has simplified this linear hierarchy in his film while preserving the basic outlines. Resembling the plot of the book, the film follows Curtis Everett (Chris Evans) taking the place of the graphic novel's Proloff as he makes his way forward through the train and away from the abject misery of the rear-most cars. In the name of cinematic simplification, however, Bong has dispensed with the middle-class cars. His train consists primarily of the two extremes of the train's impoverished tail section and luxurious front section.

In the place of the more developed class commentary in the graphic narrative, Bong substitutes two descriptive monologues by the enforcers of social structure in the film's community within the speeding train. The first is by Mason, "a ruthless Margaret Thatcher stand-in with a prosthetic overbite" (Zacharek 2014), who responds to the incident of a subaltern passenger throwing a shoe at an aristocrat with a memorable oration about the social order: "We must all of us on this train of life remain in our allotted station. We must each of us occupy our preordained particular position. Would you wear a shoe on your head?"

(Bong 2013). Referring to the man as a shoe, she informs him that his "allotted station" is "on a foot," whereas she, being a hat, belongs "on a head." Her speech provides the blueprint for the social order that ties the train together in a single body politic, a social order that Mason will keep in place with the help of the armed guards who flank her during her speech. And, as she gives it, the audience sees the enactment of such law enforcement in the ritual of the shoe-throwing tail-ender's brutal public punishment, the freezing off of his right arm, which his punishers have immobilized and extended outside into the bitter cold through a hole in the side of the train.

When we hear a similar speech toward the film's conclusion, it is Wilford (Ed Harris), the train's creator and symbolic engineer, who delivers it from his luxury suite in the train's engine.[5] By this point, Curtis has completed his journey through the length of the train, having passed with Namgoong Minsoo's help through the many armed gauntlets and locked gateways that Wilford and Mason have placed as barriers between the tail-enders and any hope of social advancement in the forward cars of the train. Once Wilford has Curtis—his captive audience—before him, he says, "We are all stuck inside this blasted train. We are all prisoners in this hunk of metal. . . . And this train is a closed ecosystem. We must always strive for balance. Air, water, food supply, population must always be kept in balance" (Bong 2013). All of this is a preamble to Wilford's big reveal that he and Gilliam (John Hurt), the seemingly kind leader of the tail-section, have collaborated to maintain the balance within the train by orchestrating a series of violent uprisings in order to reduce the population of passengers. Wilford's reference to the train as a closed ecosystem that requires constant maintenance nicely echoes Wolfgang Schivelbusch's argument that, as railroads developed in the nineteenth century, they became a machine ensemble: "The machine ensemble, consisting of wheel and rail, railroad and carriage, expanded into a unified railway system, which appeared as one great machine covering the land" (Schivelbusch [1977] 2014, 29). In *Snowpiercer*, the machine has symbolically grown outward to contain the entire world, or, at least, the entire world of its passengers, and this expansion has made this world vulnerable to a single accident, as described in John Urry's theory of railroad mobility: "The powerful system can crash when a small part of it malfunctions" (2007, 94).

The film has produced some discussion of its potential political influence in at least one scholarly article titled "Living, Again: Population and Paradox in Recent Cinema," in which Keith Clavin argues that, in various discussions of threats posed by anthropogenic climate change, there has been a turn against serious consideration of overpopulation and remedies for overpopulation. He argues that this fear of discussing overpopulation is evident in two films: *Snowpiercer* (Bong 2013) and *Mad Max: Fury Road* (Miller 2010). Ethical anxieties about the topic have refocused the conversation on the topic of overconsumption: "The result is that overpopulation, despite its obvious links to the embodied, physical world, has been removed from our intellectual view" (Clavin 2016, 49). Clavin's concern is that, in the film, "it is the *villains* who are presented as sustainably-minded, especially in respect to population issues. Those with ultimate control over the tail section use that power to reduce and manage the population's size via violence and deception" (54; emphasis in original). Clavin's interpretation of *Snowpiercer* is quite different from mine; I would suggest that the film's manner of addressing overpopulation is not the accidental oversight that Clavin suggests it is. In contrast, the film's dystopian premise actively critiques a dark history of remedies for overpopulation. *Snowpiercer* satirizes those who in the past have opportunistically used concerns about overpopulation to provide an ideological cover of scientific objectivity over a program that is actually more about class warfare and ethnic cleansing. Clavin's analysis omits the detail that Wilford and Gilliam's population-control scheme was to end before the violence had reached the front section of the train, where it would endanger the upper classes. The film astutely satirizes the notion that sacrifices will be necessary to keep the population of the train in check, as long as such sacrifices remain solely the burden of the tail-section subalterns. Like most dystopian regimes, that of Wilford and Gilliam indulges in fantasies of social control that fail to correlate with the messy realities of social interactions within large populations, and their fantasies reinforce class divisions, thereby accelerating the course of destruction of the overall community. Whereas Clavin presents population control measures as a means of staving off the apocalypse, the film argues that such measures hasten the apocalypse because they reinforce the hubris that has led humanity down the destructive path of the control of human nature and of nature itself. Wilford and Gilliam's failed population control project thus finds its analogue in the failed climate control project that produced CW-7 and froze the Earth in the first place.

Noah's Ark

In the opening title card of Bong Joon-ho's film, he has established the context for events in his film by writing, "Soon after dispersing CW-7 the world froze. All life became extinct. The precious few who boarded the rattling ark are humanity's last survivors" (Bong 2013), and the term "ark" is of particular interest. It links events in this story back to another ocean-going vessel from a much earlier era than Melville's, that of the Old Testament. If Noah's ark is among the earliest imaginings of the technology of transportation in the Western tradition, then the story reminds us that, from the very beginning, this technology was an element of the apocalypse. And, like the Snowpiercer, the ark pushes the bounds of scientific reality by cramming an unreasonable quantity of people and animals into extremely tight quarters for a long time. The technical details of ark construction as they appear in the Book of Genesis (Revised Standard Version) are remarkably precise: "Make yourself an ark of gopherwood; make rooms in the ark and cover it inside and out with pitch. This is how you are to make it: the length of the ark three hundred cubits, its breadth fifty cubits, and its height thirty cubits" (Gen. 6:15). As God's commands continue, He elaborates on added dimensions and details and, as is well known, instructs Noah, "of every living thing of all flesh, you shall bring two of every sort into the ark, to keep them alive with you; they shall be male and female" (Gen. 6:19).[6] Allusions to Noah's ark are evident in Lob's graphic narrative in the specification that the Snowpiercer is 1001 carriages in length. The film does not mention the train's length, but Curtis's revolutionaries pass through various cars filled with plants and animals, most memorably a sumptuous aquarium car in which they stop for a bite of sushi made from the local sea life. The function of wildlife on the train to sustain the wealthier passengers, of course, differs from the function of the animals on Noah's ark, but the visual effect of an ark full of the Earth's various creatures is a common thread tying the two works together.

Unlike any other ship, Noah's enormous ark would have lacked a propulsion mechanism. After all, it was not so much means of transport as it was a means simply of staying above the floodwaters. As an ark, the Snowpiercer of Bong Joon-ho's film likewise refrains from playing the role that one would typically associate with trains, which is that of getting its passengers to a destination. This makes it an extremely perverse train, one that has itself become a sort of mobile destination for its passengers. The train does, of course, go places, but the film offers contradictory explanations of the terrain across which the train moves. Namgoong Minsoo sees the fuselage of a crashed plane beneath the tracks every year on the same day, and his daughter uses a similar mental calendar to anticipate a long tunnel that plunges the passengers into darkness at a climactic moment in the film. This suggests that the train completes one rotation around its circular route per year, and it is highly suggestive of a globally circumnavigational track for the train. However, in the train's classroom car full of eager schoolchildren, a short video describes the train, and its route briefly becomes visible. Instead of circumnavigating the globe equatorially, the train squiggles across six inhabited continents in a wildly different trajectory, as if to cover as many different regions as possible. It goes everywhere and nowhere, as, one supposes, any ark would. It moves for the sake of moving, and not to actually transport its passengers. Just as Noah's ark keeps its passengers afloat in the flooded world, the Snowpiercer ensures its passengers' survival above an equally cataclysmic frozen flood.

Destruction

Among the *Snowpiercer* film's more dramatic departures from the graphic novel is the destruction of the train at the film's conclusion. Lob and Rochette's Snowpiercer continues on its journey at the end of Volume 1 with Proloff running the engine in the graphic novel, but Bong Joon-ho opts to derail the train and bring its journey to a sudden end soon after Curtis completes his journey from the train's tail to its engine. This directorial decision suggests an impulse to deliver an explosive finale to a formulaic action movie. The train derails because of an onboard explosion resulting from various outbreaks of violent combat between passengers caught up in "The Great Curtis Revolution." Somewhat arbitrarily, as violent battles rage, Namgoong Minsoo's daughter Yona (Ko Ah-sung) blows the door off of the engine with a wad of the explosive substance Kronole, which is also a mind-altering drug, and this triggers an avalanche in the surrounding mountains that knocks the Snowpiercer off of its rails. It is one of the film's more significant implausibilities. Considering that the train has been noisily rumbling through this snowy, mountainous setting for eighteen years, it is, at the very least, an incredible coincidence that this little explosion in the engine, just after Curtis has reached the front of the train, should be the trigger to a train- and humanity-ending catastrophe. Indeed, the utter implausibility of this turn of events suggests that Bong Joon-ho was motivated by the spectacle of the destruction of the train onscreen and reveals his fascination with another element in the genealogy of apocalyptic trains: the train accident itself as an icon of large-scale calamity.

History is replete with fiery railroad accidents onscreen and off, but one of the most powerful occurs in Steven Spielberg's 2005 film *War of the Worlds* in a scene that strongly echoes an event in H. G. Wells's original 1898 novel by the same name. In Wells's novel, the protagonist notices a destroyed train in a landscape devastated by a Martian invasion. As this unnamed protagonist looks out over a neighborhood near the train station at Woking, he sees an alarming sight: "The light upon the railway puzzled me at first; there were a black heap and a vivid glare, and to the right of that a row of yellow oblongs. Then I perceived this was a wrecked train, the fore part smashed and on fire, the hinder carriages still upon the rails" (Wells [1898] 1999, 50). At this moment in Wells's novel, his unnamed protagonist surveys the destruction wrought by the invading Martians, and the wreckage of the railroad looms in the foreground of this panorama. This now-disabled human transport technology motivates the protagonist to expand his understanding of the invaders as entities that may share with humanity a cyborg-like, intricate relationship with machines: "I began to ask myself what they could be. Were they intelligent mechanisms? Such a thing I felt was impossible. Or did a Martian sit within each, ruling, directing, using, much as a man's brain sits and rules in his body? I began to compare the things to human machines, to ask myself for the first time in my life how an ironclad *or a steam engine* would seem to an intelligent lower animal" (Wells [1898] 1999, 51; emphasis added). In moments like this, Wells makes it clear that he means his Martian invasion to serve as allegorical variant on the technologies of industry and military conquest that have enabled Western powers to subjugate much of the rest of the world in the nineteenth century.

In his film version, Spielberg includes an analogous scene as the protagonist (Tom Cruise) and his two children attempt to flee to safety across the Hudson River from New Jersey. As they approach the ferry landing, they must cross some railway tracks, and the crossing gate suddenly descends before them. In one of the most haunting scenes of the film, an Amtrak train races through the crossing, and it is in flames. In his mostly negative review of the film, Roger Ebert singles this scene out as one of the few effective ones: "There is an unforgettable image of a train, every coach on fire, roaring through a station" (2005). Critic Todd Alcott provides a plausible explanation for what makes this scene so uncanny when he writes, "The train passing through town is *on fire*. It rockets through the center of town and the crowd, who has seen plenty of weird stuff in the past 24 hours, *pays no attention to it*. No one comments, no one even gives it a second look" (2008; emphasis in original). It is, however, also important that this train, like the train in the opening of *The Day After*, is an icon of the vast machine ensemble of the Industrial Revolution. This singular flaming train instantiates the destruction of the entire system. In this brief moment, the viewer must wonder how many fail-safes would have malfunctioned to allow a train to catch on fire and continue to speed down the track. More hauntingly, the rival machinery of the alien invaders has coopted the train and given it a new, mysterious purpose that is independent of the human volition of the people who had once controlled it. Humanity's industrial-era technology has given it incredible control over its environment, but at this moment the risk of cooption overshadows that power. Any hostile force could turn such technology against its own creators as the flaming train in *War of the Worlds* foretells.

Ruin

The final scene of Bong Joon-ho's *Snowpiercer* leaves viewers with an image of the wrecked train strewn across a snowy, mountainous expanse while the accident's only two survivors make their way into a forbidding landscape. The train, it seems, will lie there for eons to come, and mark the catastrophe that has accompanied humanity's final gasp. This element finds a precedent in Cormac McCarthy's 2006 novel *The Road*, which famously depicts the apocalypse with reference to the automotive transportation indicated in the title. It frequently mentions the accoutrements of highway travel—roadmaps, highways, gas stations, and so on—as the unnamed protagonist and his son slowly walk south across a mostly depopulated wasteland. At a certain point in the narrative, McCarthy's main characters come across a train, and, in a few terse paragraphs, McCarthy turns the train into an emblem of a decayed assemblage of formerly moving parts, Schivelbusch's already mentioned machine ensemble. For McCarthy's protagonist and his son sitting in the engine's cab, the train's immobility provides a powerful symbol of the collapse of the entire system: "After a while they just looked out through the silted glass to where the track curved away in the waste of weeds. If they saw different worlds what they knew was the same. That the train would sit there slowly decomposing for all eternity and that no train would ever run again" (McCarthy 2006, 180). Because the railroad is such a massive and complex system, all hope of reconstructing it is lost. The immobile corpse of a train manifests the smaller-scale breakdowns that have doomed its passengers and all future passengers: "This is probably where they ran out of fuel" (179). The protagonist imagines a small group of people desperately setting this train in motion in a futile effort to escape the unnamed disaster that has destroyed their world. The train fails them by running out of fuel, reminding readers that, in a large, complex system, the failure of one component can produce systemwide failure. Thus, severed from the larger context that once made movement possible, the train stands as a ghastly remnant, a ruin, a monument to the industrial order that these characters have lost.

An even more intricate monument to this order emerges at the end of China Miéville's 2004 novel *Iron Council,* which is the final work in his Bas-Lag trilogy. The first of Miéville's steam-punk works takes place in the massive city of New Crobuzon, and the second onboard a ship; the third explores the open, untamed expanses of territory surrounding New Crobuzon, a territory across which the leftist Iron Council constructs its peculiar railroad. The whimsical and allegorical characteristics of Miéville's steam-punk universe compel readers to regard their own present-day realities with new eyes, and trains make up a key element of Miéville's challenge to readers' expectations. In our world, the existence of a persistent, rooted nation-state is a necessary precondition to the construction of a railroad network, but, in Miéville's twisted allegory, the Iron Council, a tiny splinter group of revolutionaries, is able to coopt the railroad as a platform for a counter-government insurgency. As the train roams across the wastes outside of New Crobuzon, the Iron Council's members dismantle rails in the train's wake and assemble new track in front of the train, and this liberates the train from any larger network or dependence on a larger nation-state, making it, arguably, a fictionally transnational distortion of an otherwise nationalist enterprise. In other words, Miéville has created a train that is as unreasonable as the Snowpiercer, devoid of the functions and limitations that one would typically associate with trains, all for the purpose of presenting readers a playful allegorical commentary on what rail travel represents by defining it in the negative.

Like the Snowpiercer in Bong Joon-ho's film, the Iron Council's train stops moving at the work's end. In one of Miéville's bolder and more perplexing narrative feats, his major character Judah constructs a time golem, a mystical, vaguely anthropomorphic entity that erupts around the train as it makes its way on a suicide mission to retake the city of New Crobuzon. Judah wants to prevent his friends on the Iron Council from the certain death that awaits them if they continue their mission, so his time golem surreally removes the train from time, leaving it completely immobilized on the track near the city: "The perpetual train. The Iron Council itself. The renegade, returned, returning and now waiting. Absolutely still. Absolutely unmoving in the body of the time golem. The train, its moment indurate" (Miéville 2004, 542). As a result of this magical incursion, the Iron Council's train promises to be, for ages to come, a static monument to a machine and its support system that once moved so many people and goods across the planet. Miéville's novel thus joins McCarthy's novel to provide the final piece of the assemblage that produces the apocalyptic train at the heart of Bong Joon-ho's *Snowpiercer,* which is the static monument to annihilation.

Representations of the apocalypse, as James Berger has noted, will always exist in a contradictory space. If an apocalypse is complete, then there will be no one around to remember it, so apocalyptic fictions must resort to imaginative anticipation to convey "the idea of post-apocalypse, of modes of expression made in the wake of catastrophes so over-whelming that they seem to negate the possibility of expression at the same time that they compel expression" (1999, 5). Bong Joon-ho's film leaves its viewers with the image of an apocalyptic monument in the form of the wrecked Snowpiercer, a monument that yokes the railroad's transformative power to its destructive potential in one contradictory amalgam of movement and stasis. This monument is one that, by the terms of the film, nobody is likely ever to see. The film itself is, of course, another such monument. It harnesses the power of allegory to enable viewers to bear witness to the aftermath of the apocalypse from the more comfortable vantage point of the pre-apocalypse. This game of perspective is, thus, what ultimately allows the film to transcend its sci-entific and narrative inconsistencies and to captivate viewers with im-agery that is uniquely suited to an age obsessed with its own decline and annihilation.

John D. Schwetman is associate professor of English at the University of Minnesota Duluth, where he specializes in twentieth-century liter-ature. He has recently published an article on Kazuo Ishiguro's *Never Let Me Go* and book chapters on American authors John Steinbeck and Ernest Hemingway. His article "Harry Beck's Underground Map: A Convex Lens for the Global City" appeared in the spring 2014 issue of *Transfers: Interdisciplinary Journal of Mobility Studies*, Special Issue on Rails and the City. At present, he is working on a book on regionalism in the twentieth-century US road novel titled *Far from Home*, address-ing works by John Steinbeck, Jack Kerouac, Zora Neale Hurston, and Vladimir Nabokov.

Notes

1. Peter Sobczynski (2014) writes that the film "is never less than stunning." A.O. Scott (2014) writes favorably of the film's "volatile blend of humor and horror that pays tribute to the source material while coloring its themes with the direc-tor's distinctively perverse and humane sensibility." Not all critics are united in favor of the film, however. Stephanie Zacharek (2014) writes, "Even as dystopian dramas go, the picture is arid and lusterless in its more serious moments and unpleasantly kitschy when it tries to soar over the top."

2. In his review of *Snowpiercer*, critic Scott Ashlin of the website *1000 Misspent Hours and Counting* supports my claim that a train is a less logical haven from

climate devastation than a dome would be. Ashlin (2014) argues that the decision to situate events on a train is integral to Bong Joon-ho's goal to use his film
to critique Ayn Rand's *Atlas Shrugged*, which likewise revolves around futuristic
high-speed trains, and he makes a persuasive point that the character Mason
(Tilda Swinton) is a caricature of Rand herself.

3. For more information on this conflict, see Rayns (2014).
4. Bong Joon-ho says this in "*Transperceneige*: From the Blank Page to the Black
   Screen" (Castro-Ortega 2014), a film documentary directed by Jesús Castro-
   Ortega about the adaptation of the graphic novel into the film.
5. In Lob and Rochette's graphic novel, the engine takes on an even loftier status
   because of a cult of engine worshipers who venerate the very front of the train,
   dubbing it "Saint Loco" (Lob and Rochette [1982] 2014, 47).
6. In an analysis of the role of apocalypse in the film *Children of Men* (Cuarón
   2006), Marcus O'Donnell establishes intriguing links between Biblical apocalypses such as the one that compels Noah to construct the ark, and the secular
   apocalypses of films like *Snowpiercer*. O'Donnell suggests that Alfonso Cuarón's
   influential film ends with its own sort of ark: a ship called *Tomorrow* that provides "a productive place where worldmaking is still possible" (2015, 27).

References

Alcott, Todd. 2008. "Movie Night with Urbaniak: *War of the Worlds, What Does the
Protagonist Want?*" 24 May. http://www.toddalcott.com/?s=war+of+the+worlds.
Accessed 12 April 2017.

Anderson, Michael, dir. 1976. *Logan's Run*. Metro-Goldwyn-Mayer, Beverly Hills, CA.

Ashlin, Scott. 2014. "*Snowpiercer: 1000 Misspent Hours and Counting*." http://www
.1000misspenthours.com/reviews/reviewsn-z/snowpiercer.htm. Accessed 30
April 2017.

Berger, James. 1999. *After the End: Representations of Post-Apocalypse*. Minneapolis:
University of Minnesota Press.

Bong, Joon-Ho, dir. 2013. *Snowpiercer*. CJ Entertainment, Seoul, South Korea.

Castro-Ortega, Jesús, dir. 2014. "*Transperceneige*: From the Blank Page to the Black
Screen." Disc 2. *Snowpiercer*. DVD. Beverly Hills, CA: Anchor Bay.

Clavin, Keith. 2016. "Living, Again: Population and Paradox in Recent Cinema." *Oxford
Literary Review* 38, no. 1 (July): 47–65.

Cuarón, Alfonso, dir. 2006. *Children of Men*. Universal Pictures, Universal City, CA.

Divall, Colin, and George Revill. 2005. "Cultures of Transport: Representation, Practice
and Technology." *Journal of Transport History* 26, no. 1: 99–111.

Ebert, Roger. 2005. "*War of the Worlds*." RogerEbert.com, 28 June. www.rogerebert
.com/reviews/war-of-the-worlds-2005. Accessed 19 April 2017.

Ezra, Elizabeth, and Terry Rowden. 2006. "General Introduction." In *Transnational
Cinema: The Film Reader*, edited by Elizabeth Ezra and Terry Rowden, 1–12.
London: Routledge.

Hannam, Kevin, Mimi Sheller, and John Urry. 2006. "Editorial: Mobilities, Immobilities
and Moorings." *Mobilities* 1, no. 1: 1–22. DOI: 10.1080/17450100500489189

Kenan, Gil, dir. 2008. *The City of Ember*. Playtone, Santa Monica, CA.

Khagram, Sanjeev, and Peggy Levitt, eds. 2008. *The Transnational Studies Reader:
Intersections and Innovations*. New York: Routledge.

Lawrence, Francis, dir. 2013. *The Hunger Games: Catching Fire*. Color Force, West Hollywood, CA.

Lob, Jacques, and Jean-Marc Rochette. (1982) 2014. *Snowpiercer, Volume 1: The Escape*. Translated by V. Selavy. London: Titan Comics.

Lucas, George, dir. 1971. *THX 1138*. American Zoetrope.

McCarthy, Cormac. 2006. *The Road*. New York: Vintage Press.

Melville, Herman. (1924) 1986. "Billy Budd, Sailor." In *Billy Budd, Sailor and Other Stories*, 287–385. New York: Penguin.

Meyer, Nicholas, dir. 1983. *The Day After*. ABC Circle Films, New York.

Miéville, China. 2004. *Iron Council*. New York: Del Rey Press.

Miller, George, dir. 2010. *Mad Max: Fury Road*. Warner Brothers, Burbank, CA.

O'Donnell, Marcus. 2015. "*Children of Men*'s Ambient Apocalyptic Visions." *Journal of Religion and Popular Culture* 27, no. 1: 16–30.

Rayns, Tony. 2014. "Blockage on the Line." *Sight and Sound* 24, no. 1: 38–40.

Schivelbusch, Wolfgang. (1977) 2014. *The Railway Journey: The Industrialization of Time and Space in the Nineteenth Century*. Berkeley: University of California Press.

Scott, A. O. 2014. "Stuck in Steerage for the Apocalypse." *New York Times*, 26 June 2014. https://www.nytimes.com/2014/06/27/movies/in-snowpiercer-the-train-trip-to-end-all-train-trips.html. Accessed 19 April 2017.

Sobczynski, Peter. 27 June 2014. "*Snowpiercer*." *RogerEbert.com*. http://www.roger ebert.com/reviews/snowpiercer-2014. Accessed 19 April 2017.

Spielberg, Steven, dir. 2005. *War of the Worlds*. Paramount Pictures, Hollywood, CA.

Urry, John. 2007. *Mobilities*. Cambridge, UK: Polity Press.

Vonnegut, Kurt. (1963) 1991. *Cat's Cradle*. New York: Dell Press.

Wells, H. G. (1898) 1999. *The War of the Worlds*. Norwalk, CT: Heritage Press.

Zacharek, Stephanie. 2014. "After the Crash, Grim *Snowpiercer* and Its Trains Keep Grinding Along." *Village Voice*, 25 June. http://www.villagevoice.com/film/after-the-crash-grim-snowpiercer-and-its-trains-keep-grinding-along-6442259. Accessed 19 April 2017.

CHAPTER 4

Dangerous Borders

Modernization and the Gothic Mode in
Pánico en el Transiberiano *(1972)* and Howl *(2015)*

Fernando Gabriel Pagnoni Berns and Juan Juvé

The horror film is one of the most subversive texts since it is inherently critical of traditional values and is a disruptor of societal structures. Furthermore, the horror genre is "the struggle for recognition of all that our civilization represses or oppresses, its reemergence dramatized, as in our nightmares, as an object of horror" (Wood 2004, 113). Using the figure of the repressed, horror film (and horror fiction in general) intersects with the Gothic: a genre, an aesthetic, and a narrative mode that highlight the Freudian notion of the uncanny and resist scientific reason, seemingly innocuous social progress, and the unstoppable advance of technology. Both the fantastic and the Gothic "invert perceptions, create ambivalence, and transgress binary oppositions by acknowledging the repressed negative within every positive" (Morris 2001, 188).

Horror fiction and the Gothic illustrate how modern thought, advancements in technology, and a global world cannot erase the old, uncanny imagination filled with monsters and fears. In this sense, the Gothic is the dark companion of the dreary advancement of technology and its potential for alienation and destruction. Furthermore, Gothic is transnational in nature: it works through the notion of borders (inside and outside, past and present, night and day, normal and abnormal, etc.), but its heart lies in the blurring of them. Through the Gothic, borders collapse, and with them, all hierarchies. The possibility of being revolutionary for the Gothic is the possibility of the disruption of the boundaries marking difference. In this scenario, the transnational aspect of modernization, shrinking time and space, works to enhance the Gothic. Nobody is safe from rubbing shoulders with different classes, races, religions, and cultures. Otherness becomes fascinating in modernity and, as such, dangerous, owing precisely to its power to attract. Both the Gothic and modernity (and within modernity, transnational travel) work against the closed body. In this sense, "Gothic fiction is understood as part of a broader cultural history in which the circulation of fictional fears takes place within a range of institutional contexts" (Botting and Townshend 2004, 16).

Anxieties about the wholeness of the collective body—what constitutes the human race, the nation-state—become anxieties about the idea of subjectivity. The problematic of transgression at the level of flesh and blood parallels the concerns about the protection of a culture's boundaries (Cavallaro 2002, 200). Thus, transgression of borders features prominently within Gothic fiction. Euro-horror, an ambiguous, incoherent, and open body of diverse films constructed in a transnational way through the politics of coproduction between European countries, can thus be deemed Gothic in nature. Transnational films always speak about anxieties about borders, citizenship, and national belonging. It is really hard to pinpoint where one nation and culture end and where the next begins within a concrete coproduced film.

The term "transnational" is a useful tool for studying the cinema of small nations and Euro-horror films especially, since many of the filmic productions under this umbrella were, as mentioned above, funded by two or more countries. Nataša Ďurovičová establishes interesting distinctions among geographical and theoretical definitions. For her, the term "transnational" has since the late 1980s shifted from signaling the permeability of borders to become a replacement for the adjective international. "In contradistinction to 'global,' a concept bound up with the philosophical category of totality" (like ambiguously belonging to the entire world), and "in contrast with 'international,' predicated on political systems in a latent relationship of parity, as signaled by the prefix 'inter-,' the intermediate and open term 'transnational' . . . implies relations of unevenness and mobility" (2010, ix–x). Here, we find an interesting intersection with the Gothic: rather than privileging one part and the limits delimiting it, the Gothic, modernity, and the transnational mode of coproduction among countries enhance openness. Rather than just reflect some concrete social and cultural context, the monstrosity and social anxieties illustrated in a given film ambiguously respond to more complex modes of production, circulation, and reception. As Paolo Boccagni argues, the transnational mode implies "an inbetweenness of social practices linking different local contexts, but not strictly reducible to any of them" (2012, 120), thus provoking a downplaying of geographical hierarchies.

The presence of trains and long-distance travel as important narrative devices in transnational films can work to enhance this Gothic and transnational structure. Framed by a fantastic framework, discussions about mechanization, modernization and social class are turned into a dark fantasy about uncanny trains and fears of obsolescence, both human and mechanical. As Tomasik (2007) argues, railways, always attached to precision, mechanization, and progress, are equally attached, in a negative way, to the efficiency of the Final Solution and, in consequence, to horror and annihilation. Also, the passage from animal power as the source of mobility in favor of steam or combustible was experienced as "loss of the sense of space and motion" (Schivelbusch 1986, 23), thus enhancing the feeling of ethereality so akin to the Gothic: indeed the "annihilation of space and time was the early-nineteenth-century characterization of the effect of railroad travel" (33). This process of annihilation granted by transnational travel, arguably, is one of the ultimate effects of the Gothic mode and aesthetics. In this sense, the tropes represented in the Gothic mode coincide with the claims of philosophical transnationalism, which assumes an ontological and epistemological position according to which the world is mainly transnational. While not denying the existence of frontiers, borders, and identities, transnationalism highlights their ephemeral nature as mere human social and ideological constructs. The figure of the train was fundamental to both modernity and the Gothic, since the development of railroad travel diminished time and space, leading to new perceptions of reality. "The space between the points was destroyed . . . they lost their sense of local identity, formerly determined by the spaces between them" (Schivelbusch 1986, 38).

Euro-horror often features trains as a backdrop. While some films use the figure of trains and travel as a minor feature, such as the Spanish-Portuguese coproduction *La Noche del Terror Ciego* (*Tombs of the Blind Dead;* Ossorio 1972) or the Italian film *Non ho Sonno* (*Sleepless;* Dario Argento, 2001), other films place trains and transnational travel at the core of the story. In this chapter we will analyze two examples of Euro-horror films that play on the enclosed, claustrophobic space of the train, long-distance travel, and an uncanny, feral exterior.

Pánico en el Transiberiano (*Horror Express;* Martín 1972) takes place in 1906, in Manchuria, when a British anthropologist (Christopher Lee) discovers a frozen prehistoric creature and decides to transport it to Europe aboard the Trans-Siberian express. During the trip the monster thaws out and starts to kill the passengers one by one. As a coproduction between Spain and the United Kingdom, the film highlights trans-nationality and a sense of Otherness. While trains, like other systems of mobility, "significantly played their part in institutionalizing the stratified class system" (Urry 2007, 104), the film also evokes scientific progress—forensic science, anthropology, the train itself—against a backdrop of blind obscurantism (especially illustrated in religion and in feudal political systems), and the supernatural. Many decades later, the British film

Howl (Hyett 2015) tells the story of a series of rail passengers facing the attack of werewolves lurking in a forest after their train breaks down under a full moon. One of the film's themes is the clash of civilizations: the modern train squares off against barbaric forces represented by the forest and its atavistic beasts in a context in which railway culture has become a common element in the daily life of Europeans. By examining the role of modernization and globalism in these two horror films we show how the archaic mind appears here as the twisted Gothic reflection of modernity and transnationality.

Transnational Railway Cultures in *Pánico en el Transiberiano*

It is not by chance that the story of Martín's *Pánico en el Transiberiano* (1972) takes place at the turn of the century in a setting marked by signs of modernism and technological prowess. The fin de siècle setting recalls an era dominated by uncertainty and a fear "so great and ominous" (Hogle 2001, 153) of what could come. The turn-of-the-century Gothic laid claim to the geographies occupied by late nineteenth-century science through its depictions of technological wonders like the train. In fact, "the image of the trauma of modern civilization was closely associated with the train at the turn of the century" (Gilman 1995, 125) and the train became an embodiment of the malaises that came with the acceleration of modern life. The railroad and railway accidents can be seen as causes of hysteria and mental problems. One of the first films in the history of horror cinema, Austrian-German coproduction *Orlacs Hände* (*The Hands of Orlac,* Robert Wiene, 1924) revolves around the hysterical trauma, loss of confidence, and murderous urges that result from a train collision involving the main character. Wolfgang Schivelbusch mentions how anxiety about the experience of train travel was a haunting transnational part of new pathologies in the nineteenth century. New, continuous mechanical vibrations produced "persistent pains" and a "feeling of weakness and numbness" (Schivelbusch 1986, 115) in workers and passengers alike. The rapidity of the trains caused fatigue in the sense organs "to a much greater degree than did pre-industrial travel" (117) and an increase in psychological stress. Travelers suffered from chronic fatigue as a consequence of recurrent use of train travel and the victims of railroad accidents were affected both physically and emotionally by enduring shock. "By the end of the 1880s, the concept of 'railway spine' had been replaced by that of 'traumatic neurosis'" (136). The fact of traveling by train was itself, regardless of the circumstances, a cause of neurotic fatigue and other pathologies.

Martín's transnational travel in *Pánico en el Transiberiano* (1972) forms the setting for a horrifying encounter with national, cultural, and scientific boundaries that, once transgressed, have their very existence called into question. Martín's representation of a hallucinatory and angst-ridden transnational ride foregrounds mechanization and technology, and the presence of the flâneur—a distinctive figure of modernist subjectivity (Duffy 2009, 141)—marks the film as modern. We argue, however, that it also connects to the Gothic tradition through its use of characteristic Gothic tropes, such as monstrosity and vampirism, and its preoccupation with different types of "blurred boundar[ies] with the foreign and a softened hierarchy" (Riquelme 2015, 120). These are crucial generic signposts directing straight to a powerful Gothic legacy at work, which is not surprising if we keep in mind that the United Kingdom, part of the coproduction along with Spain, is a country with strong roots in the history of the Gothic.

Fears over the porosity of borders framed the real history of the planning and construction of the Trans-Siberian, a transnational venture. Unlike most of Europe, "which had slowly embraced liberalism to accommodate the different needs of industrial growth and developments of technology," travel in Russia was "circumscribed by the state to such an extent that rail passengers needed internal passports to travel around the country" (Wolmar 2013, 17). The act of opening frontiers to the transnational involved passengers, and also fostered the circulation of ideas, a considerable concern for a poverty-stricken feudal monarchy as Russia was at the time. Although the tsars "wanted to strengthen Russia through closer economic relations with the rest of Europe, they feared that nineteenth-century Europe's increasingly volatile mixture of democratic, nationalist, and Marxist ideas would infect Tsarist society" (Parrot and Kudelia 2011, 221). Thus, the trespassing of borders, turned more vulnerable thanks to technology, was a real cause for concern. As a technology, mobility was a way of revealing, or opening up Russia to the world. The idea of "opening to the infection" of democratic ideas if distances are shortened and boundaries softened follows closely on the Gothic fear of infection as a symptom of imperial decline "detrimental to modernity" (Hoglund 2014, 146).

Also, Russia was not a society particularly interested in the railways (Wolmar 2013, 27), so there was little sense of urgency in building the Trans-Siberian. As an 1868 article appearing in *The Railway News and Joint-Stock Journal* argued, Russia suffered "unpardonable carelessness" at the moment of fomenting the building of railways ("Railways in Russia" 1868, 511). There was another problem: the severe climate typical of the territory of Siberia offered little to attract potential immi-

grants who would be needed to justify the substantial cost of constructing the railway. Even though Western European notions of Siberia as
dominated by freezing-cold temperatures is, in fact, slightly misleading
(Wolmar 2013, 20), average figures could fall to −25°C or worse. To accompany this idea, the opening shot of *Pánico en el Transiberiano* is
that of a desolate, alien landscape of ice and frozen mountains. With this
introductory image, the film establishes both the geographical location
and a sense of solitude framing the film. Schivelbusch argues that the
empirical reality observed from a window's train was perceived as belonging "to another world" (1986, 24) as the old perception of landscape
and motion answered to the slow power of animals which followed
the contours of the terrain rather than "discipline" it as technology did.
The "unnatural" (24) feeling, arguably, was enhanced by the progression
into transnationality as people stepped, in fact, into foreign worlds. One
thing is left clear for audiences: if there is horror within the train, there is
no escape to the outside, a motif that the film shares with *Howl* (Hyett
2015). In both, the passengers are a far cry from any concept of civilization. They are snobbish, misogynistic, and cruel to each other, but the
outside—made up of frozen landscapes or haunted forests populated by
werewolves—does not give shelter to humanity either. The train, thus,
whether magnificent (*Pánico en el Transiberiano*) or modern (*Howl*), is
unable to contain or protect from the horror of the outside. Here, we
observe the vulnerability of a hierarchy: the opposition inside/outside is
proven vulnerable, as both spaces are coopted by horror.

Martín's film (1972) begins in Szechuan, in Manchuria—a contested
geographical borderland where China, Russia, and Japan were the main
competitors—in the year 1906. According to Anthony Heywood, the
epic construction of the Trans-Siberian railway tends toward exotic im-
agery (1999, 16). The latter is expressed in the film when Doctor Wells
(Peter Cushing) argues that his presence aboard the Trans-Siberian is
due to the simple fact that he loves strange places, without further elaboration. His interest lies clearly in transnational exoticism. *Pánico en el
Transiberiano* begins with a voiceover (Christopher Lee, as geologist
Alexander Saxton) that sustains a scientific framework: Saxton speaks
directly to the British society of geology, to whom he will relate the
events surrounding the expedition that took place in the Manchurian
landscapes. There, an expeditionary group led by Saxton found a frozen corpse, seemingly of a prehistoric man, in a cave. The corpse is
boxed up and transported to the station and the Trans-Siberian. Cut to
the station in Beijing (called Peking in the film). It is interesting that the
film establishes in just two scenes a set of opposites that go from the
prehistoric as a signpost of the past (the frozen creature) to the new era

of scientific inquiry. The latter is embodied not only in the geological expedition but also in the image of the train, which figures prominently in wide shots that emphasizes its size and powerful presence. The film has compactly foregrounded many topics running through the story: the Gothic trope of the legacy of the past and its burden on the present in the figure of the frozen corpse, and a sense of impending doom— Saxton, in the introduction, specifies that the expedition and the discovery ended terribly badly for everyone riding the train. As Xavier Aldana Reyes argues when speaking of the legacy of the Spanish Gothic (and it can be argued that *Pánico en el Transiberiano* belongs to the Spanish Gothic), "Developments in science and technology produced a small strand of mad science tales" (2017, 26). At its core, Martín's film is a tale about mad science aboard a train, itself an emblem of modernism.

Faithful to Western imagery, Beijing (as part of an exoticized Asia) is presented as unkempt and lawless, a ruthless place. Saxton reserved a seat aboard the Trans-Siberian months ago, but the reservation has been lost. Even so, the ticket "miraculously" shows up when it is revealed that Saxton works for the tsar. Meanwhile, Doctor Wells gets a ticket by bribing the authorities, saying, "In America we call this method technique" (Martín 1972). Furthermore, a man trying to break into Saxton's boxes is found dead, his eyes turned completely white, but nobody seems to be interested in investigating the issue to any extent. He was just a pickpocket, his life and death of no concern for the authorities. In contrast with this "barbaric" place, the modern, towering train containing two prominent scientists (geologist Saxton and Wells, an expert in bacteriology) and a count named Petrovski (Jorge Rigaud) represent a marked difference from the "backward" Asian region.

It must be noted, however, that the Trans-Siberian train itself was a complex figure. Trains and railway culture were considered the tip of modernity's spear, and so by uniting many territories the Trans-Siberian could demonstrate that Russia was the equal of any great power of Europe, able at last to compete with them in terms of modernization. The train itself, however, was far from an illustration of the rationale of modernity. The railway was constructed slowly and painfully. The lack of workers, particularly skilled workers, was the greatest source of difficulty for the contractors, since there was little mechanization in Russia at the time (Wolmar 2013, 50). The landscape was extremely hostile to any project of modernity due to harsh climates and endemic violence (Bisher 2005, 9–10). The train itself was framed by corruption, incompetence, and shoddy workmanship (Wolmar 2013, 59). At the end, the completed Trans-Siberian that emerged at the turn of the century "was not a gleaming new railway exemplifying the cutting-edge technology of the age. It was, rather, a meandering, single-track line with more curves than an average mountain pass and more rickety than a rope bridge" (62).

The Trans-Siberian was railway travel at its most basic, with little, if any luxuries. It was a huge architectonic creature representing the coming of modernization to feudal Russia, but the creature was slow and shoddy, a never-ending catalogue of failings. The promise of unfolding technological progress, and an unambiguous step toward the future was muddied by resistance to that modernity. The men of science traveling aboard the Trans-Siberian face primitivism and horror, an illustration of the disjointed and far-less-than-perfect modernity that the Trans-Siberian represented in both real life and in Martín's film (1972).

In the film (Martín 1972), the fear of what the future could bring encompasses more than advancements in technology. Wells presents his companion, Miss Jones (Alice Reinheart) as an expert in bacteriology, one of the best minds in this discipline. She quickly retorts that she is good enough "for being a woman" highlighting changes in gender roles. Women could become leaders in science, and traditional ways of thinking had become increasingly obsolete. This sense of obsolescence captures the era and the Trans-Siberian itself: the train, supposedly a marvel, was in fact obsolete in comparison to other trains and railways of its time. The train held a liminal nature: it was modernity but not quite modern, pointing to the rapidly changing nature of the times in which, as Engels and Marx famously stated in *The Manifesto of the Communist Party* (1848), and as echoed by Marshall Berman (1993), "All that is solid melts into air." The Trans-Siberian was *born obsolete*, the late product of an obsolescent autocratic state. The doubleness of modernity, its dark reflection, is the rapid obsolescence of its technological ethos. The return of the repressed is the fact that mechanization comes to die quickly, at the hands of better science that refutes and eliminates the previously celebrated.

Martín's film (1972) combines the shoddy modernism of the Trans-Siberian and the presence of the man and woman of science with elements taken from the irrational. Riding the rails, technology and science are accompanied by religion and monstrosity. Father Pujardov (Alberto de Mendoza), a monk serving Count Petrovski, is the embodiment of religion and the mistruth of old values toward science. Pujardov sees the presence of the devil in the train and in any circumstance around him. He sees Satan's machinations when a thief is found dead in the station, and also feels Satan's presence in the old fossils that Saxton carries with him. Though a superstitious man, he is clearly right when pointing at the contents of Saxton's boxes as evil. Pujardov uselessly tries to draw a cross with a piece of chalk on the box containing the prehistoric man: the chalk does not leave any discernible mark. The devil seems at work, indeed, even though the prehistoric man will be revealed to be an extra-terrestrial being who had come to Earth many millennia ago. There is no reason, thus, for the inability to draw a Christian cross on the box containing the remains of an alien, a being presumably beyond Christian eschatology. This ambiguity about the real nature of the frozen creature illustrates the failure of categories: the spheres of science and religion, commonly considered mutually exclusive, interact and blend together, and the borders between the one and the other fade. In a later scene, when Saxton mentions Darwin's theory of evolution, a woman exclaims that this way of thinking is immoral. "Gothic as negative modernity expresses alienation engendered by theories and systems that undermine humanist and commonsense perception" (Morris 2001, 188), as exemplified by the rise of Darwinism. In addition, a painting representing Jesus Christ falls from the wall at the presence of the monster, suggesting a connection between its monstrosity and religion. Blurring distinctions between normal and abnormal, and religion and science, the uncanny erodes binary logics.

The alien itself can be analyzed as a complement to the Trans-Siberian. If the machine contradictorily embodied two eras (obsolescence and modernism), the monster rejects easy categorization, as its nature as a creature from the infinite corners of space and a prehistoric being collapse together.

One of the conditions of monstrosity is a hybrid state: such beings are neither one thing nor the other. Monsters are anomalies between and in contrast to existing categories of normality, and their very nature is "to destroy structure, to resist classification" (Baumgartner and Davis 2008, 2). In Martín's film (1972), the monster's condition as a man from another planet codes him as a being with superior intelligence, even if his hairy body points to the dawn of humanity. Once the monster awakes, he will be unstoppable. He starts killing all the passengers riding the Trans-Siberian, emptying and vampirizing all the minds of his victims, his purpose to collect all the intellect of those aboard the train to acquire knowledge about Earth. Vampires as parasitic beings and the violation of the body are Gothic tropes, highlighting porous surfaces and inherent vulnerability (Bloom 2010, 182).

Pánico en el Transiberiano (1972) magnifies this parallelism between creature and train. For example, when Saxton opens the lock of the box containing the creature to look on it, the camera frames the key opening the lock in close shot. A rapid cut to the train's chimney comes next, announcing the train's departure. The next shot is of the monster's face.

Finally, a close shot of the train's wheels. The alternating images unite monstrosity with the ambiguous image of progress (the train) through a Gothic frame in which technology is debased because it contains, within its bowels, a monster. Both the alien creature and the train are monsters that defy limits.

Compartmentalization is also typical of modernism. According to Ian Carter, characteristic elements of the British culture—such as the neatly drawn stratification of social classes—sustain British railway culture and the segmentation of passengers. In turn, the railway introduces new jobs that mimic military hierarchies and elements of the industrial capitalist system (Carter 2001, 10). Trains mobilize social classes, all of them perfectly compartmentalized and separated to avoid any potential blurring of categories. Class and race are clearly differentiated within the Trans-Siberian, even if repressed tensions lurk. Upper-class passengers may relate to each other without problems, but that does not mean that there are not anxieties caused by the blurring of transnational frontiers. When Countess Irina (Silvia Tortosa) meets Saxton, they exchange words of courtesy, she as a Polish woman, Saxton as a representative of England:

Countess: (dreamily) Oh yes, England, Queen Victoria, crumpets, Shakespeare. . . .

Saxton: I admire Poland, Madame, I believe that there is a bond between our countries.

Countess: (with a hint of irony in her voice) My husband, the Count Petrovski, says that in the 15th Century, your King Henry betrayed us to the Russians, hmm. (Martín 1972)

This brief exchange speaks of the historical grudges that surface when people of different nations interact in transnational travel. Transnational encounters imperil strict borders, always on the verge of collapse when passengers from other classes (or races) decide to cross invisible lines. Just as the Gothic favors the hybrid natures and the fall of borders, uneasy, transgressive encounters proliferate in *Pánico en el Transiberiano*.

The Trans-Siberian is not the only element pointing to modernism and the scientific mind: an engineer presents himself as a man of science, autopsies are made aboard the train, and an odd experiment is performed on the eye of the monster. Through a microscope, Saxton and Wells observe that the creature's eye contains images of the things observed through the course of the monster's life. They find images of brontosauruses and pterodactyls, indicating that the creature has been on Earth since before the arrival of humans. The idea of eyes containing images of past events runs parallel with the idea of science as a way of disclosing the secrets of life, time, and space, and also mirrors the Gothic idea of the vulnerability of the body. The eye is also the key to distinguishing between those possessed by the monster from those not, so both men of science begin to investigate all the passengers. Anyone is suspect, and the situation exacerbates the uneasy convergence of people of different cultures and nations cohabiting the space of the transnational train. When the blurring of hierarchies—both Saxton and Wells, men of science, investigate alongside the count, a figure for Europe's feudal past—and nationalities is perceived, there is disconnection, disjointedness, and, ultimately, fear and paranoia.

The sense of alien sensibilities intensifies toward the end of Martín's film (1972), when the most "barbaric" passengers board the train. Cossacks led by Kazan (Telly Savalas) form a middle ground between the humanity of the passengers and the completely alien nature of the monster. Cossacks, "the mounted shock troops of the Russian army known for their hardiness" (Wolmar 2013, 77), were "unruly, barely disciplined but fiercely loyal horseman-warriors of Russia's periphery" (Patrikeeff and Shukman 2007, 34), and an indispensable part of the formation of the empire. Even so, with the advent of the railway a variety of characteristics of empire came into question, including the place of the Cossacks in the further evolution of Russia (35). As the Trans-Siberian reduced the length of distances, traveling harsh territory on horseback become irrelevant.

Everyone aboard the Trans-Siberian in Martín's film (1972) hates the Cossacks, their rudeness heavily contrasting with the upper class and the scientific ways and thinking of the main characters. When the rudeness of Kazan upsets Irina, she exclaims her desire to see the Cossack sent to Siberia as a punishment. Amazed, Kazan exclaims, "But I already live in Siberia!" (Martín 1972), pointing to the incommensurable gap between cultures.

Martín's remarkable Gothic conflation of modernism and the irrational mind made it a deeply disturbing text that highlighted realities of the circumstances of the Trans-Siberian at the turn of the century. Filmed and then screened at a time when Spain was on the verge of major political and social upheaval lent it a further degree of resonance. In spite of its Russian setting, *Pánico en el Transiberiano* (1972) owes much to the tradition of Spanish Gothic. Even if Aldana Reyes calls Martín's film one of the "most international and less Spanish-looking of the fantaterror era" (2017, 17), *Pánico en el Transiberiano* is a (co-) Spanish film, with a Spanish director and many Spanish members of the cast as well.

The film was made in the first years of the 1970s, a period that saw the dictatorial regime of Francisco Franco tighten control of tourism after a pronounced openness to transnationalism in the previous decade.

Indeed, in the 1960s, "Spain began to diversify its economy through tourism at first designed to attract foreigners to a Spain that was considered 'a country of Europe, but not "European"'" (Frey 1998, 241). Franco had not supported opening Spain to the rest of Europe and the world, since that would mean the potential "infestation" of foreign ideas like democracy and freedom. Just as in feudal Russia, tourism and travel run the risk of bringing on the contagion of dangerous ideas. As mentioned, however, a breakthrough came in the 1960s, "when foreign tourism to Spain not only expanded most rapidly in quantitative and economic terms, but began to make an imprint on the national consciousness as well" (Pack 2006, 83). The opening of Spain to foreign eyes may delineate some of the obsessions with travel, trains, the clash of cultures and the importance of eyes in *Pánico en el Transiberiano*. "The human body and the home are transformed, as proximity and connectivity are imagined in new ways . . . [and] the nation itself is transformed by these mobilities" (Hannam, Sheller, and Urry 2006, 3).

Depopulation also favored the restructuring of the railway network through the 1960s and 1970s. "Some of the railway lines stopping at rural stations were not profitable as a consequence of the small economic and demographic size of rural communities" (Collantes and Pinilla 2011, 94). Small communities slowly realized that trains will not stop anymore in their stations, as migrations to the city increased year after year. It is striking that two horror films featuring trains came together in 1972, the first years of the 1970s marking a return to the closing of borders after a decade of mass tourism.

La Noche del Terror Ciego (Ossorio 1972) tells the story of Templar knights who lived in the thirteenth century. To live forever, they offered sacrifices to Satan. However, their dreadful deeds come to an end when the Holy Inquisition hangs them in public. Several centuries later, in the 1970s, two friends, Virginia (María Elena Arpón) and Betty (Lone Fleming) go on a trip together with Roger (César Burner) aboard a train bound for the countryside. After a scene of jealousy, Virginia jumps off the train. Landing in the middle of nowhere, she finds shelter in some lost ruins. The site also shelters the frightening Templar knights, who come back to life as zombies every night.

Trains are central to the narrative, as the machines take the main characters to the ruins of old Spain—modernity touring the Spanish past. In the 1960s, the past became "a foreign country with a booming tourist trade" (Frey 1998, 241), as little medieval villages (like those where horror lives in Ossorio's film) could be visited and appreciated through the democratizing benefits of mass transit.

Both *Pánico en el Transiberiano* and *La Noche del Terror Ciego* end on a dark note. The Moscow authorities cause the train to crash, the only way of preventing the monster from reaching the city, even if everyone aboard could perish. Many survive, including the main characters, but the last shot (Martín 1972) shows the Trans-Siberian burning to ashes. *La Noche del Terror Ciego* ends with the zombies, embodiments of the past, hijacking the train and killing all its passengers. That film's final shot (Ossorio 1972) shows the train arriving in the city carrying its deadly cargo. The potential contamination produced by alien ideas carried by trains figures in both films. As travel is enhanced by railway cultures, lurking behind the films are the risks of openness to foreign eyes and ideas—a source of anxiety for both feudal Russia and Francoist Spain—and a Gothic blurring of boundaries. By the time *Howl* (Hyett 2015) opened in theaters, globalization had become a reality. In addition, the luxury of train travel had become available to middle and lower classes. However, some things had not changed, like the unease associated with the mixing of social classes and the concept of a horrifying outside.

Howl and the Global World

Throughout the nineteenth century, railway expansion and developments in the technology of mobility granted better and faster travel (Hobsbawm 1995, 239). This accelerated tourism, a practice that had for long been reserved solely for elites. Through the postwar era, however, tourism developed into a mass activity, as middle classes and working classes gain access to leisure. As Mimi Sheller and John Urry argue, "All the world seems to be on the move. Asylum seekers, international students, terrorists, members of diasporas, holidaymakers, business people, sports stars, refugees, backpackers, commuters, the early retired, young mobile professionals, prostitutes, armed forces -these and many others fill the world's airports, buses, ships, and trains" (2006, 207). Transnational mobility became a common social and cultural condition of living.

Contemporary railway culture in Europe is a complicated amalgam of the traditional role of trains (e.g., mobility and leisure) with new social strata (e.g., working classes, transnational workers, etc.) while remaining expensive enough to be considered a luxury item. Still, the train's role as signpost of modernity and technological development remains, as traditional equipment is replaced in Europe by ever-higher speed machines. The current thinking that proposes a decrease in the use of private cars in favor of public mobility has led to a radical new conceptualization of the use of trains. Long-distance travel was traditionally considered part of family leisure time, particularly during weekends, holidays, or vacations. In the contemporary global world, however, it is possible to observe two characteristics changing this traditional view. First, the politics has shifted away from private car use to public transportation. Public concerns over traffic jams complement more pressing matters such as the environmental impacts of "rising road traffic and loss of countryside from road building" (Haywood 2009, 2–3). Among a host of recommendations, environmental concerns gave rise to calls "for a significant modal shift from road to rail for passenger and freight traffic" (Haywood 2009, 2–3). The growing congestion on road networks forced people to look for alternative modes of locomotion, to the point that, in the United Kingdom, rail passenger traffic grew considerably in the late 1990s and continues to grow still (Haywood 2009, 303). Trains were increasingly important to mass mobility. Even more recently, the internet has made the provision of tickets and timetable information much easier, favoring the use of public transportation as never before.

Second, globalization has changed the nature of corporations and relationships within the workforce. People in one nation can work for a corporation with offices in another, so the daily passage across borders is a part of the workday. Part of the new paradigm of mobility studies investigates this transnational flow as a "state's nation-state sovereignty has been replaced by a single system of mobile power, of 'empire': a 'smooth world,' deterritorialised and decentred, without a centre of power, with no fixed boundaries or barriers" (Sheller and Urry 2006, 209). Trains maximize the efficiency of public transportation through regional, interregional, and international routes. Continental railways were expected to "transform the relationships between men and things, to bring province closer to province and people to people" (Nilsen 2008, 27): our analysis of *Pánico en el Transiberiano* (Martín 1972) demonstrates that this assertion is as relevant today as at the turn of the century. The main difference lies in the fact that the railways initially served as a centralizing tool for the modernist political purposes of nationalism, while in the globalized context trains serve transnational purposes. If train travel in Martín's film is a solemn event confined to the upper classes, in *Howl* (Hyett 2015) travel is open to any social class. Contemporary passengers are not afraid of foreign states and nations but are excited, as knowledge about what lies beyond national frontiers circu-

lates easily. In this sense, Erik Cohen argues that "many of today's tourists are able to enjoy the experience of change and novelty only from
a strong base of familiarity, which enables them to feel secure enough
to enjoy the strangeness of what they experience" combining thus "a
degree of novelty with a degree of familiarity" (1972, 166–67).

   Howl (Hyett 2015) emerges as a twisted mirror of this new context
of train travel. The film has two kinds of mobilities at its core: that of
social class and that of travel. Young Joe (Ed Speleers), security guard
for an international British train (Alpha Trax Trains), is vying for a pro-
motion to the position of supervisor. In the film's first scene, Joe's so-
licitude is rejected, which is only the first of the young man's many
misfortunes to come. The lack of social mobility contrasts heavily with
his role as guard, accompanying people traveling in and out of the
United Kingdom primarily for business. Joe's atonal and dispassionate
enumeration of the different stations of the night train reveals part of
the new social condition of railways: rather than an exciting adventure
transporting people through Europe, high-speed mobility has turned
the journey into routine. There is no excitement in Joe's voice, nor in
the different passengers. For all of them, railway experience is an extension of work.

   In *Howl* (Hyett 2015), Joe's last train for the night is bound for East-
borough, carrying a small complement of passengers. It is noteworthy
that, despite the late hour, almost every person aboard is there on business. Kate (Shauna Macdonald) is a young executive who takes this train
every day of her life to go to her job. As she later says, she practically
lives on the train. The long distance that she has to travel to her job
makes the train a kind of second home, revealing some aspects of the
globalized world where people can find work in neighboring provinces
and countries rather than locally. All the other main passengers travel
for business as well: Nina (Rosie Day) is a young model returning home
after a photo shoot, Adrian (Elliot Cowan) is a yuppie who has the "survival of the fittest" as his personal motto, while young Billy (Sam Gittins)
goes home after a business meeting. The exception to this rule is the elderly couple, Ged (Duncan Preston) and Jenny (Ania Marson), who still
dress elegantly for their journey, a throwback of sorts to a bygone era of
train travel. A homogeneous group of businesspeople have replaced the
men of science and royalty, and the Cossacks of Martín's film (1972) as
long-distance trips are now synonymous with business trips.

   Trains are inextricably linked to the idea of modernism, even in the
new millennium. This mechanical figure points to divisions among
classes and barriers, strict schedules, and constant technological devel-

opments. As Sara Haslam argues, the train is a "modern totem" (2002, 190), a symbol of the death knell of what is old and obsolete, and is a reference to urban modernity. The increase in velocity parallels the frenzy that drives contemporary life, as the quest for velocity became an important characteristic of modernity in general. Hence the Gothic mode lies behind the shiny surface of the modern trains of *Howl* (Hyett 2015).

The Gothic surfaces in the film (Hyett 2015) in two ways, both of them related to the politics of modernism. On the one hand, the forests circling the train represent the opposite of culture. Both spaces are engaged in parallel—albeit contrasting—productions of nature and its savagery, and of culture and its technology. In this sense, the film's first shot is that of a moon that quickly turns, through superimposed images, into the electronic button that opens the train's electric doors. Nature blends into domesticated culture. In the film, nature is presented at its most brutal. The dualism of nature and culture constitutes and sustains the mythology of modernity (Graham 2011, 36), and here all the mysterious life of the wilderness is made metaphor in the figure of the werewolf, that most savage of monsters. *Howl* presents the wilderness of the forest as a space that reveals the other, demonic side of "civilized" human nature. The forests safeguarding the monsters represent the primitive mind still lurking in the era of high-speed trains.

Societies formed according to the dominant model of modernity are marked by an alienating individualism as technological developments separate people and eliminate any sense of community: denial of our internal relatedness to the past, detachment from homeland/nation, alienation from each other. Arguably, in *Howl* (Hyett 2015) all the characters on the train aside from Joe are mean and unkind to him and each other. Kate loses her ticket and blames Joe for having to pay the penalty. Adrian does not even offer his ticket to Joe. Nina too, who mocks the young employee while accusing him of "looking at my tits." Nobody pays any respect to Joe when the young man collects the tickets. For the passengers, he is just a worker undeserving of respect, the once prestigious ritual of travel now turned into daily business, with the erasure of hierarchies of reverence. This differentiation is clearly shown in studies on mobility, since they identify how mobility is stratified along social and cultural institutions and structures. "Mobility also are caught up in power geometries of everyday life" (Hannam, Sheller, and Urry 2006, 4).

In this respect, the Gothic destroys the categories of individualism. Unlike in common horror film tropes, in which a group of people get stuck in a closed location and start bickering and fighting with each other, *Howl* (Hyett 2015) privileges the opposite: everyone begins to be-have in a friendlier way once the attack on them is unleashed. Moments after the werewolves try to break into the train, the different passengers start to care for the safety of each other (with the exception of Adrian). As the attacks unfold, the passengers exchange names, recognizing each other as people within a community under attack that will sur-vive only if they work together. Even so, the group is doomed, with the creatures opening their way through the train, which is sitting immobile in the middle of a forest, an empty shell. Finally, the hierarchies fall and the savage, primitive outside wins over the modern, metallic inside. The feral triumphs over the human side, as the werewolves bite and spread their curse through the passengers.

Railroad trains running through the forests or frozen landscapes may be seen as the conquest of the savage land by the modern mind, as rail-ways split open the unknowable and make it visible. The Gothic genre, however, is a celebratory exploration of the unknowable, so trains run-ning through alien landscapes are always at risk of being swallowed up by the uncanny. The Gothic also privileges hybridism and porous bor-ders, and the European Gothic is a transnational reflection of the com-plexity of the transgression of frontiers and hierarchies, disjointedness, and lack of a cohesive body.

Conclusion

The question of a cohesive European body may be seen at stake in both the Gothic mode and the progressive construction of a railway culture, the former privileging disjointedness, the latter searching for cohesive-ness. Both *Pánico en el Transiberiano* (Martín 1972) and *Howl* (Hyett 2015) work on this complex interlinking of frontiers, modernity, and the Gothic. *Pánico en el Transiberiano* mirrors two historical moments framed by a posture of openness toward the outside world. The histor-ical moments when Russia built the Trans-Siberian and Spain chose to favor tourism may be seen as mirrors of each other, as both countries engaged in an adventure that promised modernism but also brought potential threats, as frontiers were transgressed by foreign ideas and national, cultural, and racial Otherness. In Martín's film, Russia and Spain run parallel, both diminished in comparison to more-developed Euro-pean countries of their time. In this sense, it is interesting that, even though made by a Spaniard the film's characters representing science and modernity—as well as the actors who portray them—are British (Cushing and Lee).

As trains gained speed, they also lost charm, becoming more a tool for business in a globalized world than a vehicle of leisure. The railway culture of speed wins over the flâneur. The dangers of transgression of borders are greater than ever, however, as people take the trains in increasing numbers to reach their workplaces. *Howl* (Hyett 2015) depicts the ultimate transgression, as the forest accomplishes its revenge, and nature and monstrosity hold the upper hand. It is noticeable that the film ends with Joe, the main hero, turned into a feral monster. If the young man was the aim of each act of mockery from the beginning, *Howl* ends with him as the ultimate alpha male. In fact, everyone within the train seems to gain emotion only after the attacks. Before that, they were undistinguishable from the train itself: emotionless and mechanical, technological products of modernity.

The Gothic mode in both films is concerned with modernity's strengths and weaknesses: railway culture is remarkable, but also potentially alienating; it enhances the transgression of borders and puts different cultures and nations in closer proximity to one another. With the future of railway culture essentially unpredictable in a world at once increasingly globalized and walled off in the interests of security and rising nationalisms, Gothic narratives, specters of modernity, will likely haunt trains forever. As modern trains travel at higher speeds, the countryside is an ever-greater blur, thus more effectively hiding its monsters. Yet they are lurking there all the same.

Fernando Gabriel Pagnoni Berns (PhD) is professor at the Universidad de Buenos Aires (UBA)—Facultad de Filosofía y Letras (Argentina). He teaches courses on international horror film. He is director of the research group on horror cinema, Grite. He has authored a book about Spanish horror TV series "Historias para no dormir" (Universidad de Cádiz, 2020) and has edited a book on Frankenstein bicentennial (Universidad de Buenos Aires) and one on horror director James Wan (McFarland).

Juan Juvé holds an MA in social sciences from the Universidad de Buenos Aires (UBA)—Facultad de Ciencias Sociales (Argentina). He has published in books such as *Science Fiction and the Abolition of Man: Finding C. S. Lewis in Sci-Fi Film and Television,* edited by Mark J. Boone and Kevin C. Neece; *Bad Mothers: Regulations, Representations, and Resistance,* edited by Demeter Press; *Requiem for a Nation: Religion, Politics and Visual Cultures in Post-war Italy (1945–1975),* edited by Roberto Cavallini; and *The Rwandan Genocide on Film: Critical Essays and Interviews,* edited by Matthew Edwards; among others.

References

Aldana Reyes, Xavier. 2017. *Spanish Gothic: National Identity, Collaboration and Cultural Adaptation*. New York: Palgrave Macmillan.

Baumgartner, Holly Lynn, and Roger Davis. 2008. "Hosting the Monster: Introduction." In *Hosting the Monster*, edited by Holly Lynn Baumgartner and Roger Davis, 1–10. Amsterdam: Rodopi.

Berman, Marshall. 1993. *All That Is Solid Melts into Air*. London: Verso.

Bisher, Jaime. 2005. *White Terror: Cossack Warlords of the Trans-Siberian*. London: Routledge.

Bloom, Clive. 2010. *Gothic Histories: The Taste for Terror, 1764 to the Present*. New York: Continuum.

Boccagni, Paolo. 2012. "Rethinking Transnational Studies: Transnational Ties and the Transnationalism of Everyday Life." *European Journal of Social Theory* 15, no. 1: 117–132.

Botting, Fred, and Dale Townshend. 2004. "Introduction." In *Gothic: Eighteenth-Century Gothic: Radcliffe, Reader, Writer, Romancer*, edited by Fred Botting and Dale Townshend, 1–18. New York: Routledge.

Carter, Ian. 2001. *Railways and Culture in Britain: The Epitome of Modernity*. Manchester, UK: Manchester University Press.

Cavallaro, Dani. 2002. *Gothic Vision: Three Centuries of Horror, Terror and Fear*. New York: Continuum.

Cohen, Erik. 1972. "Toward a Sociology of International Tourism." *Social Research* 39, no. 1: 64–82.

Collantes, Fernando, and Vicente Pinilla. 2011. *Peaceful Surrender: The Depopulation of Rural Spain in the Twentieth Century*. Newcastle upon Tyne, UK: Cambridge Scholars Publishing.

Duffy, Enda. 2009. *The Speed Handbook: Velocity, Pleasure, Modernism*. Durham, NC: Duke University Press.

Ďurovičová, Nataša. 2010. "Preface." In *World Cinemas, Transnational Perspectives*, edited by Nataša Ďurovičová and Kathleen E. Newman, iv–xv. 2010. New York: Routledge.

Engels, Friedrich, and Karl Marx. 1848. *Manifesto of the Communist Party*. London: Workers' Educational Association.

Frey, Nancy. 1998. *Pilgrim Stories: On and Off the Road to Santiago*. Los Angeles: University of California Press.

Gilman, Sander. 1995. *Freud, Race, and Gender*. Princeton, NJ: Princeton University Press.

Graham, Nicole. 2011. *Lawscape: Property, Environment, Law*. New York: Routledge.

Hannam, Kevin, Mimi Sheller, and John Urry. 2006. "Editorial: Mobilities, Immobilities and Moorings, Mobilities." *Mobilities* 1, no. 1: 1–22.

Haslam, Sara. 2002. *Fragmenting Modernism: Ford Maddox Ford, the Novel and the Great War*. Manchester, UK: Manchester University Press.

Haywood, Russell. 2009. *Railways, Urban Development and Town Planning in Britain: 1948–2008*. Farnham, UK: Ashgate.

Heywood, Anthony. 1999. *Modernising Lenin's Russia: Economic Reconstruction, Foreign Trade and the Railways*. New York: Cambridge University Press.

Hobsbawm, Eric. 1995. *The Age of Capitalism 1848–1875*. London: Abacus.

Hogle, Jerrold. 2001. "The Gothic at Our Turn of the Century: Our Culture of Simulation and the Return of the Body." In *The Gothic*, edited by Fred Botting, 153–79. Cambridge, UK: D. S. Brewer.

Hoglund, Johan. 2014. *The American Imperial Gothic: Popular Culture, Empire, Violence*. New York: Routledge.

Hyett, Paul. dir. 2015. *Howl*. Borehamwood, UK: Starchild Pictures.

Martín, Eugenio, dir. 1972. *Pánico en el Transiberiano (Horror Express)*. DVD. California: Severin Films, 2011.

Morris, Nigel. 2001. "*Metropolis* and the Modernist Gothic." In *Gothic Modernisms*, edited by Andrew Smith and Jeff Wallace, 188–206. New York: Palgrave Macmillan.

Nilsen, Micheline. 2008. *Railways and the Western European Capitals: Studies of Implantation in London, Paris, Berlin, and Brussels*. New York: Palgrave Macmillan.

Ossorio, Amando de, dir. 1972. *La Noche del Terror Ciego (Tombs of the Blind Dead)*. DVD. Oregon: Sinister Cinema, 2001.

Pack, Sasha. 2006. *Tourism and Dictatorship: Europe's Peaceful Invasion of Franco's Spain*. New York: Palgrave Macmillan.

Parrot, Bruce, and Serhiy Kudelia. 2011. "Russia: European or Not?" In *Europe Today: A Twenty-first Century Introduction*, edited by Ronald Tiersky and Erik Jones, 219–56. Lanham, MD: Rowman and Littlefield.

Patrikeeff, Felix and Harold Shukman. 2007. *Railways and the Russo-Japanese War: Transporting War*. New York: Routledge.

"Railways in Russia." 1868. *The Railway News and Joint-Stock Journal*, vol. 10 (December). London: The Office of the "Railway News."

Riquelme, John Paul. 2015. "Gothic." In *A Companion to the English Novel*, edited by Stephen Arata, Madigan Haley, J. Paul Hunter, Jennifer Wicke, 117–31. Malden, MA: Wiley Blackwell.

Schivelbusch, Wolfgang. 1986. *The Railway Journey: The Industrialization of Time and Space in the 19th Century*. Berkeley: University of California Press.

Sheller, Mimi, and John Urry. 2006. "The New Mobilities Paradigm." *Environment and Planning A* 38, no. 2: 207–26.

Tomasik, Wojciech. 2007. "The Auschwitz Terminus: Driverless Trains in Zola and Borowski." In *The Railway and Modernity: Time, Space, and the Machine Ensemble*, edited by Matthew Beaumont and Michael J. Freeman, 191–200. Bern, Switzerland: Peter Lang.

Urry, John. 2007. *Mobilities*. Malden, MA: Polity.

Wolmar, Christian. 2013. *To the Edge of the World: The Story of the Trans-Siberian Express the World's Greatest Railway*. London: Atlantic Books.

Wood, Robin. 2004. "An Introduction to the American Horror Film." In *Planks of Reason: Essays on the Horror Film*, edited by Barry Keith Grant and Christopher Sharrett, 107–39. Lanham, MD: Scarecrow Press.

CHAPTER 5

Anachronism, Ambivalence, and (Trans)National Self-Reference

Tracking the English Literary Chunnel from 1986 On

Heather Joyce

The Chunnel is an obvious touchstone for cultural critics who seek to interrogate the extent to which the nation-state continues to be a useful political and cultural category moving forward in the twenty-first century. At the same time it seems to presage a "state of postnational borderlessness" (Apter 2002, 287), it is insistently territorial, encompassing contending and contradictory claims of "*extension*" and "abrogation of sovereignty" by the nations it connects (Hadfield-Amkhan 2010, 91). The view the Chunnel offers, then, is compatible with philosophical transnationalism, which takes as its starting point the premise that "social life is transnational to begin with" but crucially promises to reveal "why certain boundaries arise" and "how" they are "reproduced and perpetuated" (Khagram and Levitt 2008, 8). Accepting a "transnational ontology," according to Sanjeev Khagram and Peggy Levitt, means taking the approach that "the local, regional, national, and global are not automatic, taken-for-granted social arenas but categories to be investigated as constructed and often-contested social facts" (8–9). The multilevel coordination that construction of the Chunnel entailed sheds light on the necessity of moving to "excavate the interaction" between the "layer[s]" Khagram and Levitt describe (9). On one hand, this entails interrogating new affiliations the Chunnel engenders as "links between Kent and Calais" and also Europe are forged (Darian-Smith 1999, 163); on the other hand, it involves recognizing that, along "with the increasing connections between people and places on either side of the Channel, new boundaries are emerging and old divisions are being redefined" as Kent, for example, "experienc[es] a need to reclaim its own identity and to assert its own independence as a region within England and a borderland with France" (165).

The Kentish dilemma emerges on a national level as the Chunnel acts as a powerful reminder that cultural identity is "embedded in and influenced by cross-border and cross-boundary phenomena and dynamics" (Khagram and Levitt 2008, 8). In a climate in which Thatcherism succeeded at authorizing and directing a prevailing postwar narrative of British crisis toward Englishness, it is unsurprising, then, that the continual struggle over the Chunnel—particularly its symbolic value—reveals a concomitant negotiation between Britishness and Englishness to take place alongside the brokerage of British and French and European relations. This is borne out through how, though it has largely been absorbed into the national imaginary, literary representations show the cultural topography of the Chunnel to be overwritten by an "uneasy history" (Hadfield-Amkhan 2010, 90) that has tended to be shaped by the role it has played and continues to play in enabling the nation to imagine itself politically and culturally; in effect, the Chunnel has come to function as an ambivalent signifier that is capable of reflecting a dynamic political landscape. At the same time that it invites an outward-looking gaze, the Chunnel forcibly turns the national historical gaze within.

The Chunnel functions as a predictable site of struggle based not only on how it promises to reshape the political and social geography of the nations it joins but also over how movement through it is to be regulated; in doing so, it shows how "issues of movement, of too little movement or too much or of the wrong sort or at the wrong time, are central to many lives, organisations and governments" (Hannam, Sheller, and Urry 2006, 1)—particularly on the British side as the island nation grapples not only with becoming conjoined to the continent but also with what it means to be a postimperial nation. The Chunnel is also a powerful reminder that "mobilities cannot be described without attention to the necessary spatial, infrastructural and institutional moorings that configure and enable mobilities" (3); "detachment" entails "reterritorializations" in part because of how the Chunnel itself draws attention to "re-arrangements of place and scale" (3) by virtue of how it is implicated in a "nexus" of travel—"an expanding system" that "makes places relational" (Urry 2007, 101) and is also bound up with a symbolic "shift from land to landscape" (102) that critics associate with rail travel.

Mapping how political and cultural scripts converge in the Chunnel on the British side, then, entails unravelling the representational value it has accrued through its close association with railways. Notably, the rhetoric of Eurostar picks up on the "drive to speed" and the "timetabling of social life" that are legacies of the "nineteenth-century railway" that continue to "cast long shadows over the forms of movement that emerge in subsequent centuries" (Urry 2007, 100). The Rail Europe website notes that Eurostar "specialises in speedy travel" and provides "sleek and efficient service" as it connects London to "Amsterdam, Brussels and Paris" via the Channel Tunnel (Rail Europe, 2021). This discourse of modernity and the tacit promise to enact a new spatiality that defines the Eurostar experience take on a specific and complex inflection on the British side because of how, since their inception, railways have been signposts for politicians and public figures who seek to shape the nation's (modern) understanding of itself.

Beyond debate about the regulatory requirements that "public movement" requires (Urry 2007, 92), railways have long functioned as sites where struggles over Englishness and Britishness have played out. In fact, representations of railways often function as shorthand for the English nation's historic understanding of itself simultaneously as throw-back and throw-forward—a mode of self-understanding that is submerged in larger narratives of Britishness. Recognition of the denaturalizing function of railway travel facilitates this view. Literary representations of railways in works by poets such as Philip Larkin and John Betjeman exploit the altered perspective of the landscape that travel by rail seems to offer even as they interrogate the extent to which these insights can be lasting. What these writers ultimately register is how this mode of travel closely mirrors the process whereby "history, in English post-Enlightenment tradition, absorbs revolutionary fervor by first using it to create, and then forgetting that it has created, a parallel story of the past, named English history or heritage" (Summers-Bremner 2005, 273). The difficulty of precisely defining the cultural value railway travel accrues is exacerbated by how railways are complexly implicated in the nation's understanding of itself as modern.

The tendency for writers to evoke the Chunnel as a covert frame of reference in their thematic treatments of Englishness speaks to how the "narrative Chunnel" that critics envisioned does not overwhelmingly predominate (Apter 2002, 287). For Emily Apter, the promise of the "narrative Chunnel" to become heir to the "literary channel" rests in how it seems to offer a "paradigm" distinct from transnational understandings because of how it elides boundaries (287). She explains, "The Chunnel imaginary assimilates Britain to Europe and connotes Europe to Europe or intra-European narrative forms that, at their most radical, obfuscate national borders in the Isles and on the Continent" (287); from this perspective, Apter argues, "In contrast to transnational literature . . . Chunnel literature points to a state of postnational borderlessness that sublates regionalist and minority claims in the future history of the novel" (287). What representations of the Channel Tunnel in British literary works from 1986 on insist on, however, is that the symbolic value of the Chunnel in fact rests in how it continues to function as a complex and highly symbolic "transnational paradigm" against Apter's vision and, in so doing, provides access to (English) narratives that have been "forcibly excluded" from the nation's historical self-understanding (Said [1993] 1994, 67).

The breaking of ground on the Chunnel in the late 1980s seemed to rehearse anew the nineteenth century promise of a "new, reduced, geography" that railways offered (Schivelbusch 1986, 35). At the same time that the Chunnel promised to link nations to an unprecedented extent, it brought into sharp relief the "defensive exclusivism" that underwrites the late twentieth and early twenty-first centuries' political and cultural nation (Hall 1997, 25); in other words, the defensive territoriality the Chunnel provoked finds its symbolic correlative not only in embattled Britishness but, more specifically, in defensive formulations of Englishness that proliferated as England was forced to conceive of itself as distinct from Britain in the heyday of empire. Reading contrapuntally— that is, opening a text "both to what went into it and to what its author excluded" (Said [1993] 1994, 67)—reveals works by poets such as Carol Ann Duffy and Patience Agbabi and prose writers such as Julian Barnes, Nicola Barker, and Ben Okri to take up and engage with the specific political and cultural conjunctures that led to the construction of the Chunnel; in doing so, they begin to reveal how the same (post)imperial scripts of nationhood that informed debates regarding the constructions of the railways continue to underwrite the nation's (post)modern understanding of itself politically and culturally.

To Chunnel or Not to Chunnel?

Although public debate surrounding the construction of the Chunnel at the end of the twentieth century seemed an almost anachronistic repetition of the political and cultural debates that the first railways in Britain provoked, it was, in fact, the continuation of a discussion broached in the eighteenth century, but begun in earnest in the nineteenth century: "In 1751 the Amiens Academy held a competition to explore new ways of crossing the Channel, while the first serious tunnel proposal came from the French engineer Albert Mathieu in 1802, a project favored by Napoleon" (Barnes 1995, 286). From the nineteenth century on, the prospect of building the physical link continually resurfaced in a cycle that proved responsive to shifting political and cultural moods on both sides of the Channel.

It is worth noting, however, that "in the first half of the century the initiatives for a fixed link crossing came mainly from the French" (Gourvish 2006, 1), a trend that speaks to how the responsiveness of successive

Figure 5.1. W. K. Haselden, political cartoon. *Daily Mirror* (21 September 1914).
(Original work published 18 February 1907.)

politicians and governments to the public mood on the British side has tended to reflect how "boundaries and borders" in fact "emerge at particular historical moments" (Khagram and Levitt 2008, 5). W. K. Haselden's political cartoon ([1907] 1914), published 18 February 1907 in the *Daily Mirror*, illustrates the "simple xenophobia, the dislike of strengthening links with Europe" (M. R. Bonavia quoted in Hadfield-Amkhan 2010, 90) that dampened enthusiasm and delayed construction of the Chunnel on the British side for so long (see figure 5.1). In three frames, Haselden depicts the increasing ingenuity and relentless determination of an invading French army. In the first frame, the image of soldiers concealing themselves in barrels transported by railway supports the incendiary caption, "Watchfulness will not prevent the enemy getting through concealed." In the second, men thwart the provisions meant to mitigate risk: "No use flooding the tunnel, he will come through in diving suits." And in the final frame, the viewer bears witness to the fanciful depiction of the army being sent over, hyperbolically, "in a few minutes." The panels give credence to the "military opposition" (Fetherston 1997, 46) that long thwarted attempts to build the tunnel.

The publication of the same cartoon seven years later speaks to how public sentiment about the Channel Tunnel reflects the dynamic political landscape, however. When it was republished on 21 September 1914, the new caption, "What do Channel-Tunnel phobes think now?," anticipated how the war would be "of particular assistance to the tunnel": "During the war, military of several nations concluded that a tunnel would have aided the Allied effort in the conflict—a conflict that Britain entered, after initial reluctance, when Belgium was invaded and the other side of the Dover Strait and the Channel seemed likely to fall into unfriendly hands" (Fetherston 1997, 48). "The insights of the war did not long endure" (48), however, and construction of the Chunnel was again deferred. "After the Second World War the military objections to the tunnel became progressively weaker" (Gourvish 2006, 16) in part because "the Channel Tunnel that the Victorians had rejected as a technological threat to the nation now seemed sadly old-fashioned" (Fetherston 1997, 54). Nonetheless, "political and economic" concerns continued to defeat proposals to build a fixed link between nations (Gourvish 2006, 17).

Margaret Thatcher's surprising endorsement of the Chunnel in the 1980s could be explained by her recognition of its potential to symbolize the nation's "relationship with Europe" and "the newfound strength of the private sector, following . . . five years of Thatcher government" (John Noulton quoted in Fetherston 1997, 101). The Chunnel was not only "an entrepreneurial project" capable of "inculcating recent ideals of British national sufficiency and regional growth (rather than earlier ideas

of English survival)" (Hadfield-Amkhan 2010, 91), but also an achievement to be absorbed into the longer historical record. Emphasis on
these qualities countered fears and reassured the public that construction of the link would mean "an *extension* rather than an abrogation of
sovereignty" (91). Evidence both of Thatcherism's sophisticated understanding of the role symbolic identifications play in forging political and
cultural identities and its strategic deployment of Britishness, Thatcher's
support for the project also speaks to how a complex negotiation of national self-understanding is bound up with the Chunnel's construction
in a cycle that has continued even after it became operational.

Twenty years after its official opening in 1994, the Chunnel was taken
to be a familiar and unremarkable part of the cultural landscape as British
journalist Benedict Brogan observed. "Taken for granted," Brogan (2014)
mused, the Chunnel shows "how easily" Britain's—and more immediately England's—inhabitants "have adjusted to the idea of being linked
to the Continent." Although it is an iconic symbol of "new transnational
contexts" (Darian-Smith 1999, xiv), it has not been immune to the postcolonial melancholia that Paul Gilroy diagnosed in the early 2000s. Gilroy cites the nation's "inability even to face, never mind actually mourn,
the profound change in circumstances and moods that followed the
end of the empire and consequent loss of imperial prestige" (2005, 90),
as well as "the apprehension of successive political and economic crises, . . . the gradual breakup of the United Kingdom, . . . the arrival of
substantial numbers of postcolonial citizen-migrants, and . . . the shock
and anxiety that followed from a loss of any sense that the national
collective was bound by a coherent and distinctive culture" (90), as root
causes of a political and cultural morbidity afflicting the nation that
manifests, in part, in a symptomatic fixation on (lost) Englishness. In addition to the more benign expressions of nostalgia that are provoked by
the nineteenth-century associations travel by rail continues to conjure,
the Chunnel has occasioned overt expressions of "defensive exclusivism" (Hall 1997, 25) that derive from the repression Gilroy describes and
that center on the mobility the Chunnel makes possible.

For Gilroy, "once the history of the empire became a source of discomfort, shame, and perplexity, its complexities and ambiguities were
readily set aside" (2005, 90). In part, this is because at the root of the
"contested history of its difficult relationships with its colonial subjects"
is the "greatness of the British nation" (94). The construction of the
Chunnel was not incidentally taken to recapture this sense of "greatness," given its nineteenth-century associations. It is unsurprising, then,
that even before its construction the Chunnel acted as a symbolic locus
for the "hostile responses to strangers and settlers" and the formulation

Figure 5.2. S. Franklin, political cartoon. *Daily Mirror* (23 February 1968).

of "intractable political problems that flow from understanding immigration as being akin to war and invasion" (Gilroy 2005, 94) that mark the postimperial British landscape and often uphold notions of threatened Englishness. Stanley Franklin's polemical political cartoon published in the *Daily Mirror* on 23 February 1968 picked up on the mood of Enoch Powell's infamous "Rivers of Blood" speech delivered two months later on 20 April 1968. In the cartoon, a line of exoticized, non-White immigrants forms even as ground on the Chunnel is beginning to be broken on the French side. The quintessentially English sign that they stand before—a sign that reads "Queue here"—tacitly places the blame for this expected incursion at the feet of British politicians (see figure 5.2).

This same sentiment is expressed in Brian Adcock's political cartoon that responds to the Calais crisis (see figure 5.3). In the cartoon, published almost fifty years later in *The Guardian*, a Border Control dog corners David Cameron as the agent apologizes, saying, "Sorry Mr. Cameron. He's trained to sniff out desperate people struggling with immigration." Adcock makes use of the language of crisis that was omnipresent in the headlines of July 2015, as tensions in Calais came to a head, to bring to light how Cameron's own language dangerously replicated

Figure 5.3. B. Adcock, political cartoon. *Guardian* (1 August 2015).

the "swamping" rhetoric of earlier politicians when he "vowed to throw more illegal migrants out of Britain as a deterrent, blaming the Calais crisis on 'a swarm of people' trying to escape north Africa in an attempt to come to the UK [United Kingdom]" (Taylor, Wintour, and Elgot 2015). Here, the Chunnel reveals how the "potential for mobility" becomes a "crucial dimension of unequal power relations" (Hannam, Sheller, and Urry 2006, 3) as the ability to cross borders is granted some and denied others. Both political cartoons reflect how "conflict" is based on "both the actual and the imagined movement of people from place to place" (4), which is complicated in the present moment by contemporary interrogations of what it means to be British as well as the changing nature of British-European relations.

Although Groupe Eurotunnel was able to reassure potential passengers and investors on the heels of Brexit that "the British vote in favour of leaving the European Union 'will not affect the activity of the Channel Tunnel concession'" ("'Brexit' Will Not Affect Channel Tunnel" 2016) because of the roles private enterprise and regional cooperation have played in its construction and continuation, the changing political landscape will inevitably alter symbolic representations of the Chunnel and reflect altering conceptions of both Englishness and Britishness. For one cultural commentator, the vote to leave the EU is another symptom of the melancholic nation. In an opinion piece for *The Guardian*, Anne Perkins (2017) stressed that "the leave vote was about a complex web of issues to do with a sense of powerlessness, nostalgia, and a mistrust of people in general and experts in particular." She adds, "It is not, however, an accident that immigration has come to stand as shorthand for all of the above." This is particularly true given how "ongoing tension[s] between national modes of historic self-reference and the influence of modernity in a specific government initiative" (Hadfield-Amkhan 2010, 90) seem to intersect in the Chunnel.

Minding the Chunnel

It is clear that the Chunnel has long been "more than a mere engineering project" (Gibb 1994, 1). As early as the 1960s, Chunnel historians argued it was "a 'state of mind'" (1). For Richard Gibb, P. Whiteside summed this up best in 1962 when he described the pervasive "feeling that somehow, if England were to be connected by a tunnel with the Continent, the peculiar meaning to an Englishman of being English would never be quite the same again" (1). The focus on Englishness here is key and, indeed, examination of the Chunnel begins to expose the complex political maneuvers that underlie political and cultural constructions of Britishness even as it functions as the "symbolic step forward in the development of Europe" (Came 1994) that François Mitterand and Margaret Thatcher ostensibly envisioned.

Literary preoccupation with the Chunnel is traceable to its capacity, like railways, to function simultaneously as "a tangible technology of 'connection' and a symbolic metaphor" (Darian-Smith 1999, 3). According to Eve Darian-Smith, these signifying functions "together form a dynamic 'field' that represents shifting attitudes in England at national, regional, and local levels, to the experience of an ever-encroaching EU" (3). For writers who make use of this "dynamic 'field,'" these shifting attitudes are not solely directed toward the EU. If "any discussion of the Channel Tunnel and how it relates to issues of nationalism, sovereignty, or citizenship in the English imagination necessarily links the postcolonial condition with globalization, transnationalism, and modernity" (4–5), it is because the symbolic value the Chunnel accrues is based on how it facilitates the English nation's conception of itself as modern even as the Chunnel challenges that understanding.

Occasional Poems

In "Translating the English, 1989," published in her 1990 collection *The Other Country,* Carol Ann Duffy tacitly positions the decision to build the Chunnel as an offshoot of the cultural mood the poem registered after a decade of Conservative rule. The title of the poem simultaneously evokes linguistic and cultural translation. "The English" refers to both the language and the people. Here, then, the two strands Michael Woods reads in her work as "literal translation involved in changing from one language to another" and "metaphorical [translation]," which, in this case, involves the "political transformation of Britain since 1979" (2003, 169), come together to allow her to assess the state of the nation.

The truncated language of the poem and the speaker's play with syntax and verb tense in lines such as "Also the weather has been most improving / even in February" strongly imply that English is not the speaker's first language (Duffy 1990, 11). Despite this, there are clear indications that it is the speaker who performs the role of translator. The speaker's proud proclamation "We have here Edwina Currie / and The Sun newspaper" (11), which evokes the public scandal that came to a head in December 1988 when Currie, then minister of health, "provoked outrage" by suggesting that "most of Britain's egg production" was "infected with the salmonella bacteria" ("1988: Egg Industry Fury Over Salmonella Claim" 2008), indicates that he or she is a cultural insider. A few lines later, Duffy reinforces this when the speaker uses cultural shorthand to allude to the controversial minister's statements, warning, "Don't eat the eggs" (1990, 11).

The aphorisms and clichés the speaker uses are repetitions that denaturalize political rhetoric; their recontextualization constructs a view of the country that is very much tongue-in-cheek. "All very proud we now have / a green Prime Minister. What colour yours?" the speaker asks (Duffy 1990, 11). The shifting tone of the poem and the symbolic signifiers the speaker marshals to welcome the reader to his or her "country" reveal an ambivalent relation to cultural Englishness that alters its scope. For Woods, the tension in Duffy's forthright condemnation of how "England" has "been debased under the then Tory government" (2003, 172) can be traced to how the "voice" of the "persona of this monologue" is "commut[ed] to that of the tack-spitting poet" (173). However, the speaker's yoking together of incontrovertible national markers such as "Rule Britannia" and base crimes such as "child abuse" is indicative that he or she exemplifies a more complex expression of modern national identity than Woods allows for (Duffy 1990, 11). To some extent, Woods's reading of the poem participates in the narrative that Duffy's speaker tacitly critiques. It is not so much a fallen England that the speaker represents, but rather a vision of the modern nation laid bare.

The Chunnel appears in this poem as one of a chain of ambivalent cultural signifiers. Immediately following his or her evocation of the Channel Tunnel, the speaker says "You get here fast no problem to my country / my country my country welcome welcome welcome" (Duffy 1990, 11). The reference to the speed of entry anticipates the jibe François Mitterand made when the Chunnel opened: "Visitors who had sped through France, he [Mitterand] observed, would have plenty of time to appreciate the beauty of the English countryside as they trundled towards London" (Brogan 2014). It would not be until 2007 that the "new 68-mile high-speed link" would "join Europe's ever-growing network of 300kph (185mph) electric railways" (Glancey 2007). In the context of the poem, the speed of arrival is counterpoint to the backwardness of the ostensibly modern nation that the speaker depicts.

The speaker's positioning of the contested Chunnel as a gateway that enables entrance into instead of exit from England evokes the fears of ingress that underpinned objection to the project from the nineteenth century on. Through her speaker, Duffy tacitly registers how the Chunnel's close connection with railways threatened the larger narrative of greatness even as it seemed poised to recapture it. Eve Darian-Smith points out that "railways historically symbolized England's imperial power, and the EU's role in promoting the fast train thus suggests England's potential colonization by the New Europe, echoing the nation's past" (1999, 194). The resurrection of colonial discourses is undercut, however, by the state of the nation that the poem expresses. The view of the nation that Duffy's speaker offers counters the very conception of a pristine nation that will be despoiled by being connected to the continent. Here, the Channel Tunnel functions as a quintessential—if ambivalent—signifier of Englishness that facilitates the denaturalizing gaze of the speaker and that also incites the reader to interrogate what "my country" constitutes (Duffy 1990, 11).

Like Duffy, Patience Agbabi implicitly registers how postimperial scripts find expression through the signifying properties of the Channel Tunnel. The occasional nature of Agbabi's poem makes it unsurprising that the speaker in her sonnet offers a more positive view of the transnational possibilities the Chunnel has been taken to symbolize, though, like Duffy's poem, it stops short of a postnational vision. Included in *Jubilee Lines: 60 Poets for 60 Years*, an anthology that marks significant moments in Her Majesty's reign, Agbabi's poem, "Chunnel/Le Tunnel sous la Manche" (2012), overtly situates the Chunnel's construction within a longer historical narrative.

It soon becomes clear that the first-person speaker of the work is the Channel bed itself, a hard-won romantic conquest that has preoccupied men's minds even as they have fallen in love with the sea: "Moi, j'étais difficile, unyielding, hard to get / The men, they craved me more, too dangerous, too dear" (Agbabi 2012, 89). Agbabi's poem is a predictable and to some extent nonpartisan celebration of modern achievement: men on both sides are able to overcome the obstacles that make the tunnel difficult to forge. Their accomplishment and meeting soon take on mythical overtones, however. The link bridges nations but also historic cultures; it is forged from "Shakespeare Cliff" on the English side and constructed by "Europa's sisters" on the French (Agbabi 2012, 89). The speaker strategically positions the construction of the Tunnel within a longer Western cultural narrative on both sides. Even as the construction of the Chunnel implies forward-looking progress, interpretation of this accomplishment entails looking back.

Penetration of the Channel is not the object of desire, however. Instead, romantic fulfillment comes through the symbolic meeting of those who "carved down deep": "They first kissed here" (Agbabi 2012, 89). The speaker's representation of the construction of the link as both inevitable and desirable—an act that inspires the "reborn" Channel to declare "And now I am complete"—is reinforced by the speaker's effortless movement between French and English throughout the poem. Agbabi's tacit recognition of the complex signifying potential of the Chunnel emerges as the speaker describes the (un)natural movement "from cliff to breath" that takes place. In the context of the occasion it is meant to celebrate, the speaker's imperative plea for the listener to "put history on ice" and "salute me in two tongues" pays tribute to the idealism that led to its construction. It is not incidentally a vision that naturalizes the view that "social life is transnational to begin with" (Khagram and Levitt 2008, 8). The speaker's use of the colloquialism also foreshadows how the Chunnel will come to challenge teleological constructions as a symbol of temporal suspension, if perhaps only temporarily. Presumably, the ice will melt. The Channel Tunnel in Agbabi's poem is both "structure" and "sculpture" (Agbabi 2012, 89), a link that not only enables literal passage but also functions as a vessel of symbolic exchange that paradoxically elides even as it pays tribute to the construction and subsequent suspension of national difference.

Both poets capture how the Chunnel emerges out of but also comes to stand as a quick reference point for the specific political and cultural conjunctures that made its construction possible. Duffy and, to a greater extent, Agbabi insist on locating the Chunnel within a wider teleological historical narrative even as they show how the symbolic associations it takes on disrupt it. The Chunnel in Duffy's poem is implicated in an articulation of Englishness that resonates with the cultural morbidity Gilroy describes. Even in Agbabi's more hopeful depiction of the modern accomplishment that the Chunnel represents, the speaker insists that to look forward the nations must look back. Both poems speak to the wider symbolic implications of the Chunnel itself as a site in which modern and postmodern national and postnational scripts—and to some extent even prenational scripts—unsettlingly converge, creating unease.

Post (Chunnel) Scripts

From the outset of Julian Barnes's short story "Tunnel," published in his 1996 collection *Cross Channel,* the protagonist's contemplation of how the Chunnel—once so resisted—has become part of the general landscape signals his interrogation of the altered national community in which he claims membership. The elderly passenger's musings as he travels from King's Cross to Gare du Nord are offered during a journey that is habitual: "He reflected, as he did every time, on the surprising banality that within his lifetime Paris had become closer than Glasgow, Brussels than Edinburgh" (Barnes 1996, 191). For the narrator, the normalization of travel by Chunnel is emblematic of a more insidious alteration to the national character that is symbolized by how "wary camaraderie" has replaced the genuine communication of yesterday's traveling communities (196)—though even this notion is itself a nostalgic legacy that is belied by the fact that, though "rail travel involved new sociabilities" (Urry 2007, 105), passengers sought to find ways to "[maintain] . . . social distance" (106).

The transnational ideals that the Chunnel seems to exemplify are called into question by the presence of "fences" near the tunnel's entrance; the "unsullied concrete" that the elderly gentleman describes similarly configures the space as a historical no-man's-land (Barnes 1996, 199). What comes into view here, then, is how passage through the tunnel is an extension of the landscape the new experience of travel provides access to. The "inappreciable descent, . . . suave blackness" (199) that the narrator experiences is emblematic of the "homogenized Europeanism" that the Chunnel heralds (Apter 2002, 288). "On arrival," the narrator observes, "He had scarcely noticed the journey: countryside projected behind glass, twenty minutes of tunnel, then more projected countryside" (Barnes 1996, 208). What we see here is not only the homogenization of travel but of culture that Barnes also warns against in his own account of the Chunnel's opening.

Writing as London Correspondent for the *New York Times* in 1994, Barnes, in his coverage of the Chunnel's inauguration, argued for the importance of maintaining "the experience of transition" (1995, 294) that construction of the Chunnel has dramatically altered. "You do not have to be anti-European or xenophobic to like the idea of the frontier," he declares. "On the contrary" he continues, "the more Europe becomes integrated commercially and politically, the more each nation should confirm its cultural separateness" (294). Barnes's insistence on the importance of maintaining cultural distinctions derives from the same nostalgic and exclusivist structures of feeling that attend the end of empire. Though perhaps unfashionable, his resolve that cultural difference must be preserved signals the importance of intervening in a prevailing national narrative where even the most liberal narratives support cultural morbidity. For Barnes, like his narrator, the threat of the Chunnel is not so much the threat of transnationalism but rather the threat of a postmodernist cosmopolitanism that overwrites long-held distinctions.

Just beyond the Frame of Reference

Similarly, in Nicola Barker's *Darkmans* (2007), which focuses on Daniel Beede, "a lifelong Ashford resident whose victory against the Channel Tunnel's destruction of a local landmark took a Pyrrhic turn" (Ness 2007), the Chunnel is to some extent a period-bound signifier, "a vision of a moment" (Said [1993] 1994, 67) that is homogenizing and postmodern. Its very presence remolds the landscape around it into a pastiche of cultures as space becomes overtly "relational" and is configured as a passage that is "on the way to, or on the way from, somewhere else" (Urry 2007, 101). *Darkmans* opens at a "vulgar, graceless licensed 'family restaurant'" that is "thoughtfully constructed to service the adjacent Travel Inn, which had, in turn, been thoughtfully constructed to service the through-traffic from the Channel Tunnel" (Barker [2007] 2008, 3). Called the French Connection, the restaurant is a "prefabricated hut, inside of which a broad American roadhouse mentality rubbed up against all that was most intimate and accessible in Swiss chalet-style decor" (5). Here, the "homogenized Europeanism" (Apter 2002, 288) that Barnes's narrator fears—itself reshaped to become an "Americanized Euro-culture" (288)—is writ large against the English landscape. Proximity to the Chunnel begins to remake the nation.

Nonetheless, Barker is insistent that the Chunnel's meaning derives from "the various revisions" that it "provoke[s]" (Said [1993] 1994, 67). The Chunnel itself distills the paradoxical timeliness and untimeliness of Barker's novel that critics seeking to make sense of *Darkmans* (2007) have argued is typical of her treatment of history. Alissa G. Karl, for example, argues that, "set in a contemporary British town that overlaps with the medieval past," the novel "is from the outset concerned with re-thinking historical periodisation, causality and teleology" (2015, 337). Barnes paves the way for conceiving of the symbolic value of the Chunnel in this novel with the tongue-in-cheek description he offers in his own role as cultural translator for the *New York Times*: "What we have now … is the ultimate nineteenth-century project completed just before we enter the twenty-first century" (1995, 296). From this perspective, the achievement the Chunnel represents is belated. "Perhaps the Channel Tunnel has come too late," he says (295): "Imagine if it had been built a century or more ago. … Then it would have been a marvel: it might even have changed history, instead of merely adjusting it" (295–96). For Barker, it is precisely this anachronistic quality that captures the English historical view.

Even though the Chunnel itself is just beyond the reach of the characters who inhabit Barker's novel—and is largely outside the reader's purview—its construction drives the narrative action. Beede's attitude toward the "imminence" of the Chunnel affirms his status as English Everyman: he is "studiously phlegmatic" (Barker [2007] 2008, 6), a quintessential English stoic. This is with good reason, the narrator explains, based on how the plans for—and deferral of—the tunnel's construction "informed (and seasoned) his own childhood in much the same way that it had informed both his parents' and his grandparents' before them" (6). The naturalization of a relationship to the Chunnel that is agonistic and antagonistic in turn produces ambivalence; the continual threat of and reprieve from an altered sense of proximity is what Beede—and the English—became accustomed to, and to some extent it is this largely unacknowledged sense of being in a continual tension with otherness that is taken to define the national character. This insistence on duration speaks to the role the Chunnel has played from the nineteenth century on in acting as a barometer of, even as it shapes, the nation's cultural understanding of itself as modern. Amelia Hadfield-Amkhan makes this point when she argues that "the objections to the completion of the tunnel in 1994, while absorbing new political realities, still echoed the strain of those of 1882" (2010, 90).

The narrator's itemization of the aspects of the Chunnel's construction that underlie but do not precipitate Beede's sense of betrayal—the substance of the novel itself—is a catalogue of local, parochial concern. He is "passingly concerned about the loss of the rare Spider Orchid (the site of the proposed Folkestone Terminal was one of the few places it flourished, nationally)" and "the currently endangered great crested newt" (Barker [2007] 2008, 6); he is "aware . . . of what the true (and potentially devastating) implications of a Channel link would be on the Kentish shipping industry" (6); and he "harboured serious fears . . . that many of the employment opportunities of the project would pass over local people" (6–7). Barker's focus on the regional concerns—the "headaches—and terrible heartache" experienced by "East Kent" (7) is a faithful depiction of objections that arose as construction of the Channel Tunnel began.[1] If these concerns have since been absorbed into the present day of the nation—the narrator observes in a parenthetical aside that the Chunnel is "now a source of . . . unalloyed national complacency and pride" (7)—it is because of how these transformations have been uncritically reabsorbed.

Beede's relationship to the Chunnel is instead changed because of his awareness of his complicity in—and consequent denaturalization from—a more complex narrative of nationhood that the Chunnel allows for but also disavows. "When the developer's plans for the new Folkestone Terminal were initially proposed" (Barker [2007] 2008, 7), the narrator explains, it became clear that "the access road from the terminal to the M20 was due to cut a wide path straight between Newington and Peene" (7). Beede "maintained . . . a strong sense—however fallacious—that the union of these two places (like the union of his two parents) was a critical—almost a *physical*—part of his own identity" (7–8). Although this reshaping of the English landscape initiates Beede's involvement with the Chunnel's construction—and seems to affirm his Englishness based on the role that landscape plays in his sense of self—it is in fact his involvement in the creation of the "hard-won Alternative" (8) that sees the access road rerouted that comes to be the driving force behind his actions.

His involvement with the preservation and relocation of the "beautiful, ancient properties" that are "sacrificed" to keep Newington and Peene together (Barker [2007] 2008, 8) is undertaken not out of a sense of outrage at "The Newington Hit List" (9) but out of a sense of obligation borne from Beede's involvement in the revised plan. In a parenthetical aside, the narrator focalizes through Beede to observe, "Didn't he owe the condemned properties that much, at least?" (9). This interjection, like the "italicised running commentary (sometimes from specific characters, sometimes not)" contributes to the reader's sense that "the text never rests in any conclusive form" (Karl 2015, 348). Alissa Karl explains, "The thought-processes of narrator, character, and reader are perpetually under revision and hence in a state of decontainment" (348) that has the effect also of "undermin[ing] the notion of a cumulative temporality" (349)—an effect not incidentally produced by the attempt to preserve the properties that Beede is involved in.

The reconfiguration of geographical space and the expectation that Beede's sense of self will be renegotiated or at least reaffirmed with his victory are displaced. Instead, Barker's novel seems to support Emily Apter's argument that, in the Chunnel, "time supplants place as the measure of subjective experience" and, furthermore, that "antihistoricist chronotypes displace the map, implicitly disorienting historical memory" (2002, 289). Instead of offering a "posthistorical, postnational" (289) view that overwrites even a transnationalist perspective, the disorientation that Apter describes spills over onto the landscape that surrounds the Chunnel in Barker's novel and is what ensures the continuation of historical scripts of Englishness.

The conditions for preservation are imposed by Eurotunnel and are based on what can be determined to have "real historical significance" (Barker [2007] 2008, 9); the fact that the mandate allows for the partial preservation of sites foreshadows Barker's complication of the terms "historical" and "modern," which are themselves political signposts. The candidate for preservation that Beede is linked to—the Mill House—is one such palimpsestic site; its credentials that "meet Eurotunnel's high specifications" are based on its duration, but also subsequent modifications: it "had been mentioned in the Domesday Book and had a precious, eighteenth-century timber frame" (9). The Mill House lays bare the structures that led to its production and guaranteed its preservation up until the point of the Channel Tunnel's construction. The very modifications that ensure that it is a likely candidate for preservation ensure its destruction, however. "At some point (and who could remember when, exactly?) it became distressingly apparent that recent 'improvements' to the newer parts of Mill House had seriously endangered the older structure's integrity" to the extent that "the old mill might never be able to function independently in its eighteenth-century guise; like a conjoined twin, it might only really be able to exist as a small part of its former whole" (10). With this revelation, distinctions between Beede's past and the present time of narration increasingly erode. Italicized interjections—"Now hang on— . . . .What are you saying here, exactly?"—disrupt the present time of narration (10). The collapse of temporal distinctions, here, intimates that the way that Beede experiences time is irreparably altered.

For Beede, the Mill metonymically comes to stand for history itself: "He had pushed his ear up against the past and had sensed the ancient breath held within it. He had gripped the liver of history and had felt it squelching in his hand" (Barker [2007] 2008, 10). Beede's personification of history confirms that it is far from static—and far from anonymous. It is imperial in its demand for conquest and survival. He feels the liver *"Expanding—Struggling"* beneath his hand (10). These last gasps are resonant with the rhetoric of expansion that sold the Chunnel to the British people. This personification of history also paves the way for a further act of transference. Beede himself comes to share the symptoms of the sickened Mill: "He was so stressed—felt so *invested* in his thwarted physicality—that he actually thought he might be developing some kind of fatal disease" (11). Like the Mill, "Pieces of him stopped functioning" (11). Beede's hyperbolic account of when he "saw History *die*" (11) is a reaction, in part, to the exposure of and destruction of a composite—a convergence of time periods that the historical narrative of Englishness covers and conceals; it is also a reaction to the breakdown of his own sense of Englishness.

Beede's obstinate fidelity to the idea of authenticity nonetheless means that when the "salvageable parts of the mill" such as the "ancient Kent Peg Tiles" that had been "preserved . . . maintained . . . entrusted" are lost (Barker [2007] 2008, 11–12), he becomes a "vengeful tsunami of history" (13). From Beede's perspective "Progress, *modernity*" have thwarted his attempt to salvage even "a semblance of what had been" (12). His decision to take revenge against the person he believes stole the tiles nonetheless affirms his (nostalgic) allegiance and fidelity to the notion of authenticity that the Mill House challenges.

At the same time, his actions make him an agent of postmodernity. After arriving at the conclusion that local resident Tom Higson "was behind the theft of those tiles from the old mill" Kane explains, "Beede resolved to duplicate his life. To turn everything he touched—everything he cared about—into a lie" (Barker [2007] 2008, 821). Beede's plan to replicate the quotidian items that fill Higson's home, taking possession of the originals himself, is not straightforward. Artist and forger Peta confesses that she "was instructed to build a tiny fault into each piece" of his life that she replicates in order "to help generate" an "indefinable sense of unease" (821). The crux of Beede's revenge—a series of repetitions with a difference—metonymically represents his altered conception of history, which is revealed indirectly through his admission, early in the novel and focalized through the narrator, that the effect the Mill House has on him is that "nothing—*nothing*—had felt the same, afterwards" (12).

Beede's revenge is complicated when his son, Kane, discovers that the artist and forger Beede has commissioned to construct simulacra is the person for whom the tiles were stolen and, more importantly, when Peta admits she has perpetrated a "double-bluff" (Barker [2007] 2008, 823). That is, Peta "swapped . . . *back*" (823) the items that she created, surrounding Beede with the repetitions with a difference meant to provoke unease. As Kane points out, this is an ironic repetition that violates Beede's assumption that she will assist him in "good faith" (823). It is also a move that re-implicates Beede as an unwitting participant in the process of forgetting that underlies historical modes of Englishness.

Kane's own attempt to understand Beede's actions is similarly based on self-interest; he is attempting to make sense of the scripts that he feels are converging around him. If, for Peta, "Life is just a series of coincidences, accidents and random urges which we carefully forge . . . into a convenient design," for Kane a "sense of . . . *connectedness*" tempers individual agency (Barker [2007] 2008, 824). It is no accident that what Peta describes mimics the amnesiac process by which England and Englishness have historically operated by constructing and "then forgetting that it has created, a parallel story of the past" (Summers-Bremner 2005, 273). Peta explains, "It doesn't serve our purpose to see the whole picture. And the parts that we do see? . . . They're often the same parts. And how we keep it fresh is that we constantly re-create them, then conveniently forget them, then suddenly rediscover them anew, own them anew" (Barker [2007] 2008, 825). The process of reclamation that Peta describes is undercut, however. Peta's sense that the crisis that Beede experiences is personal rather than social is too reductive from Kane's perspective. Against Peta's view that "it was never about the tiles . . . It was only ever about Beede and what he felt. Or maybe—more to the point—what he *couldn't* feel" (826), Kane introduces another possibility. He notes, "Perhaps you underestimate him. . . . Perhaps Beede actually knew something—all along—that you didn't" (826). Kane's staunch defense of his father at this juncture of the novel positions him as the modern heir of the brand of Englishness that Beede represents—the recognition of which is provoked by and embodied by the Chunnel even as it lies just outside the frame.

Railing the Chunnel

Ben Okri's *In Arcadia* (2002), like Barker's *Darkmans* (2007), presents itself as a search for meaning in a ruthlessly postmodern context. Though the Chunnel is also at the forefront of Okri's quest narrative, unlike Barker, Okri—like Barnes in "Tunnel"—makes explicit use of the symbolic implications of railway journeys to contemplate the individual's relationship to history, memory, and community. The first-person narrator, television presenter Lao, foreshadows how the "literal journey" to find Arcadia will come to "[suggest] . . . a metaphorical one" (Fox 2005) the speaker describes the train that will bear them across the Channel toward France as it is "poised to set off, poised to rush past the countryside, beneath the waters, at wonderful speed designed to postpone time" (Okri [2002] 2014, 62).

The suspension of time that the speaker anticipates is a characteristic trope in railway literature, wherein passage by rail performs a denaturalizing function. What comes into view at the outset of the journey is a familiar iteration. The landscape is overtly Larkinesque: "We watched our own lives go past in the shape of the suburban houses, the drab back gardens, the houses that seemed sadder and more monotonous as we sped on" (Okri [2002] 2014, 70). What the group is in fact experiencing, the narrator explains, is "the back view of [their] lives. The way it seems to strangers, never to us" (71). The speaker's evocation of the language of Philip Larkin's "The Whitsun Weddings" suggests that an intimate view of modern Englishness encapsulated by the "suburbia" that "spe[eds] past" (74) is on offer here. What is connotation in Larkin's poem is denotation here, however. The speaker spells out the mundane existence the passengers seek to escape. Alistair Fox explains, "In the course of the work, Okri represents and interprets the condition of the contemporary world, which is found to be unsatisfactory, and contrasts it with an alternative condition that is viewed as being an antidote to the first one" (2005). As with Duffy, Okri challenges the notion of an unspoiled England and Englishness that underwrote anxieties about the Chunnel's construction at the same time that the search for an alternative that he introduces upholds the ideal.

In Okri's novel, it is travel through the Channel Tunnel itself that forces confrontation with the self. The narrator explains that it "makes us see inward, against our will" (Okri [2002] 2014, 77) and, furthermore, it prepares the individual for "dislocation, for paradox" (79). This dislocation, as in Barker's novel, is predicated on how the Chunnel seems to privilege temporal over geographical reorganization and affiliation. In short, the Chunnel itself stands as an exemplar of the postmodern that is borne out by how the high-speed rail alters the experience of railway travel even as it promises escape from it. If modern railways are associated with modernity, travel by high-speed rail seems to stand in for a postmodern experience rooted in ambivalent and anachronistic repetitions.

The dislocation that Okri's characters experience reveals Arcadia to be a contradictory concept that "can only come out of reality, not an ideal" (Okri [2002] 2014, 201); this is true for Englishness as well. At the end of the novel, in a reversal, Okri positions his passengers as the object of the gaze. As the occupants "[stare] . . . wistfully out of the window of the train," the "world looking in" reads them as "inscriptions" (291). This reversal functions as a self-conscious declaration that the characters are morbidly implicated in the orienting narrative they struggle against.

Arrival and Departure

Barnes's and Okri's depictions of railway travel perform a similar function to the role comparable journeys played in "nineteenth-century novels as an event of travel and social encounter" (Trachtenberg 1986, xiv). The description of the link as a "hi-tech triumph of ideology" (Came 1994) upon its opening not only conveys the metonymic importance it holds as a fraught symbol of the future of transnationalism but also captures how the mobility it makes possible has come to be taken to be an apposite site for the interrogation of modernity and postmodernity in turn as Okri's novel, especially, shows.[2] "At bottom," however, railway journeys were "an event of spatial relocation in the service of production" (Trachtenberg 1986, xiv). The literary works under consideration in this essay lend themselves to periodization: they register the public and political mood. In part, this is due to how the anachronistic qualities of rail direct attention to the covert struggle over Englishness that is played out through the Chunnel. Like railways that "[connect] that which is routine with that which is exceptional in such a way as to transform our sense of the commonplace" (Revill 2012, 54), literary representations of the Chunnel denaturalize its absorption into the contemporary landscape. Attending to the symbolic connotations of the Chunnel means acknowledging that politically mobilized crisis narratives have a longer and more intimate provenance that is bound up with how the nation has and continues to historically understand itself.

Heather Joyce received her PhD from Queen's University in Kingston, Ontario, in 2011 and is now teaching at Grande Prairie Regional College. She specializes in modern and contemporary British literature and has taught courses in short fiction, modern prose fiction, and postcolonial studies. Her current research derives from her interest in mapping intersections of culture, power, and politics.

Notes

1. Political cartoons by Mac published in the *Daily Mail* in 1989 and 1993 depict the arbitrary and destructive reformulation of the landscape and hint at the regional divisions that construction of the Chunnel exposed.

2. These associations are captured by the split focus of Yuko Kondo's commission for Euro Rail (Kondo 2017)

References

"1988: Egg Industry Fury Over Salmonella Claim." 2008. On This Day: 3 December 1988." BBC News. http://news.bbc.co.uk/onthisday/hi/dates/stories/december/3/newsid_2519000/2519451.stm. Accessed 16 April 2021.

Adcock, Brian. 2015. "Political Cartoon." *The Guardian*, 1 August.

Agbabi, Patience. 2012. "Chunnel / Le Tunnel sous la Manche." In *Jubilee Lines: 60 Poets for 60 Years*, edited by C. A. Duffy, 89. London: Faber and Faber.

Apter, Emily. 2002. "Afterword: From Literary Channel to Narrative Chunnel." In *The Literary Channel: The Inter-National Invention of the Novel*, edited by M. Cohen and C. Dever, 286–93. Princeton, NJ: Princeton University Press.

Barker, Nicola. (2007) 2008. *Darkmans*. London: Harper Perennial.

Barnes, Julian. 1995. "Froggy! Froggy! Froggy!" In *Letters from London*, 282–96. New York: Vintage International.

Barnes, Julian. 1996. "Tunnel." In *Cross Channel*, 189–211. New York: Alfred A. Knopf.

"'Brexit' Will Not Affect Channel Tunnel, Says Eurotunnel." 2016. *Railway Gazette*, 24 June. http://www.railwaygazette.com/news/policy/single-view/view/brexit-will-not-affect-channel-tunnel-says-eurotunnel.html. Accessed 16 April 2021.

Brogan, Benedict. 2014. "Twenty Years of Chunnel Vision." *The Telegraph*, 3 May. http://www.telegraph.co.uk/news/worldnews/europe/10804227/Twenty-years-of-Chunnel-vision.html. Accessed 16 April 2021.

Came, Francois. 1994. "Two Nations Linked by Blood, Sweat and Toil." *The Guardian*, 6 May. https://www.theguardian.com/travel/1994/may/06/railtravel.wonders.channeltunnel. Accessed 16 April 2021.

Darian-Smith, Eve. 1999. *Bridging Divides: The Channel Tunnel and English Legal Identity in the New Europe*. Berkeley: University of California Press.

Duffy, Carol Ann. 1990. "Translating the English, 1989." In *The Other Country*, 11. London: Anvil Press Poetry.

Fetherston, Drew. 1997. *The Chunnel: The Amazing Story of the Undersea Crossing of the English Channel*. New York: Times Books.

Fox, Alistair Graeme. 2005. "In Search of the Postmodern Utopia in Ben Okri's *In Arcadia*." *PORTAL: Journal of Multidisciplinary International Studies* 2, no. 2.

Franklin, Stanley. 1968. "Political Cartoon." *Daily Mirror*, 23 February.

Gibb, Richard. 1994. "The Channel Tunnel Project: Origins and Development." In *The Channel Tunnel: A Geographical Perspective*, edited by R. Gibb, 1–29. New York: John Wiley and Sons.

Gilroy, Paul. 2005. *Postcolonial Melancholia*. New York: Columbia University Press.

Glancey, Jonathan. 2007. "The Miracle of St. Pancras." *The Guardian*, 11 October. https://www.theguardian.com/society/2007/oct/11/communities.architecture. Accessed 16 April 2021.

Gourvish, Terry. 2006. *The Official History of Britain and the Channel Tunnel*. London: Routledge.

Hadfield-Amkhan, Amelia. 2010. *British Foreign Policy, National Identity, and Neoclassical Realism*. Lanham, MD: Rowman and Littlefield.

Hall, Stuart. 1997. "The Local and the Global: Globalization and Ethnicity." In *Culture, Globalization and the World-System: Contemporary Conditions for the Representation of Identity*, edited by A. D. King, 19–40. Minneapolis: University of Minnesota Press.

Hannam, Kevin, Mimi Sheller, and John Urry. 2006. "Editorial: Mobilities, Immobilities, and Moorings." *Mobilities* 1, no. 1: 1–22.

Haselden, William Kerridge. (1907) 1914. "Political Cartoon." *Daily Mirror,* 21 September. (Original work published 18 February 1907.)

Karl, Alissa G. 2015. "The Zero Hour of the Neoliberal Novel." *Textual Practice* 29, no. 2: 335–55.

Khagram, Sanjeev, and Peggy Levitt. 2008. "Constructing Transnational Studies." In *The Transnational Studies Reader: Intersections and Innovations*, edited by S. Khagram and P. Levitt, 1–22. New York: Routledge.

Kondo, Yuko. 2017. "Rail Europe." http://www.yukokondo.com/works/rail-europe. Accessed 8 June 2021.

Ness, Patrick. 2007. "A Roar, a Titter, and a Tee-hee-hee." *The Guardian,* 5 May. https://www.theguardian.com/books/2007/may/05/featuresreviews.guardianreview3. Accessed 16 April 2021.

Okri, Ben. (2002) 2014. *In Arcadia*. London: Head of Zeus.

Perkins, Anne. 2017. "May's Brexit Focus on Immigration Will Have Catastrophic Consequences. *The Guardian,* 18 January. https://www.theguardian.com/comment isfree/2017/jan/18/theresa-may-brexit-immigration-focus-catastropic-conse quences. Accessed 16 April 2021.

Rail Europe. 2021. "Eurostar Train Tickets." https://www.raileurope.com/en-ca/trains/eurostar. Accessed 8 June 2021.

Revill, George. 2012. *Railway*. London: Reaktion Books.

Said, Edward W. (1993) 1994. *Culture and Imperialism*. New York: Vintage Books.

Schivelbusch, Wolfgang. 1986. *The Railway Journey: The Industrialization of Time and Space in the 19th Century*. Berkeley: University of California Press.

Summers-Bremner, Eluned. 2005. "Family at War: Memory, Sibling Rivalry, and the Nation in *Border Crossing* and *Another World*." In *Critical Perspectives on Pat Barker*, edited by S. Monteith, M. Jolly, N. Yousaf, and R. Paul, 266–82. Columbia: University of South Carolina Press.

Taylor, Matthew, Patrick Wintour, and Jessica Elgot. 2015. "Calais Crisis: Cameron Pledges to Deport More People to End 'Swarm' of Migrants." *The Guardian,* 30 July. https://www.theguardian.com/uk-news/2015/jul/30/calais-migrants-make-further-attempts-to-cross-channel-into-britain. Accessed 16 April 2021.

Trachtenberg, Alan. 1986. "Foreword." In *The Railway Journey: The Industrialization of Time and Space in the 19th Century*, by W. Schivelbusch, xiii–xvi. Berkeley: University of California Press.

Urry, John. 2007. *Mobilities*. Cambridge, UK: Polity Press.

Woods, Michael. 2003. "'What It Is Like in Words': Translation, Reflection and Refraction in the Poetry of Carol Ann Duffy." In *The Poetry of Carol Ann Duffy: "Choosing Tough Words,"* edited by A. Michelis and A. Rowland, 169–85. Manchester, UK: Manchester University Press.

CHAPTER 6

Crossing Borders on and beyond the Train in *Joan of Arc of Mongolia* (1989)

Steven Spalding

The transnational ambitions of German director Ulrike Ottinger's *Johanna d'Arc of Mongolia* (*Joan of Arc of Mongolia*) (1989)—a film that features famed French actress and activist Delphine Seyrig (playing the character of Lady Windemere)—are in evidence from the start of the film. Seyrig's Windemere accompanies a small group of female characters as they travel out of Europe, across Soviet Russia and into Mongolia, first on the Trans-Siberian Railway—noteworthy as the longest train line in the world—and then on the Trans-Mongolian Railway. Roughly one half of Ottinger's playful narrative takes place entirely on trains, while the second unfolds on the Mongolian plains, where the female European travelers find themselves roaming on camelback and sleeping in yurts as the gently handled captives of a Mongolian princess (the film's titular character). This two-part structure underpins the importance of this film to the present collection: its first part is entirely devoted to examining the meanings and experiences of the transnational train journey, while the second part departs from the train's confines in order to explore a dramatically different experience of intercultural exchange. The train is shown to be limiting—a rolling museum of sorts of train history and the West, a space for sharing stories and song in fairly lavish comfort—and, by becoming separated from its trajectory, the group is able to face a different mode of transport, one with its own mode of spatial use. Most importantly, they can then confront representatives of a radically different Other. Thus, the putative vehicle of transnationalism falls short in the characters'—and the film's—project of crossing borders and encountering cultural differences. In having its characters leave the train behind and experience the cultural rites and rituals performed by the Mongolian characters on the steppes, *Joan of Arc of Mongolia* underscores the limits of the train as a context for getting beyond a certain set of cultural references and practices and facing intercultural experience. Just like her character Windermere, Ottinger's transnationalism has this oft-cited ethnographic ambitiousness; I would add, however, that it is utopian as well. Ultimately, part 1 appears to turn a jovial, light comical eye toward the interactions among the European train travelers, and the train seems less a space of liminality and more a rehearsal of the familiar, isolated, and insulated from the rail journey itself (on liminality and train travel, see Despotopolou [2015, 95, and infra]). Through what has been aptly named a postmodern lens that skillfully mixes irony and Romanticism, Ottinger imagines what a genuine encounter of cultural differences in the contemporary era might look like (An 2018, 130). Her choice of the train as starting point is a remarkably evocative one since it puts into play cultural meanings that the train as trope mobilizes, in turn allowing the Mongolian detour to have an even greater effect of *dépaysement* (change of scenery)—of separation and crossing of borders into difference. This reading of *Joan of Arc of Mongolia* has as primary focus to tease out many of the train meanings referenced in part 1 of the film, and to connect these to the film's second part. I then discuss the outcomes described at the end of the film for each of the main Western characters to explore further the significance of the Mongolian journey. This project seeks to illustrate how Ottinger's film offers an insightful critique of modern mobility and conventional notions of the transnational. In making the case for going beyond the train—itself too easily a prolongation or projection of Western comforts across time and space—*Joan of Arc of Mongolia* offers a compelling, ethically performed, and visually stunning representation of an encounter with a cultural Other.

This reading of *Joan of Arc of Mongolia* departs from much of the scholarship on Ottinger's (1989) film. Scholars have tended to read the first half of the film as essentially preparation for seeing an equivalence between the performance of Western cultures on the train and that of the Mongolian culture the film's characters witness in part 2 (ChaiWalla 2010). This view emphasizes the train sequences as intended to initiate the viewer in Lady Windemere's perspective, to become attentive observers to the acting out of cultural roles. Lady Windemere's role as cultural ambassador and narrator remains consistently important throughout both parts of the film, and viewers do not need to see the first part in order to understand that she is serving as guide through the women's sojourn on the steppes. I argue that there is more to part 1 than just this. Taking our cue from Khagram and Levitt's definition of philosophical transnationalism, which puts forward the premise that our social lives are inherently transnational (2008, 2), I read Ottinger's train as a critique of international train sociality, even voicing an argument about the long-term outcomes of the projection of a limited and limiting Western international monoculture.[1] The first part of the film is vital for capturing a cultural experience of Western train travel and its limitations, so as to articulate the conditions that a productive encounter with cultural difference (such as occurs in part 2) entails. To exit the train altogether is also to step away from the cultural signs and frames of reference it embodies and sustains.

Ottinger's endeavor is a feminist one not because of any dogmatic or programmatic adherence to feminist politics[2] but rather because the interruption of the train's mastery of space and time creates a symbolic separation from the linear, masculine teleology of Western train travel and sets the film's group of female protagonists on a detour through uncharted spaces and unregulated time. John Urry identified the creation of railway time as the introduction of a new regime of time, both regimented and commodified; here, the presupposed punctuality of the train's timetable gets lost in the long distances traveled; the timetable is then altogether abolished when the women leave the train (2007, 98). Release from the bonds of the train's path and rhythm marks the film's initial crossing of borders, and prepares the terms of an intercultural encounter that will change the lives of the travelers meaningfully. The film manages to accomplish a number of deliberate and fascinating symbolic movements—all with a gentle, wry, and ironic sensibility rather than an expressly political one. It portrays and parodies stereotypical European and international train travelers, Russian peasants, military officers, and train service personnel and the interactions among these heterogeneous groups, and it debunks the legendary mythos around the Trans-Siberian as a tsarist (and male) legacy and accomplishment. A gentle and whimsical sensibility is no doubt in evidence when, in the second part, the train—along with its attendant symbolism—has been defeated by that least likely of antagonists, a peaceful band of nomadic Mongolian women on horseback and their brightly decorated leader. This same sensibility might explain the choice of Seyrig's character's name, which is borrowed from an Oscar Wilde play that had—by the 1970s—been adapted to film seven times, and even more times to television. Written in 1891, *Lady Windermere's Fan* was Wilde's first major success in the theater, initiating his audience to his signature blend of humor and serious themes. Taking the character's name from Wilde pays homage to that source, while extricating the female lead from her entirely domestic setting—indeed, Ottinger's setting for her Lady Windermere is anything but domestic, and is a world apart from the potential adulterous misdeeds of men. Throughout the film, Seyrig's Windemere plays the crucial role of intermediary figure for characters and audience alike, helpfully smoothing the edges of the film's critical pivot from observing the at-times sterile, at other times bombastic introspection on board the train to creative and vibrant engagement and exchange with the Mongolian community away from the rails. While fully anchored in a strongly postmodern reflexivity, and betraying no illusions about itself as construction, Joan of Arc of Mongolia revels in its performances of cultural difference and ritual. This reflexivity affords the film's so-called natives—the Mongolians performing a traditional Mongolian nomadic lifestyle—greater agency than as mere props to the Western characters' journey.

In the film's initial sequence, where each of the main female characters is presented in her place on the train, the introductions of Lady Windermere and Frau Vohwinkel seem especially important in terms of preparing the film's commentary on the train and its own narrative direction. The film's opening shots are of Lady Windermere, sitting in her luxurious train car, crowded in by artistic and historical artifacts. Windermere's voice-over narration accompanies the camera's leisurely, meandering pan around the compartment—termed appropriately as sumptuous by Galt (2011, 282)—and displaying the Orientalist-themed artwork (paintings, printed screens, dolls, vases, and masks) and the imperial-era furnishings of the train car, evoking the colonialist past and origins of Western train travel. Unlike the other characters, Windermere does not speak on screen; one hears her voice only in-off, which accords her an elevated authorial status and voice. Coupled with the aristocratic furnishings around her, Windermere has from the very beginning a detached aspect; an ethnographer of sorts by pastime, she is not of the aristocratic world of the objects around her, but rather inhabits that world ironically, even whimsically. Indeed, she appears to be constantly scrutinizing the behavior—and performances—of everyone around her as well as herself. Against this backdrop and as a kind of theoretical preamble, Windemere's voice-over identifies many of the Western cultural tropes of the railway journey that the film will, in turn, play on. These include the notion of the train as a technological subduing or taming of wild and uncharted places, and fantasies of the East and of pushing limits, of penetrating uncharted territory and planting marking signs of civilization. The train is an instrument of seeing, mapping, penetrating, and taming, simultaneously finding, identifying, and situating the Other in an assigned space. Windemere's voice-over speaks of the fearful myth of the void:

> Yermak Timofeyevich crosses the border between Europe and Asia and beholds for the first time the unending verdant expanses, the myth of the green void. Once only the bravest of the Chinese travelers and merchants

dared to venture this far, into the utter void. Inventing artistic means, they created signs in the land of the void. An initial attempt to tame the raw wilderness with the aid of cultivated nature. The made clearings in the shape of huge, written signs in the forests of conifers, in which they then planted oaks. Their signs changed color with the seasons and could be seen from afar. An attempt to place a sign in the void, to leave a mark. The fears of the travelers were ... for a moment allayed. And now, much more than a sign, this line leading into the heart of the slumbering wilds, the Transsiberian follows this line as simply and as easily as a finger follows the path on a map from Europe to Asia. (Ottinger 1989)

In this description, the ease and speed of train travel has transformed the notion of the border and the transnational, and has put fears of the limitlessness of the green void to rest. The train is, in this sense, itself also a kind of act of narration, of making clearings and filling them with signs. While on its surface Windemere's voice-over addresses the first perceptions of Asia by European travelers, from this inaugural moment of the film's journey viewers understand that this train trip is also an evo-cation of and deliberation on the origins of the train and its meanings in Western culture, and that culture's sense of limits and boundaries. Additionally, there is a deliberation on the Lumière brothers' *L'Arrivée du train en gare de La Ciotat* (Arrival of a train at La Ciotat station) that famous piece of Ur-film at the origins of the cinema itself.[3] Furthermore, Windemere will retain the authorial role of a kind of infra-diegetic voice-over narrator, putting the other travelers' transcultural experiences into words—or as one critic puts it, "she functions to bring things into the realms of the verbal" (ChaiWalla 2010). For Windemere, then, the "green void" has more to do with the solicitousness or invitation of the blank page, on which to record, document, recount, and examine the stories of self and Other.

Where Lady Windermere's introduction offers a conceptual intro-duction to the film, Frau Vohwinkel's introduction adds a few familiar, traditional symbolic dynamics and meanings of train travel to the film's preamble. Just after Lady Windermere is introduced, Frau Vohwinkel (at 3'18") is shown pacing back and forth, alone in her compartment, reading aloud from her Baedeker's guide about the construction of the Trans-Siberian Railway, framed by photos from the construction on the wall behind her. Her Baedeker denotes conventional European tourism, and the authority of that father of modern tourism who tells travelers all they could need to know throughout their journeys, insulating them from misunderstandings, misadventures, getting lost, or losing time. In-troduced as a schoolteacher, Vohwinkel initially comes across as a cari-cature of the bored housewife stereotype, who will be most challenged by the transnational and transcultural journey of the film. The focus in what she reads and then expounds on is on the train itself as modern technological and logistical marvel, and only in an incidental way is the terrain traversed given mention. She says,

> At times up to 70,000 workers were engaged in building the Transsiberian Railway. When you consider . . . just the task of organizing . . . the transportation, food supply, lodging, medical care, sanitary facilities. . . . Back then everything which today is done by machines or calculated by computers had to be performed by engineers and workers. An incredible feat! . . . A triumph of the human will! I admire this energetic, thorough Sergei Yulyevich Witte—a German—well it says here "on his father's side," at least. My God, I would be lost here without my Baedeker. . . . This way at least . . . I know the relevant facts behind all this greenness. (Ottinger 1989, 3'18"–4'33")

The greenness threatens to engulf civilization, so the narration in her Baedeker of the train's history of conquering the terrain and reducing it to something forever off in the distance out her train car window is Frau Vohwinkel's instrument of civilization. In addition to her bourgeois tourist's notion of travel—one that hinges on the purchase of the guidebook as the primary means of acquiring the travel experience—Frau Vohwinkel appears to reveal a nationalistic prejudice when she discovers lead engineer Witte's part-German origins. Her exuberance at recounting these facts is an almost infantilizing naïveté; the female consumer marveling over the male accomplishment of the Trans-Siberian signposts her as not much emancipated from traditional patriarchal Western ideas.[4] Indeed, in this Frau Vohwinkel embodies a strong contrast to the three other female characters who embark on the Mongolian adventure together: Lady Windemere, Fanny Ziegler, and Giovanna. Reticent to welcome new experiences not already programmed on her itinerary and weary of others (especially Others), Vohwinkel must overcome her fear of the green void in order to cross self-imposed traditional national borders and limits in a liberating process of self-discovery.

This part of part 1 illustrates the ways in which Ottinger's critique of the train dovetails with observations made by Wolfgang Schivelbusch ([1977] 1986) in his *Railway Journey: The Industrialization of Time and Space in the 19th Century.* In examining the early history of the train in Europe and North America Schivelbusch characterizes the train as a networking of the industrial city into the landscape of the nation and forever transforming the spatial meanings and relations of those regions. In "losing their inherited place" Schivelbusch writes, they also lose "their traditional spatio-temporal presence, or as Walter Benjamin sums it up in one word, their 'aura'" ([1977] 1986, 41). Elsewhere, Schivelbusch describes how the transforming power of the rail network resulted in the creation of new kinds of landscapes, "a producer of territories," particularly as a function of the use-value the urban economy could assign to those regions (91). For Vohwinkel the train is a projection of familiarity into the unknown, into territories that have not yet been incorporated into the Western urban network and economy. Like the "sign in the void" of Windermere's introductory voice-over, the train imperiously forges a network, producing a territory out of the various economies, timetables, and consumable landscapes through which it traverses.

Vohwinkel's introduction thus adds a different layer of class perspective to what Lady Windemere represents: that of the traditional bourgeois consumer of travel, for whom train travel is a mode of consumption, much as she consumes the narratives in her travel guide. She later criticizes Giovanna's way of being a tourist when she insists to her that, because the young backpacker is traveling without a guidebook such as Vohwinkel's, she is traveling with "insufficient knowledge" and "too lightly in every respect" (49'08"–49'10"). Just as she mentions the greenness above, Vohwinkel echoes several times the way in which nearly every character on the train refers to the tundra or void outside the train; indeed, during the lengthy dining car party scene, Vohwinkel refers to the green inferno. This is akin to the "loss of landscape" Schivelbusch identifies in descriptions of early train travel; the new "panoramic perspective" of high-speed train travel involved separating the first train travelers from their relationship to the land, flattening the world into a blurry panorama of one-dimensional impressions ([1977] 1986, 61 and infra). Ottinger's characters' disappointment with the "colorless aridity" (Katz's terms; Ottinger 1989, 50'12") outside the train car windows expresses a longing for something more that—for all its entertainments and comforts—the train cannot provide. Fanny Ziegler, in her first words in the film, in a singsong voice, says "melancholy, monotony, monochromy." If it is true that the world outside the train car windows—though coded as invitation by Windemere, and source of fear by Vohwinkel—has little else to offer in part 1 of *Joan of Arc of Mongolia,* that is as much owing to the nature of train travel itself as it is to Ottinger's very clear aesthetic choice to avoid entirely the intersplicing of external shots from and of the train. Unlike the very familiar cinematic tropes of trains shot at a distance as they wind through dramatic terrain or of shots out windows at moving landscapes—or even Hitchcock's well-known train-entering-tunnel shot from *North by Northwest*—up until it is stopped by the Mongolian nomads the train in *Joan of Arc of Mongolia* is something of an existentialist *huis clos* (behind closed doors). This subtle enclosure of the narrative within the train in the first part of the film serves a purpose that is critical to the film's argument: namely, it allows the narrative to dwell on the train as a microcosm of a Western pluralist or internationalist culture that, while endlessly entertained and self-entertaining, is separate and alienated from the world outside of the train. As such, the train is not the vehicle of transnational and transcultural exploration one might have hoped for. The shift in part 2 from the train to the characters traveling the steppes on foot and on pony becomes all the more necessary.

As a microcosm of a broad Western culture the train in part 1 of *Joan of Arc of Mongolia* is a space of performance, interaction, and even festivity; across the gender divide that underlines most of part 1, it is apparent that the train fails to facilitate the crossing of cultural borders. Rather, *Joan of Arc of Mongolia* plays with and discards traditional train narrative tropes in favor of pursuing a study of the characters, their cultural habits and rituals, and the relationships they forge—or, in the case of the male characters, the relationships they do not forge. As Lynne Kirby has documented in *Parallel Tracks* (1997), the train has had a special connection to the cinema and to certain genres from very early on in its existence. *Joan of Arc of Mongolia*'s playfulness is apparent from the end of the title and credit scroll, the last screen of which presents a comical, yet incomplete table of contents underscoring the exotic journey ahead. Among the topics the film will deliver are included "Wives of impoverished Russian nobles," "Strong Mongolian wrestlers," "Female lance riders on fast riding-camels," and "Mongolian families on the highway," among other intriguing subjects. In lieu of adventure or an exploration of such exotic and strange topics, the first part of *Joan of Arc of Mongolia* stages the social interactions of the main female characters— Lady Windermere, Frau Vohwinkel, Fanny Ziegler, and Giovanna—and a secondary set of characters that includes the Kalinka Sisters, a singing trio; Mickey Katz, a Jewish cabaret singer; and Alexander Muraviov, a Russian military officer with aide-de-camp in tow. As the principle set piece of part 1, the dining-car party scene takes up fully thirty minutes of runtime. In it, the viewer is given to observing the characters' behaviors and interactions; foremost among the noteworthy details, the contrast between Mickey Katz's ordering of a lavish *zakuska* (a traditional Russian and Eastern European course of dozens of different appetizers) and the humble "touristen Menu für paschal Reisende" (tourist meal for travelers heading East) that Vohwinkel and Ziegler have books of small tickets for. Katz's order is lavish, but so is his performance of ordering, which goes on well past the point at which the server stops listening and heads off to the kitchen. Katz's order is inspired by the painting on

Figure 6.1. A feast for one and his audience. *Joan of Arc of Mongolia* (1989). Screen capture by Steven Spalding.

the wall behind his head, and is itself a colorful and complex portrait of culinary extravagance. Do the train chefs, Katz wonders, even "possess the proper knowledge and skills required . . . are you proficient in the arts of collage, of mounting, of mosaic, of sculpture, painting, color composition, and taxidermy?" (Ottinger 1989). Done properly, his *zakuska*—like Katz's own rhetorical performance while ordering it— should be an exercise of high art and technical accomplishment. Katz savors the poetic comparisons he makes with each ingredient he lists as if he were already indulging in his one-man feast. When the *zakuska* is ready to be served in what is essentially a procession, the lights in the dining car are dimmed, the Kalinka Sisters provide a dramatic soundtrack, and the camera executes a series of shots and reverse shots centered on the enormous stuffed swan that serves as centerpiece to the banquet-sized order that is unique in the film. When the *zakuska* has been all laid out, there is a point-of-view shot from Katz's perspective (26′50″; see figure 6.1) in which nearly everyone in the dining car is arranged in a semicircle around Katz's feast and the swan; even the servers to Katz's right are at pains to get in the shot, bending down to get their faces in the shot at upper right. The Kalinka Sisters cannot be seen, but are heard continuously. The group applauds the presentation of the *zakuska*, and then goes immediately silent as Katz is shown silently gesturing to the servers to come serve him. His hat sits cocked slightly back, like a crown. This absurdly crowded-in shot is something of a visual crescendo within part 1: where the slow-moving sideways tracking shots replicating a train easing in along the platforms of a train station captured crowds as well, they move across the field of vision in measured quantities. In this shot, the comical folly of Katz and his *zakuska* are in plain view.

Like the figure in the painting behind him, Katz makes himself the focal point of the scene—one full of warmth and humor, such as when Katz suggests that the *zakuska* he has just ordered should be a "sufficient antidote to [his] epicureanism" (19'18"). Nonetheless, there is something highly excessive about the entire *zakuska* ritual, from Katz's rhetorical performance to its delivery and appreciation by the crowd, and its focus on the consumption of the exotic in service of only the ego of Katz, the consumer. Serving such a lavish banquet for one on a train stretches the logic of the train as a kind of height of Western achievement to where it breaks. Moments later, Vohwinkel and Ziegler are advised by the train staff that, in order for the meal service to accommodate Katz's eating habits successfully ("He is a good eater"; Ottinger 1989), they will not be receiving the meals they had preordered but must make do with kosher trays. Katz's opulence is at a price paid by the other passengers; furthermore, his performance in this instance is entirely self-serving.

Katz's meal performance is followed shortly by his song performance, and in a further illustration of the film's whimsical sensibility he chooses a song that has him—and the Kalinka Sisters backing him—tooting like a train ("Toot Toot Tootsie Goodbye"). Just as the men in this scene will continue on the Trans-Siberian and the women will switch to the Trans-Mongolian—and of course later say goodbye to the train altogether—the nostalgia-laden theme of farewells is appropriate. When Katz finishes his number, the American hit from the 1920s inspires a brief exchange about cultural appropriation, internationalism, and neocolonialism in which Fanny Ziegler intimates an important piece of the film's comment on transnational cultures. She describes how "shameless and uninhibited American culture" takes the best from every culture around the world and mixes them into a "typical American musical" (38'20"). The Americans may be "characterless chameleons," in Katz's words, but he, for Fanny, is a "large, conspicuous swatch of color in our monoculture" (38'33"). This important remark points to the necessity—once again—of the experience to come. There is a need for genuine transnational experience, to expand the cultural repertory of the characters and of Western culture more broadly. The horizons of the Western cultural mixing on/of the train are limited, and there is an optimism for something beyond. As the film winds closer to the end of part 1, the women's praise for Katz is surely genuine; yet, when Katz bemoans their impending separation (54'10") none of the women offers any response.

The second part of the film, the group's Mongolian adventure, lasts roughly ninety minutes and offers crucial contrasts to the first. The visual contrast cannot be starker: for all of part 1's crowded visual field—replete with either stately antique train appointments (including a *zakuska* swan), or characters (with or without speaking parts), or both—part 2 allows a sweeping Mongolian landscape to share the screen with the characters, their animals, and their dwellings. The slow-paced camera moves of part 1 were part and parcel to the sense of enclosure on the train: there is nothing to see outside. Now, medium and long shots give life and color to the film, and the equally slow-paced camera movements mimic the slow mobility of the film's subjects, and linger over the bright contrasts of blue, green, and red, of sky, land, and vibrantly colored clothing, yurts, and bedecked animals. Only a couple sequences are filmed entirely within a yurt, which further emphasizes the spatial horizons framing the rituals and practices of the Mongolian tribe and its guests. As illustrated in figure 6.2, those spatial horizons signal a shift with respect to time as well, where in the absence of train time the movements of the characters rhythm the film. In this shot, Mongolian princess Ulan Iga is riding with her new protégée, Giovanna, in a sequence devoid of teleology like much of part 2. Spectators are not given to know where they are coming from, where they are headed, or why they are traveling. Instead, focus is on the time of the characters' movements, or their being-in-movement.

Additionally, through the individual trajectories of the four main characters and their interactions with the Mongolians, the film offers an ethics of cultural exchange that is respectful of the Other as well as transformative for the travelers without being exploitative. Inasmuch as part 2 is dominated by an ethnographic gaze—audience and character alike look to Lady Windemere for instruction, and come to observe the tribe with her same respectfulness and curiosity—it highlights the film's intriguing twist on film genre, shifting from fictional adventure story to the borders of documentary, as often cited by critics and scholars (Galt 2011; Rickels 2008). The second part of the film also addresses matters of gender that were both implicit and explicit throughout the first part, and offers a glimpse of what an excursion into a matriarchal culture would look like. Gendered meanings imposed or even articulated by men are not emphasized, with the notable exception of the message and song performed by the ambassadors of Olgi Sumiya near the beginning of part 2. The film's second part is marked especially by silences and listening, and by minute attention paid to the performance of routines and rituals in gestures, dance, stories, songs, and incantations.

Figure 6.2. The wide-open green. *Joan of Arc of Mongolia* (1989). Screen capture by Steven Spalding.

As an ethnographic adventure fiction, then, *Joan of Arc of Mongolia* presents a form of escape from Western culture—a form that is not an indulgent fantasy of escape that delivers spectators nowhere in particular. *Joan of Arc of Mongolia* puts forth a roadmap for escaping the railway grid, for crossing borders, and exceeding the national limits, and offers an image of openness to a more genuine adventure than those of the conventional film genres. It is an openness and earnestness accompanied by much self-conscious irony and humor. The joke in the film's title, for instance, can only be understood at the end of the film, when viewers realize that Giovanna, the young woman who is renamed Johanna by the Mongolian princess in charge of the tribe, shares nothing in common with Joan of Arc. Rather, the title models the film's pattern of activating certain tropes of Western cultural imagination and myth-construction only to reject those expectations (*détournement,* or derailing) in favor of something far less predetermined. The historical Joan of Arc story is one of conflict, belief, and sacrifice: Joan is captured by a hostile enemy and religious judgment is passed on her, resulting in her martyrdom. The specter of conflict does hover over part 1 of *Joan of Arc of Mongolia,* with the frequent appearance of soldiers and officers reminding viewers that this film takes place in the Soviet Union during the Cold War. Then, in part 2, characters and viewers watch as peace is concluded between warring Mongolian tribes, gifts are exchanged, and feasts are shared. Giovanna/Johanna does not make any sacrifice at the end of the film, even though at first the character announces plans to stay with the tribe and continue her life as a protégée to the Mongolian princess—a kind of sacrifice of her life to the journey east. In a final moment of generic narrative drama, the film ends with Giovanna racing on horseback to catch up to the train taking Lady Windermere on her way and climbing aboard. She rejoins Lady Windermere, thereby choosing not to stay with the tribe, and giving up Johanna for Giovanna.

As is emphasized by the voiceover narration at the end of the film, each of the sojourners would translate their Mongolian adventure into some form of successful performance for their home cultures. These outcomes for each of the women in the group put paid the promise of the "trans" in transnational: in crossing the border separating train and steppes, escaping the train's panoramic perspective, and undoing its loss of landscape, the characters enrich their cultures in definitive ways. Lady Windemere would go on to author a best-selling book on Mongolia, Fanny would star in a long-running smash musical on Broadway entitled "TransMongolia," and the Kalinka Sisters would receive awards for their work as cultural agents in "the unremitting struggle for international understanding." Giovanna is to become head server at Le Gobi, a Mongolian restaurant in Paris opened by the Mongolian princess she meets on the train at the end of the film. Of them all, it is Frau Vohwinkel who is transformed the most radically, as she will leave behind her previous life and take on an entirely new one by setting off on a pilgrimage with the "lamaistic hermit-nun" she met during her long solo walk in part 2 of the film, and joining a monastery.

In its clever articulation of cosmopolitan European traveler culture and feminist ethics, *Joan of Arc of Mongolia* twists the genre of the epic train journey into an unpredictable and unforgettable experience of mobility and immobility, and of fiction and documentary film styles. Most importantly, Ottinger's film speaks of the legacies, meanings, and practices of the train that stand in the way of a meaningful crossing of national borders and cultural frontiers into a transformative encounter with cultural difference. The characters' whimsical abduction by the Mongolian princess transforms them into more true travelers, challenged to shed the cultural familiarity and reassuring qualities of the train, to leave behind their status as passive consumers of the train journey, and to confront cultural difference head on. More broadly, the film's wringing out and eventual discarding of the train as locus of symbolic and narrative creation—that figure and emblem so strongly linked with the history of the cinema and so linked to the birth of Western cinema—amounts to an important call for a new departure of the medium: one with a new vision of a slower mobility an unaccelerated modernity, and following the tracks of Ottinger's foray into the Mongolian steppes.

Steven Spalding holds a PhD from the University of Michigan and a D.E.A. from the Université de Paris VIII. He is editor of the special section on "Railways and Urban Cultures" (2014) in *Transfers: Interdisciplinary Journal of Mobility Studies* and coeditor of the books *Trains, Culture, and Mobility* (2012) and *Trains, Literature, and Culture* (2012). After more than twenty-five years of teaching at colleges and universities in the United States, France, and Switzerland, he is an independent scholar who writes about French cultural studies, mobility studies and urban studies. His interests involve twentieth- and twenty-first-century French and francophone novels, films, and comics.

Notes

1. The term "monoculture" is spoken by the character Fanny Ziegler in a scene examined below.
2. Galt details how early feminist criticism takes Ottinger to task for this lack of dogmatism (2011, 285–90).
3. Rickels makes this same association (2008, 128). For more on Ottinger, see King (2007).
4. Her naïveté is belied by the implicit reference in her speech to Léni Riefenstahl's Nazi propaganda film, *Triumph des Willens* (*Triumph of the Will*) (1935).

References

An, Grace. 2018. "Filmmmaking at a Crossroads." Review of *Johanna d'Arc of Mongolia*, directed by Ulrike Ottinger. *Transfers: Interdisciplinary Journal of Mobility Studies* 8, no. 1: 130–33.

ChaiWalla. 2010. "Johanna d'Arc of Mongolia." *Night in the Lens*. 18 April 2010. https://voicethrower.wordpress.com/2010/04/18/johanna-darc-of-mongolia. Accessed 10 June 2017.

Despotopoulou, Anna. 2015. *Women and the Railway, 1850–1915*. Edinburgh: Edinburgh University Press.

Galt, Rosalind. 2011. *Pretty: Film and the Decorative Image*. New York: Columbia University Press.

Khagram, Sanjeev and Peggy Levitt. 2008. "Constructing Transnational Studies." In *The Transnational Studies Reader: Intersections and Innovations*, edited by Sanjeev Khagram and Peggy Levitt, 1–22. New York and London: Routledge.

King, Homay. 2007. "Sign in the Void: Ottinger's *Johanna d'Arc of Mongolia*." *Afterall* 16 (Autumn/Winter): 46–52.

Kirby, Lynne. 1997. *Parallel Tracks: The Railroad and Silent Cinema*. Durham, NC: Duke University Press.

Ottinger, Ulrike, dir. 1989. *Johanna d'Arc of Mongolia (Joan of Arc of Mongolia)*. Ulrike Ottinger Filmproduktion, West Germany: NEF 2 Filmverleih.

Rickels, Laurence. 2008. *Ulrike Ottinger: The Autobiography of Art Cinema*. Minneapolis: University of Minnesota Press.

Riefenstahl, Léni. 1935. *Triumph des Willens (Triumph of the Will)*. Chicago: International Historic Films, 1981.

Schivelbusch, Wolfgang. (1977) 1986. *The Railway Journey: The Industrialization of Time and Space in the 19th Century*. Berkeley: University of California Press.

Urry, John. 2007. *Mobilities*. Cambridge, UK: Polity Press.

CHAPTER 7

The Cosmopolitan Writer

Exploring Representations on the
Underground Railways of Buenos Aires
and Paris through Julio Cortázar

Dhan Zunino Singh

Introduction

Mobility is more than the mere physical movement between Point A and Point B; indeed, it is as much a form of "material and sociable dwelling-in-motion" (Sheller and Urry 2006, 214). Following Jensen (2009) and Cresswell (2010), mobility can be defined as a social, embodied, and meaningful practice, experienced and represented, shaping and being shaped by culture as well as by technologies. Transport, in fact, can be considered as a mediation between the material and the imaginable (Divall and Revill 2005) becoming a hybrid (human and non-human) experience. Within this assemblage of materials, practices, social relations, environment, meanings, and so on, comparative cultural analysis of transport technology—particularly but not exclusively involving literature—has become a useful tool to explore the experience of railways (Schivelbusch 1986) or the automobile (Mom 2014) in different national contexts or even beyond national borders. For instance, Schivelbusch has noticed two different kinds of sociabilities shaped by the design of wagons in Europe and the United States, while Mom shows how the development of the car and its culture was multicentered (or simultaneously produced in different locations).

Railways, tramways, cars, ships, airplanes, and bicycles are produced and consumed globally. Moreover, their invention and development were also multisituated, as the history of the tramway shows—invented in Europe, developed in the United States, and then diffused in Europe (McKay 1976). Flows and networks of experts, technologies, capital, companies, and knowledge allowed the circulation of transport to cross national boundaries. Along with the technology, the ideas and images of mobility also circulated and were consumed—even before the arrival of the technology (see Mom 2014). Therefore, a transnational approach—taking "the interconnected world as a point of departure, and the circulation of things, people and ideas" (Conrad 2016, 5)—becomes relevant to understanding globalized transport technologies like the underground railway.

Between the late nineteenth century and the early twentieth century the underground was implemented in many large cities of Europe and the Americas. Unlike railways, which tended not only to organize flows (of people and things) at the national level but also to connect the national economy with the world market, the underground was a mass transit system for the city. These undergrounds were built at municipal scale, so to speak; in fact, many of them were built by municipal governments. But the implementation of subways in each city can be understood as a global response to processes of urbanization. The boom of metro systems in the 1890s–1930s, hence, can be understood as a transnational phenomenon in which the metro became an ideal solution to urban congestion and suburbanization. Bobrick has written the story of many early undergrounds, but the history of how this technology spread around the world needs further exploration.[1] David Pike (2005), exploring representations on underground space culture in general, has also tackled different cities but, usually, the underground stories are local. Reading those underground histories, one can read a situated mobility experience, how a singular city has conceived, planned, built, lived, and represented the subway.

Although each city has developed a particular design (and subways have become an icon of the city) and a particular culture, what is important for this chapter are shared or common experiences of traveling and representing the underground beyond singularities. Following underground histories in different cities (Bobrick 1994; Brooks 1997; Pike 2005; Zunino Singh 2014), one can find that, on both sides of the Atlantic, the underground unleashed ambivalent impressions and feelings, between fascination and fear—an ambivalence that technology historians define as sublime (Nye 1994; Williams 2008). Like surface or elevated railways, the underground has shaped the way in which space-time (through the experience of speed) is perceived and gave rise to new sociabilities within a sort of public-private space. The unique aspects of the railway journey—observed early on by Schivelbusch (1986)—are altered when the train runs inside a tunnel: for instance, there is no chance of a panoramic view in the underground. One of the most shared experience it that its physical condition triggers atavistic meanings associated with hell, death, the underworld, the habitat of animals (moles), and so on.

Moreover, this technology has modified urban culture as much as culture has modeled the experience and representation of the underground. Such representations have gone global, through the production and dissemination of cultural products. There are common tropes about the underground in film, literature, songs, and so on, such as those in which trains become spaces for chase scenes (action films), spaces of mystery, secrets, and solitary souls traveling within the anonymous crowd (Pike 2005). Looking at photos from the early twentieth century, in different cities, one can identify middle-class passengers riding the subway, reading newspapers, bodies performing similar poses, and so on. These images trigger the following question: Just how similar are the practices and representations brought about by the technology of underground transit? And, if global technologies tend to favor homogeneity among cultures of mobility, to what extent are they endowed with new meanings through local cultural appropriation?

Looking at cultural representations of mobility in two different but networked cities, Buenos Aires and Paris, through the lens of Argentinean writer Julio Cortázar (Belgium, 1914–Paris, 1984) can help us address these questions, particularly because the author saw the underground as universal. For him, the London Underground, the New York City Subway, the Paris Metro, and the Buenos Aires Subte resemble one another not only because they have a similar functional map, but also because the underground creates in its own way "the same feeling of otherness that some of us live as a threat but, at the same time, as a temptation" (Cortázar [1978] 1996).

What Cortázar's statement seems to suggest is that beyond (or along with) singular features of each underground and the particular city and culture in which it is placed, there is a shared experience, an almost universal experience that we can characterize as cosmopolitan, common across local boundaries. In several short stories and interviews, Cortázar explains or reflects on his own experience as a subway traveler (and the meaning that this transport has for him) in several cities, constituting an important corpus for examining not similarities between different cities, but rather transnational representations of underground mobility.

This chapter explores the underground experience through Julio Cortázar's commentaries about the underground railway and short stories in which the Buenos Aires Subte or the Paris Metro appear. The topics that Cortázar's literature raises allow us to explore various meanings related to traveling within the crowd, anonymity, visual and embodied effects of the subway, body proximity and social distance, sociability, speed, love stories, and spatial and temporal perceptions that we can find in many other cities and historical contexts (Butcher 2011; Pike 2005; Stalter-Pace 2015; Zunino Singh 2014). This chapter focuses on four themes: first, the atavistic representation of subterranean transit space, which historians of the underground have discussed. The second section deals with the practice of the descent as a key moment in Cortázar's experience. Our analysis then turns to the story about missing passengers depicted in "Texto en una libreta" (Text in a notebook). And, finally, we take on underground mobility as a performance by exploring the effects of bodily proximity.

The analysis is mainly based on Cortázar's short stories, such as "Texto en una libreta" (1980 [1996]), "El Perseguidor" (The pursuer) ([1965] 1995), "Manuscrito hallado en un bolsillo" (Manuscript found in a pocket), and "Cuello de Gatito Negro" (Little black cat neck) (both from 1974), an article about the subway from 1978 ("Bajo Nivel," published in 1996 by the Mexican newspaper *La Jornada*), and the documentary film *Cortázar* (Bauer 1994), which includes interviews with the author.[2] The article and the interview are useful to analyze what the subway means for Cortázar because, although his fiction belongs to the fantasy genre, the use of internal monologue allows us to trace a strong link between the writer's experience and his literature.

While "Texto en una libreta" is set in the Buenos Aires Subte, the other stories occur in the Paris Metro. Cortázar, who lived for three decades in Paris, identified himself as an Argentinean writer, remembering and writing about Buenos Aires and even introducing Argentinean characters in the stories that occur in the Paris Metro—like Lucho in "Cuello de Gatito Negro." In this sense, both cities become interweaved through his stories in the underground within a wider cultural context in which Paris and Buenos Aires have been interconnected.[3] By 1910 Buenos Aires was well-known as the Paris of South America—an impression stressed by foreign visitors and an aspiration of local elites who sought to shape Buenos Aires into a modern metropolis following Paris's urban reforms. But not only architecture and urban design made Buenos Aires resemble Paris; so too did cultural consumption and the visits that the elites used to conduct in Paris, as characterized by David Viñas (1995).

A Creepy Space

The subway of Buenos Aires is known as the Subte, from the Spanish word *subterráneo* (underground). Unlike the rest of the Spanish-speaking world, where the subway is called metro, from the French *métropolitain* (metropolitan), Buenos Aires inherited the English name "underground" from the British company that built the first subway line in 1913.[4] Early on the name appeared abbreviated in magazines such as *Mundo Argentino*, which used the word "Subt" in the caption of a picture of the opening day (2 December 1913). By the end of the 1920s the word "subte" was popularized and it was common to find it the press and literature. According to the National Academy of Letters in Argentina, the abbreviation is typical of an economy of language, a product of the rapid and vertiginous movement of a large city as Buenos Aires. Julio Cortázar ([1978] 1996) used to say that Buenos Aires's inhabitants called it subte as if in shortening the name they wanted to demystify its meaning, as if they feared the meaning of the complete word.

With the construction of the world's first underground railway, the London Underground (1863), atavistic representations of subterranean space emerged and became common. If apprehension toward traveling through a tunnel placed underground was expressed before and during the construction of the first underground rail in London, it is true that the representation of hell was reinforced by the atmosphere that the steam locomotive created in that enclosed space. Nonetheless, the electrification of the subway did not signal the end of atavistic representations (Zunino Singh 2012). In the Paris Metro, the art nouveau *édicules* (subway entrances) designed by the architect Hector Guimard reinforced the association of the metro with the necropolis, especially after a fire killed eighty-four people in 1903 (Pike 2005, 52–55). The heat due to lack of ventilation in the New York City Subway also triggered representations of a hellish space. Michael Brooks (1997, 4) claims that the association of the underground railways with "dark, damp, dank, smoke-laden tunnels," or the archetypical image of a hellish underground, begs historicization in order to understand its resonance in particular locations and historical contexts.

The chief engineer of the first New York City Subway was aware of the fears that underground space created when he said that it was necessary to introduce sunlight into the subway "to destroy the popular antipathy toward the 'hole in the ground'" (quoted in Bobrick 1994, 231). Similar statements can be found in the engineering reports for the Buenos Aires Subte in 1909. The municipal engineers sought to build a shallow tunnel beneath the street, with easy access to the surface, for the sake of aesthetics, hygiene, and time. When the A Line was finished, the Anglo-Argentine Tramway Company considered it an advance on other underground systems because it not only fulfilled principles of hygiene and aesthetics, but also gave the feeling of being in the street. Reinforcing the idea of the underground as gloomy, the company said that the abundance of light (natural and electric) and fresh air circulation, "apart from being another appreciable hygienic advantage over other underground railways, diminishes the foreboding aspects of this underground" (Anglo-Argentine Tramway Company 1913).

Although popular magazines celebrated the implementation of the underground, especially through photography and articles, they also published humorous discourses and visual representations of the underground space as a place of death and animals. These discourses did not imply a rejection of the subway so much as an illustration of the recurrence of atavistic representations over and over in literature, film, comics, and popular music.

In the early days of Buenos Aires's Subte, it is possible to find expressions of and reactions to notions of progress and to the so-called destiny of humankind. As Constancio Vigil, an important journalist, put it a few days after the opening of the first underground line in 1913, "The inauguration of the underground tramway represents a notable conquest for modern man. It is absolutely impossible to say 'for man,' since many contemporaries and perhaps all the forebears will judge the idea of underground travel as an outrageous and crazy thing" (1913; translation by the author). The popular magazine *P.B.T.* satirized that the living will inhabit the place of the dead, saying, "Before only the dead were to the pit; now the living are buried and they rush above and under the ground." "Now," it continued, the underground passengers will say, "May the Earth rest lightly upon you" (Tomey 1913). The same article pointed out that the conquest of underground space signified the beginning of a new age: "The troglodytic life, after the aerial one, or both at the same time: the mole-man and the bird-man are the men of our times." The troglodytic life is a metaphor that also evokes the prehistoric era when humans lived in caves. Instead of a futuristic image of the new technological space created by modern engineering, the new underground space appeared to be working out as a shelter: "The earth's crust does not only have layers to give us shelter, but it constitutes now our umbrella and parasol. Going through it (digging), we seek for the core heat and we shelter from rain and the sun's rays." Still in the 1930s, when Buenos Aires acquired the image of a vertical city with its first skyscrapers, the soon-to-be completed underground network triggered the idea that the vertical city implied the conquest of both the aerial and the underground space: "Buenos Aires grows upward but it also grows downward: it takes roots and makes itself holes" (1937, 20).

Another metaphor that represented the change introduced by the underground in the life of the urban dweller was of the image of the mole-man. Rather than an evocation of remote times, the figure of the mole reflected the impression that humans were to dwell in the habitat of an animal as an editorial of the magazine *P.B.T.* claimed: "We have built the underground to compete with moles" ("Charlas del Pebete" 1913). This metaphor emphasized the following contradiction: occupying the underground space turns humans into animals, instead of emphasizing the transformation of the subsoil into an artificial space suitable for humans. Similar representation caused the construction of tunnels in London that, according to a critic, "is to be burrowed through and through like a rabbit-warren" (quoted in Pike 2005, 40). This view, according to Pike (40), "saw the network of animal tunnels as a nuisance threatening the stability of the human-occupied ground above."

This threat to the stability of life above that David Pike has found to be a common characteristic of the imagination of subterranean space in many cities is crucial for understanding certain of Cortázar's stories. In the short fiction "Texto en una libreta," Cortázar tells the story of subway inhabitants, passengers who never return to the surface and seem to live in the underground. They are depicted as the living dead—pale passengers, pale and sad—because they do not see the sun. The subway as the place of the uncanny is often used by Cortázar to build up an opposition between the subterranean and the street. And most important, he stresses the action of descent into the subway, the *katabasis* (descending), as a key moment of transformation or threshold. We will find in Cortázar that the underworld is the Other that disturbs the order of the life above.

The Passage: Descending as a Spatial and Temporal Change

The transformation of the subterranean space into a place to be inhabited by humans, suitable for modern urban dwellers, needed a great effort to change the atavistic representations attached to the underground. The transformations produced by the underground railways not only implied a shrinking of space and time as stressed by W. Schivelbusch in his classic *The Railway Journey* (1986) but also the material and symbolic production of a rational space—an "inorganic underground" (Pike 2005, 16). If "the cosmos of modern technology has a vertical structure," epitomized by the skyscraper, it is also represented by the hidden infrastructure that supports the city from below—what Lewis Mumford called the "physiological apparatus of the new city" (quoted in Williams 2008, 52). Nonetheless, as Pike (2005, 16) highlights, the "proliferation of the inorganic space," like the subway, "thus transformed the perceived space of the underground without thereby eliminating the traditional representational associations with the organic underground."

In this context, descent becomes a journey into another world. This is one of the most interesting meanings that Cortázar builds in his literature. It implies a transformation that the passenger can experience when he/she goes down into the subway and then returns. Descent is closely related to Cortázar's idea of passage: "The metro was always a passage for me," says Cortázar in Bauer's film (1994). The passage is a key figure for understanding, then, the connection between Paris and Buenos Aires, since the metro will work as a bridge between the two cities. In the act of descending the passage is spatial and also temporal, between day and night. The practice of roaming, that Cortázar considers to be a vital urban experience for his literature, occurs at night. It is a nocturnal mobility that resembles the wandering typical of Situationism. The night is the perfect context because it places oneself in a "privilege situation" that is contrary to ordinary life and rational events, says Cortázar in Bauer's film (1994). He also states that, "particularly during the night, I know very well that I am not the same as during the day, with a common and ordinary life."

This condition of nocturnal flâneur is stressed by the act of descending into the subway, because, as characterized by Cortázar, the underground is a night space: "In the subway everything happens at night" said the protagonist of "Texto en una Libreta" (Cortázar [1980] 1996, 352). Cortázar also stresses this idea, saying, "Like in the theatre and the cinema, in the metro it is night. But its night does not have that ordered delimitation, that precise time and that artificially pleasant atmosphere of theatres. The metro's night is overwhelming, humid (like a greenhouse in summer) and also infinite . . . we can feel it spreading out in the tentacles of the tunnels" (Cortázar [1980] 1996). The underground night is the territory of the strange. The subway, thus, becomes a fertile terrain for the author's fantastic stories where the disturbance caused by the uncanny is part of the experience of descent. That feeling of otherness expressed by Cortázar, and his fictional characters, when going down into the subway is not only a subjective change but an embodied experience. In "Texto en una libreta," the protagonist feels nausea, stomach cramps, and paralysis when he approaches a subway entrance. Such feelings are produced once he experiences strange events in the subway. He feels calm on the surface, hesitant about descending again. "The man who descends into the metro is not the same as the one returning to the surface," says Cortázar ([1978] 1996). It is important that one deserves the journey that "for the rest is merely a journey between stations" that is rapidly forgotten. "If going down into the metro means to me mild distress, a physical tension that quickly vanishes, it is not less true that leaving the metro means . . . a return to the cowardly safety of the street." Going underground as a process of transformation is also represented through a change of clothing. Like in the film *Subway* (Besson, 1985) in which the protagonists change their clothes to wear sec-ondhand outfits, in "Texto en una libreta" the author explains that the missing passengers' clothes wear out and they need to change them, and they even have a store with clothes in case of emergencies or when a new missing passenger arrives.

But it is the notion of time experienced in the subway by the protago-nist of "El Perseguidor" (Cortázar [1965] 1995). Johnny Carter (a Parisian jazz trumpeter, a character that Cortázar modeled on Charlie Parker), which better expresses the sense of the subway journey as a passage to another time, another dimension. In William Morris's *News from No-where* (1890), the protagonist also begins a temporal journey during a ride on the London Underground: he leaves the present-day London when he goes down into underground and arrives at a utopian London when he leaves the station at night. This metaphor of the subway as a threshold to another dimension, a parallel reality, to the future or the past, can be also found in the Danish film *Reconstruction* (Boe 2003) in which the reality of the protagonist changes every time he passes through Copenhagen's metro.

In Bauer's film (1994), Cortázar explains the spatial-temporal passage that the experience of the subway provokes in him in this way: "I just have to go down into the metro to enter into a totally different logi-cal category . . . logical categories where the sense of time changes. At certain moments of distraction in the metro, suddenly it is discovered that one has the impression of living a time completely different from the surface time." In "El Perseguidor," Johnny in fact says that he does not live another time when he rides the subway; rather, he experiences time. Johnny loses his saxophone during a journey in the Paris Metro (he forgets it under his seat) and realizes it when he was going up the stairs—that is, when returning to the surface. Johnny tries to explain his experience of mobility in the subway in relation to his embodied prac-tice of playing jazz, and thinks about time. "This matter of time is com-plicated, it catches me everywhere," he says (Cortázar [1965] 1995, 230). For him time is a whole, something that surrounds or envelops him, especially when he plays jazz or travels in the subway: "Sometimes I put the music into Time when I am playing. [I put] the music and what I think when I travel in the metro" (230). Then, he explains his experience to his friend Bruno, he says, "The metro is a great invention, my friend Bruno. Travelling in the metro you realize everything that could fit in a bag" (230). Johnny is frantic and seems to talk nonsense when trying to explain how he lost the instrument: "Maybe I didn't lose my saxophone in the metro, maybe. . . . One day I began to feel something in the metro, then I forgot. . . . So it repeats, two or three days later" (231).

Johnny experiences two times: while he remembers several moments from his life, he feels he has been thinking about it for fifteen
minutes though only a minute and a half has passed. "How can I think
a quarter of an hour in one minute and a half?," he wonders and states,
"To travel in the metro is like being inside a clock: the stations are the
minutes, you understand, that is your [people's] time, right now; but I
know that there is another time, and I've been thinking, thinking, . . . "
(Cortázar [1965] 1995, 233).

Spooky Passengers

The vertical order implies the rationalization of space—turning the subsoil into a tunnel suitable for humans—but also of time (speed, timetable, frequency) and mobility (the circulation of trains and of people).
The underground can be viewed as the spatialization of time—a modern and social time dominated by the capitalist economy that Lefebvre
(2004) called the lineal rhythm.

In Buenos Aires the image of the ideal commuter was symbolized
by the employee (commercial or administrative worker) who is eager
for punctuality (Zunino Singh 2014). Well-known writers rejected the
idea of the subway as a symbol of progress since it was identified with
the discipline imposed by work time. By the end of the 1920s, Roberto
Arlt (1976), in his daily sketches *Aguafuertes porteñas* (Etchings from
Buenos Aires), depicted several scenes in the subway. Although Arlt expressed fascination with new technologies and showed the subway as
a space of sociability, he also found the subway to be an instrument for
mechanization of social life and, therefore, dehumanization. Against the
figure of the employee that seeks to be on time, he uses the figure of
fiaca (laziness) as a sign of resistance or a way of contesting clock and
work time (Zunino Singh 2014, 108). Martínez Estrada ([1947] 1968) also
compares the underground mobility with the time of the city, which
is clock time, a machine that transforms the qualitative experience of
travel into *traslación* (translation): a physical displacement closer to a
mechanical movement than to a living, wished-for mobility (Zunino
Singh 2014, 109). In Cortázar's works we find similar impressions about
the subway; however, it is also an odd space. "Texto en una libreta" is a
story in which the author introduces a disturbance to that rational order
that ruled underground mobility in order to set off on a fantasy about
missing passengers.

The story begins in the summer of 1946 with a failure of the system:
the number of passengers that leave the A Line of the Buenos Aires Subte

is smaller than the number who entered. One day the system registered 113,983 passengers who left the subway but 113,987 had entered into the network. Cortázar exaggerates this failure, which seems minimal, to stress the power of and the reliance on statistics in the management of transport systems. Statistics is one of the main tools used to plan and operate the subway; travelers are counted as passengers through the journeys they make or, more precisely, passengers are counted through numbers of tickets.

People not only disappeared but on another day the number of passengers who left the subway was one person higher. The company does not publish the numbers (the anomaly) to avoid creating panic, but the protagonist (Cortázar tells the story in the first person) had heard about it from a friend and checked the information with a chief inspector of the Subte. He shares the story with another friend, who offers a ridiculous explanation (a trademark of Cortázar's fantastic literature): the decrease in number of passengers might be the result of "the atomic wear of mass," because every time the train stops or follows a curve thousands of passengers brush, scrub, and shake in the overcrowded cars (Cortázar [1980] 1996, 350).

This anomaly begins to affect the protagonist, who tries to write a report about it. He launches an investigation and immediately recalls that he had seen strange passengers in the subway. After discovering what was happening, the ordinary experience of traveling in the subway as well as the act of descent become disturbing, provoking rejection: as we noticed before, the disturbing experience is expressed through bodily symptoms like the stomach cramp.

The protagonist says he will tell the story about what happens even when it could discourage people to take the subway. He will do it, first, because it is important for Buenos Aires's inhabitants (who are always upset due to public transport) to know the truth. He has found that the missing passengers are still in the subway, living there, roaming in the trains, platforms, and stations. He would feel relief if those people were to be expulsed because it is not fair to have to ride the tramway (which is for him slow and uncomfortable) out of fear of the Subte.

The idea of missing people in the underground can be found also in *Moebius* (Mosquera 1996). In the film, the subway operators are disconcerted by a kind of anomaly and seek a topologist to investigate the case, who descends into the underground to find strange events: the train is running but it cannot be seen because it runs in another dimension created by the complexity of the network. A professor (who used to be the topologist's master) has discovered this anomaly and has used it to hijack the train. The plot is based on social as much as moral arguments that call into question life above and justify escape by train (Zunino Singh 2008).

In Cortázar's story, however, the missing passengers are not escaping but rather are dwelling in the underground. They seem to be well-organized like a community, following strict orders from a leader (that the narrator calls "The First") and resembling a secret society or clandestine commando. Those people have found a place to live in the subway as they do in *Subway* (Besson 1985), the French film that shows the life (a "countercultural life") of people who find refuge in "in the deep tunnels and corridors beneath and surrounding the vast new Chatelet/Les Halles complex" and roam within the metro when it is closed at night (Pike 2005, 67). The underground as a space of dwelling rather than passing can be also found in the Hungarian film *Kontroll* (Antal 2003). Set in the Budapest Metro, the film tells the story of the daily life of inspectors and other people who spend almost all day in the subway; the film never shows the surface.

The missing people who stay in the Subte might not be considered passengers since they are not passing—or perhaps they are perpetual passengers. Cortázar distinguishes between the subway commuters and these subway dwellers. The protagonist recognizes them in subway cars, although the anonymous crowd helps them to escape notice. Still, it is on the first and last trains of the day that he is able to spot missing passengers, since these trains are typically almost empty. The protagonist wonders why they are not detected once the train stops: "Maybe the motorman is one of them" or "they are mixed up with cleaning service staff" (Cortázar [1980] 1996, 352). He prefers to believe that they live in the abandoned tunnel under the A Line or in some room in the stations. Nonetheless, the main hypothesis is that they are in motion all the time, changing trains at the end stations to avoid traveling twice in the same train. Moreover, all those movements seem to be coordinated.

Cortázar's ([1980] 1996) narrator attempts to separate their perpetual motion from the short trips that the usual Buenos Aires commuters take: those who travel in the morning to work and return home in the evening, and those who move within the city for work and take the subway every thirty minutes. Regardless, he struggles to identify the missing passengers. One must tell them from their pale skin and sad look—a cold portrait that contrasts with the hot and sweaty bodies of the commuters, who smell like cattle—and from their behavior. They are like leukocytes, says the protagonist, stressing their paleness but also their endless circulation. He describes their emotions and behavior, which resemble the typical distance and blasé attitude of the anonymous mul-

titudes, what Georg Simmel ([1903] 2005) cited as a defining characteristic of modern city life. Yet, they seem to "forgot their instruction of
indifference and disdain when they see mothers with kids in the car"
(Cortázar [1980] 1996, 357). The protagonist depicts how two female
missing passengers left their seats to stand near the children, almost
"brushing them." "I would not have been too astonished," he guesses, "if
they touched their hair or gave them candy, things that are not done in
the Buenos Aires Subte and probably on any subway" (Cortázar [1980]
1996, 357).

Brushes and touches among passengers are an important trope of
Cortázar's literature about subway travel. In this story, the anonymity
of the subway has become a privileged space where the missing passengers can wander and hang out, without the urgency of the commuter. Cortázar also depicts them as ghost consumers, recalling Walter
Benjamin's remarks on the rhythms of Moscow's people during the
early years of the revolution, workers who stay watching a filming in
the street and arriving late to work. Benjamin (1992, 43) said that Russians still lived an Oriental time, one different from the Western rational
time that Lenin wanted to introduce through his industrialization plan.
In "Texto en una libreta," these ghost passengers seem attracted and
distracted by the aura of commodities, closer (although not exactly) to
a practice of *flânerie*. About the female missing passengers, the author
says, "Sometimes they stop at Lima or Peru station and stay browsing
the shop-windows in the platform where furniture is displayed. . . . They
look at the furniture with a humble and reserved wish, and when they
buy the newspaper or Marible [magazine] they are absorbed by ads
about sales and perfume, and by fashion sketches and gloves" (Cortázar
[1980] 1996, 357). Yet, the fact that they seem to follow instructions
makes them more akin to soldiers. They live an imposed rhythm, even
though the protagonist depicts moments of calm and, perhaps symptoms of fatigue and boredom. They sleep in the car seats for up to four
hours and know when to wake up, leave, and change trains. In this
sense, they have a rhythm that, while not responsive to clock and work
time (Lefebvre 2004), is also nonetheless a disciplined rhythm. The way
in which the author depicts their movements, what is allowed and what
is not (like eating only what they can buy in the subway shops), and the
instructions they receive, mirror the ordered movements of the vertical
city. Or perhaps Cortázar sees a new order there. The story closes on an
increase in the numbers of missing passengers and a sort of invasion:
more and more trains and stations are exclusively occupied by the pale
passengers.

The Subway Journey as Embodied Experience

Passengers' behaviors, sociability, and embodied practices are depicted in detail by Cortázar ([1980] 1996) in "Texto en una libreta" and other short stories set in the Paris Metro. The author describes scenes that are familiar to us since they are part of our daily experience of traveling and are related to the way in which we accommodate our bodies in the subway: navigating a context of physical proximity while trying to maintain a certain distance.[5] The visual perceptions, the sounds, the smells, and the atmosphere of the subway are each also part of the experience. Moreover, the bodily experience of touching becomes vital to stories about encounters between men and women.

Unlike the abstract, statistical representation of passengers referenced above, the protagonist of "Texto en una libreta" (Cortázar [1980] 1996) depicts passengers' movements, performance, emotions. Sometimes they are depicted as animals. As mentioned, the crowd is compared to cattle due to its smell ("bovine air of those who have travelled standing"; 359). This image of cattle—or perhaps meat at a processing plant—is underscored by the way in which passengers must hold on to the train car straps of the A Line.

For the same line, the poet Fernández Moreno described different modes of holding on—timidly, violently, gently—or simply trying to keep one's balance without holding on: "The floor *vacila* (sways). Some deeply trust in their constant attention, with legs wide apart and hands inside pockets. Others timidly and very gently hold onto the U straps, saying 'this is not needed at all.' Others violently squeeze it with the whole hand, with the sleeves rolled up, the forearm almost naked as if it were a bunch. Others hold on with both hands as if they wanted to lift themselves with their bare hands in a gym" (Fernández Moreno [c.1930] 1965, 63).

The cattle metaphor also refers to the poor quality of service. Overcrowded subway cars are a typical scene in Buenos Aires, now and before. This used to be a common trope in cartoons and literature about public transport, depicting the overcrowded vehicles as sardine cans. The lack of space in the subway during rush hour is a recurrent complaint in Buenos Aires. Moreover, Buenos Aires's public transport experienced a crisis of rolling stock and spare parts caused by World War II. Subway travel was depicted as insupportable, unacceptable, and shameful. In 1938 the underground cars were so packed that the newspaper *Noticias Gráficas* said that "to get a *huequito* [little space] was one of the greatest aspirations among working people" and that "to be a contortionist or to learn jujitsu is required to get a place in the car" (1938, 11).

Although the image of passengers as cattle conveys discomfort and alienation as part of the common experience of the Buenos Aires Subte, bodily contact produced by close physical proximity also represented a starting point for conversation, a sign of sociability rather than discomfort. A joke published in the magazine *Caras y Caretas* (M. L. 1914) tells the story of two young ladies in the underground car. One of them tries to take the hand of her friend to keep her balance, but after a while she realizes that it was a young man's hand. She reddens and stammers, "Sorry, I took the wrong hand." Smiling very kindly, the young man offers her the other hand. Even the abrupt movements of the underground train become an excuse for starting a conversation. The overcrowded car has the potential to build relationships, as ironically illustrated by a cartoon from 1934. In the middle of the crowd, a man says: "A splendid opportunity to strengthen relations. Isn't it, miss?" (Munson 1934). The verb *estrechar* (to strengthen) has a double meaning in Spanish: to establish a strong relationship and to narrow. Therefore, the ambiguity of the verb emphasizes both the social and the spatial proximity established in the underground car.

These features are typical of the underground journey in general, as shown by the cartoons quoted (many of them were French or American but reproduced in Buenos Aires to satirize the local experience) and also shown by Cortázar's stories. In his literature, we find ephemeral contacts between bodies that become extraordinary events. In "Cuello de Gatito Negro" (Cortázar [1974] 1996), the two protagonists (a French woman and an Argentinean man) who ride in the Paris Metro initiate an odd love story by touching hands. In fact, the narration indicates that the hands seem to act by themselves. The author tells a similar story in an interview: "The day I travelled standing in a packed subway car, and a young woman's hand rested over mine and stayed there" more than usual, before "it left" while "its owner excuses herself with a gesture and smile" (Cortázar [1978]1996). These kinds of approaches are not exclusively a subway experience but are typical of any public transport. Nonetheless, he highlights an important detail: what occurs is only possible in the subway, and not in a bus, for example: "For the simple reason that the protagonists would have been *busier* by the surrounding" (emphasis added). The lack of vision in the tunnel stresses human bonds: "the brush of hands would not have had that subtle energy transmission, that mossy electricity that touches me so deeply."

In "Manuscrito hallado en un bolsillo" (Cortázar [1974] 1996), also situated in the Paris Metro, the author tells how he is attracted by the image of a female passenger sitting near him but seen only through reflections in the train car windows. In fact, multiple images of different women catch his eye. Cortázar uses these social interactions not only to begin a story or to depict how bodies interact in the subway but also to voice a common male fantasy about public transport as a space for romance and flirting (Zunino Singh 2017). These kinds of encounters and feelings contrast sharply with the image of passengers as cattle.

Conclusion

In line with atavistic representations, the subway is for Cortázar a different space and time marked by its key spatial feature: its placement under the city. Unlike buses, tramways, and railways, which Cortázar also uses in his stories, the subterranean realm is what makes this urban train different and singular, lending it a halo of mystery. In Cortázar's literature this experience of mobility is a play marked by the tension between the lineal rhythm of commuting and that of roaming (shaped by the nocturnal atmosphere of the underground). Nonetheless, to feel lost in time like the protagonist of "El Perseguidor" (Cortázar [1965] 1995) contrasts with the synchronized and ruled movement of the missing passengers in "Texto en una libreta" (Cortázar [1980] 1996), although both, in turn, differ from the rhythm of the street. The subway experience for Cortázar is strongly conditioned by the act of descending, a vertical mobility. It is in that action where a passage takes place. It is a transitional moment that implies transformation: one cannot be the same after going down and coming back up.

This transformation is not the usual one that everyone experiences when traveling the subway. Cortázar recognizes and characterizes the subway as impersonal and anonymous, resembling what Marc Augé (2000) called nonplaces. This characterization, also typical of classical social scientists like Robert Park, has been largely criticized by the mobility scholars who see mobility as a meaningful practice (Jensen 2009). Anonymity, loneliness, and social distance are among the most common representations of daily mobility as lived experience. Schivelbusch (1986) noticed how these feelings emerge from the experience of the compartment in the early European railways. Yet, as the same author highlights, the American train coach generated another kind of experience: a more sociable interaction. Still, distance and discretion are social behaviors that help us to cope with others in public spaces (Goffman 1971).

Cortázar seems fascinated by this tension between the crowd and the individual. This characteristic of public transport allows Cortázar to use equally the Buenos Aires Subte and the Paris Metro as settings for social interactions and bodily encounters that trigger fantastic stories, mixing Argentinean and French characters. Moreover, the subway becomes a passage connecting both cities.

Cortázar's mobility experience in the underground is cosmopolitan. It allows us to see beyond the particularities of each subway to explore representations about this transport mode that have become globalized. He lived in both Buenos Aires and Paris and the subway representations do not show significant differences. In other words, the singularities of each subway do not drive different practices and representations of time, the descent, sociability, bodily proximity, and so on. Moreover, his idea that there is a universal subway experience points to a cosmopolitan experience shaped by the infrastructure itself, the basis for common or shared tropes across national and cultural borders.

Dhan Zunino Singh is a sociologist (University of Buenos Aires) with a PhD in history (University of London) who works on cultural history of urban mobilities, looking at infrastructures and experiences of mobility, particularly in Buenos Aires. He is an associate researcher at the National Scientific and Technical Research Council (CONICET) at the National University of Quilmes, Argentina. He lectures undergraduate, master's, and doctoral seminars on history, mobility, and cities. He is also an associate editor of the *Journal of Transport History* and member of the International Association for the History of Transport, Traffic, and Mobility (T²M).

Notes

1. Bobrick's *Labyrinths of Iron* (1994), nevertheless, is an important international approach.
2. An earlier analysis of this corpus has been done by Zunino Singh (2005). Except for the film, these pieces have been also analyzed by Ana Lozano de la Pola (2006) and Amanda Holmes (2007).
3. Such mix between both cities is also noticeable in Cortázar stories like "El otro cielo" (1966) or his well-known novel *Rayuela* (1963) (Schmidt-Cruz 1998).
4. The first line was built by the Anglo-Argentine Tramway Company.
5. See the idea of proxemics (Hall [1966] 2003).

References

Anglo-Argentine Tramway Company. 1913. *Subterráneo de Buenos Aires. Inauguración al Servicio Público de la Línea Plaza de Mayo-Plaza Once de Septiembre.* Buenos Aires: AATC.
Antal, Nimród, dir. 2003. *Kontroll.* Budapest: Budapest Film and THINKFilm.

Arlt, Roberto 1976. *Aguafuertes Porteñas*. Buenos Aires: Losada.
Augé, Marc. 2000. *Los no lugares*. Barcelona: Gedisa.
"Bajo tierra." 1937. *Caras y Caretas*, 6 June 1937, 20.
Bauer, Tristán, dir. 1994. *Cortázar*. Buenos Aires: La Zona.
Benjamin, Walter. 1992. "Moscú." In *Cuadros de un pensamiento*, 26–67. Buenos Aires: Imago Mundi.
Besson, Luc, dir. 1985. *Subway*. Neuilly-sur-Seine, France: Gaumont Film Company.
Bobrick, Benson. 1994. *Labyrinths of Iron: Subways in History, Myth, Art, Technology, and War*. New York: Henry Holt.
Boe, Christoffer. 2003. *Reconstruction*. Valby, Denmark: Nordisk Film.
Brooks, Michael. 1997. *Subway City: Riding the Trains, Reading New York*. New Brunswick, NJ: Rutgers University Press.
Butcher, Melissa. 2011. "Cultures of Commuting: The Mobile Negotiation of Space and Subjectivity on Delhi's Metro." *Mobilities* 6, no. 2: 237–54.
"Charlas del Pebete." *PBT*, 13 December 1913.
Conrad, Sebastian. 2016. *What Is Global History?* Princeton, NJ: Princeton University Press.
Cortázar, Julio. 1963. *Rayuela*. Buenos Aires: Pantheon Books Sudamericana.
Cortázar, Julio. 1966. "El otro cielo." In *Todos los fuegos el fuego*, 72–85. Buenos Aires: Editorial Sudamericana.
Cortázar, Julio. (1965) 1995. "El Perseguidor." In *Cuentos Completos 1*, 225–66. Buenos Aires: Alfaguara.
Cortázar, Julio. (1974) 1996. "Manuscrito hallado en un bolsillo" and "Cuello de Gatito Negro." In *Cuentos Completos 2*, 65–73, 106–16. Buenos Aires: Alfaguara.
Cortázar, Julio. (1978) 1996. "Bajo Nivel." *La Jornada* 10 March. http://www.jornada.unam.mx/1996/03/10/sem-julio.html. Accessed 17 April 2021.
Cortázar, Julio. (1980) 1996. "Texto en una libreta." In *Cuentos Completos 2*, 349–60. Buenos Aires: Alfaguara.
Cresswell, Tim. 2010. "Towards a Politics of Mobility." *Environment and Planning D: Society and Space* 28, no. 1: 17–31.
Divall, Colin, and George Revill. 2005. "Cultures of Transport: Representation, Practice and Technology." *Journal of Transport History* 26, no. 1: 99–111.
Fernández Moreno, Baldomero. (c.1930) 1965. *Guía Caprichosa de Buenos Aires*. Buenos Aires: EUDEBA.
Goffman, Erving. 1971. *La presentación de la persona en la vida cotidiana*. Buenos Aires: Amorrortu Editores.
Hall, Edward T. (1966) 2003. *The Hidden Dimension (La dimensión oculta)*. Mexico City, Mexico: Siglo XXI.
Holmes, Amanda. 2007. *City Fictions: Language, Body, and Spanish American Urban Space*. Lewisburg, PA: Bucknell University Press.
Jensen, Oleb. 2009. "Flows of Meaning, Cultures of Movements—Urban Mobility as Meaningful Everyday Life Practice." *Mobilities* 4, no. 1: 139–58.
Lefebvre, Henri. 2004. *Rhythmanalysis. Space, Time and Everyday Life*. London: Continuum.
Lozano de la Pola, Ana. 2006. "Líneas del bajo nivel. Cuando Cortázar viaja en metro." *Extravío* 1. http://www.uv.es/extravio/PDFs/A_LOZANO.PDF. Accessed 17 April 2021.
Martínez Estrada, Ezequiel. (1947) 1968. *La cabeza de Goliat*. Buenos Aires: Centro Editor de América Latina.

McKay, John P. 1976. *Tramways and Trolleys: The Rise of Urban Mass Transport in Europe*. Princeton, NJ: Princeton University Press.

M. L. 1914. "Concursos de postales." *Caras y Caretas*, 12 May 1914.

Mom, Gijs. 2014. *Atlantic Automobilism: Emergence and Persistence of the Car, 1895–1940*. New York: Berghahn.

Morris, William. 1890. *News from Nowhere*. Boston: Roberts Brothers.

Mosquera, Gustavo, dir. 1996. *Moebius*. Buenos Aires: Universidad del Cine.

Munson, Walt. 1934. "Así es la vida." *Noticias Gráficas*, 22 October.

Nye, David. 1994. *American Technological Sublime*. Cambridge, MA: MIT Press.

Pike, David. 2005. *Subterranean Cities: The World beneath Paris and London, 1800–1945*. Ithaca, NY: Cornell University Press.

"La población trabajadora tiene un problema angustioso: la escasez de transportes." 1938. *Noticias Gráficas*, 8 October 1938, 11.

Schivelbusch, Wolfgang. 1986. *The Railway Journey*. Berkeley: University of California Press.

Schmidt-Cruz, Cynthia. 1998. "De Buenos Aires a Paris: los cuentos de Julio Cortázar y la reformulación de su identidad cultural." In *Actas del XIII Congreso de la Asociación Internacional de Hispanistas*, edited by F. Sevilla and C. Alvar, 411–19. Madrid: AIH.

Sheller, Mimi, and John Urry. 2006. "The New Mobilities Paradigm." *Environment and Planning A* 38, no. 2: 207–26

Simmel, Georg. (1903) 2005. "The Metropolis and Mental Life." In *The Urban Sociology Reader*, edited by J. Lin and C. Mele, 23–31. London; New York: Routledge.

Stalter-Pace, Sunny. 2015. "Underground Theater: Theorizing Mobility through Modern Subway Dramas." *Transfers* 5, no. 3: 4–22

Tomey, Víctor. 1913. "En el Subterráneo." *P.B.T.*, 13 December.

Vigil, Constancio. 1913. "La semana." *Mundo Argentino*, 10 December.

Viñas, David. 1995. *Literatura argentina y realidad política*. Buenos Aires: Editorial Sudamericana.

Welsh, David. 2010. *Underground Writing: The London Tube from George Gissing to Virginia Woolf*. Liverpool, UK: Liverpool University Press.

Williams, Rosalind. 2008. *Notes on the Underground: An Essay on Technology, Society, and the Imagination*. Cambridge, MA: MIT Press.

Zunino Singh, Dhan. 2005. "Cortázar y los subtes. Juegos de espacio y tiempo en los subterráneos de Buenos Aires." *Bifurcaciones* 2. www.bifurcaciones.cl/002/Zunino.htm. Accessed 17 April 2021.

Zunino Singh, Dhan. 2008. "Moebius: Buenos Aires subterránea y un relato de fuga." *Bifurcaciones* 8. http://www.bifurcaciones.cl/008/moebius.htm. Accessed 17 April 2021.

Zunino Singh, Dhan. 2012. "Towards a Cultural History of Underground Railways." *Mobility in History* 4: 106–14.

Zunino Singh, Dhan. 2014. "Meaningful Mobilities: The Experience of Underground Travel in the Buenos Aires Subte (1913–1944)." *Journal of Transport History* 35, no. 1: 97–113

Zunino Singh, Dhan. 2017. "A Genealogy of Sexual Harassment of Female Passengers in Buenos Aires Public Transport." *Transfers* 7, no. 2: 79–99.

CHAPTER 8

Literary Railway Bazaars
Transnational Discourses of Difference and Nostalgia in Contemporary India

Abhishek Chatterjee

Introduction: Transnational Modernity and Imperialist Nostalgia

Railway journeys in India have long been an integral component in the sociocultural life of the millions who have to travel by train at some point or the other. This dependence on the railway system was all the more pronounced at a period when this relatively slow form of travel, which began with the inception of the Indian railway system in 1830, was the only means of mass transport, up until the incipient boom of low-cost air travel in postliberalized India beginning in the 1990s.

Train journeys evoke perennial nostalgia in India, an entity whose ontology is fundamentally transnational. As Marian Aguiar argues in *Tracking Modernity: India's Railway and the Culture of Mobility*, the railway system introduced by British colonialism "was positioned in representations as a way to assimilate an India seen as multitudinous" (2011, 8). A creation of British colonialism, enmeshed in the discourse of nineteenth-century technological modernity brought about by the railway system, the notion of India is one that has been deeply contested from its very inception by its overwhelming diversity. This chapter uses the methodological approach of philosophical transnationalism, which is "the metaphysical assumption that social worlds and lives are inherently transnational" (Khagram and Levitt 2008, 2).

The idea of transnationalism is at the core of the imagination of the entity called India, a subcontinental landmass inexorably scarred by British imperialism and, paradoxically, also birthed by it. As Paolo Boccagni observes, "Rather than Transnationalism as a noun, which suggests an indeterminate but overwhelming expanding entity, the transnational should indeed be understood as an adjective—that is, as a social attribute which may apply and be enacted to different degrees, depending on other variables which turn into the real focus of the analysis" (2012, 128).

This chapter delineates how this notion is negotiated in the context of mobility studies through the privileged lens of foreigners such as the travel writer Paul Theroux, filmmaker Wes Anderson, and the British national of Indian origin, Monisha Rajesh (2012), in a haze of complex transnational and postcolonial relationships dictated by nostalgia and difference. The element of nostalgia—from a colonial nostalgia to nostalgia for every decade of the twentieth century—foreshadows railway journeys in India, which are somehow already regarded with nostalgia.

The journey takes place in a parallel universe of timelessness, where the traveler is rocked into a lull by the frenetic motion of the train. The disorienting giddiness and corporeal fatigue can be felt even several hours post-journey. The destination is not of immediate consequence. The emphasis, rather, is on the frantic urgency to be present in the situation and partake in a communal experience with people who are mostly strangers, and who may very well steal your luggage. A train journey is a transient phase, where conversations and encounters with others happen in a cocoon; it is a phase in which passengers are brought together as characters in a compartment who shall, in all probability, never meet again.

The event of remaining seated while the unfamiliar and the exotic are presented to the eye is very similar to the process and politics of photography. As Susan Sontag writes, "Photography develops in tandem with one of the most characteristic of modern activities: tourism" (1977, 6). Photography, much like travel writing in general, seeks to capture moments for eternity by freezing them in time, rendering them devoid of both life and context. In this light, one might argue that documenting railway journeys, too, is a process of myth-making, and an appeal to nostalgia. The Indian train, then, seems like a relic from the past, one that somehow should not coexist as it does with modernity in its spartan ordinariness. In contemporary India railway travel is the primary mode of mass transport, an indispensable yet scatological and sanitary nightmare for someone like the British-raised Monisha Rajesh. The temporal incongruity in trains of the third world and modern trains in Japan and the West adds to this lament for the lost colonial world by writers like Paul Theroux and filmmakers like Wes Anderson. If Theroux takes comfort in the fact that trains in India are old-fashioned and rickety—unlike the smooth clinical operations of its Western counterparts—for Anderson it is the appeal of a hyper-real exoticism, as dreamlike and comforting as the womb for his orphaned and forlorn characters.

Marian Aguiar charts the British Empire's justification of their role as the harbingers of modernity in India by projecting the introduction of the railway network into the subcontinent as a powerful unifying tool.

She writes, "The public space of the train became a site of reform: a rational utopia that appeared to embody, in its very spatialization, ideals that would order a seemingly chaotic India" (2011, 11). The discourse of rational modernity and the subsequent culture of mobility sought to transform the transnational subcontinent into a unified whole.

The Indian Railways system has been largely credited to the benevolence of British Empire building, but in actuality was a primarily self-serving strategy to debt-finance the bankrupt East India Company's commercial and political interests under the guise of improving local lives, much like the Macaulayian minute on Indian education (Macaulay, Macaulay, and Young 1835). However, there was never a concerted mass people's movement against the railway system introduced by the British. The railway networks helped the British construct and concretize a definite idea of India out of the diverse subcontinental landmass, and the native population swiftly embraced the incentives of technological progress and easy transportation. For the Indian masses, the railways, for whatever its intended purposes, were an inadvertent boon granted by the colonial master, a piece of imported modernity in a society that had not yet transitioned from its feudal foundations. In the following section, in my analysis of select texts, I examine how the fantasy of colonial nostalgia, centered around the Indian railway network operates within the aesthetics of the filmmaker Wes Anderson, and in the genre of the literary travel book.

Nostalgia and Redemption in Wes Anderson's *The Darjeeling Limited*

In Wes Anderson's *The Darjeeling Limited* (2007), the fictional luxurious Toy Train that the Whitman brothers embark on, becomes a motif for movement, space, and memory dictated by colonial nostalgia. The film follows the journey of the three brothers who set out to experience India on The Darjeeling Limited. The train also is the location of the reunion of the estranged brothers, who are now at various crossroads in their lives. Complete with an itinerary of various temples to visit to aid their spiritual discovery, the brothers embark on an emotionally tumultuous journey into the heartlands of India's spirituality.

Released about three decades after Edward Said's pioneering work *Orientalism* (2006), *The Darjeeling Limited* is a veritable embodiment of the Oriental fantasy of India and being Indian as nursed by Western and colonial imaginations. This Other situates India as the seat of spirituality, a requiem for spiritual awakening and an antithesis to the cultural and spiritual emptiness of the West.

The train in *The Darjeeling Limited* works as a metaphor for life and spatiality that has been a recurring field of enquiry in the Western philosophical tradition. Space and the memory of it sum up the experience of travel. We move from place to place but we perceive the space and remember it according to our subjective positions. According to Edward Casey, memory is itself "a space where the past can survive and revive" (Casey quoted in Whitehead 2011, 12). The idea of *loci memoriae* (memory places) has been influential in the idea of mnemonics from the classical to the early modern period. Mnemonic landscapes served as a bridge between memory and spaces in pilgrim routes of the Middle Ages. Anne Whitehead, in *Memory*, writes how a "commemorative worship" (2009, 13) of space can be perceived in the Romantic landscapes on the mind as illustrated by Wordsworth's *Tintern Abbey* (Wordsworth and Coleridge 1798) and Proust's evocations of his childhood landscapes of Combray. An equivalent of this in contemporary times is the uncomfortable silence and reverence obvious in the countenance of visitors to sites of Holocaust memorialization. This metaphor is constantly evoked by Anderson, as exemplified in one of the stream-of-consciousness montages of images from their various lives, strung together like the compartments of a train. Anderson speaks of this shot:

> The idea of it was simple. Roman had this idea that Anjelica Huston's character would say, "Maybe we can express ourselves more fully if we do it without words." And then Anjelica was very good in this silent moment but then we wanted to find a way to visually express whatever it is they were saying to each other and we didn't want to explain it. That was our answer to that. We searched for a while to figure out how to physically express it. In the end, we took a train car, gutted it, and we built these sets all in the train car and then we set out into the desert on the train and we shot it live with this construction. (Anderson quoted in Guillen 2007)

The film is thus a journey in itself, without maps or a specific destination. The crew, including Wes Anderson, Roman Coppola, and Jason Schwartzman, traveled to India, and the script emerged out of their subjective impressions. The act of physical travel translates to the journey on screen in a world of the director's own making, and becomes an elaborate Oriental fantasy.

Similarly, self-centered and self-absorbed voyeurism marks the journey outside the train. Thirsting for a spiritual high, the brothers finally experience one after being thrown off the train for their repeated misdemeanours. Their perception of India is both impressionistic and superficial, in a manner decidedly touristic. The people of the country seem like mere props and stimuli to aid this journey of spiritual discovery. Walking down a muddy trail, beside a river, they see a boat carrying a group of boys capsize and they manage to rescue all of them but one. Carrying the dead child to his family in the village, and in the subsequent otherly exotic interactions with the natives, the Whitman brothers consume the profound experience of his funeral with a voyeur's engagement.

This experience of a funeral becomes a *loci memoriae* for the brothers to the funeral of their father at home that they could not attend because of a set of absurd, almost Kafkaesque incidents. They find peace by attending the funeral of the boy in a land where such deaths are commonplace, just another commodity to be ticked off in the list of dark tourism. As Anderson himself admits, the script largely evolved out of the experiences of Anderson and the actors who script the act of traveling through India in a drug-fueled Romanticism of Oriental otherness. Francis acts as an extension of their absentee mother figure while the brothers traverse the unfamiliar under the burden of their father's memory. The name of the father literally is a load that they are carrying in the form of the father's suitcases, bearing his initials. They finally manage to drop this burden in pursuit of another train—the Bengal Lancer—and embark on a new journey after a meeting with their mother in India. Their mother, whom they meet in a monastery near the Himalayas, has become a nun teaching native children and assisting in the hunt for man-eating tigers—an extension of colonial missionary zeal.

The lyrical quality of this journey is supplemented by the compelling Eastern rhythms of Satyajit Ray and Merchant and Ivory productions. Similarly, Anderson draws on the cultural iconography of Rabindranath Tagore, the first Nobel laureate of Asia, through the strategic use of soundtracks from *Charulata*.[1] Ray uses an immersive instrumental soundtrack that accompanies a lonely housewife's trapped gaze out the window of her house, much like Anderson's three sibling characters who stare out in wonderment at the world. The lonely, bored housewife's counterparts in Anderson's film are the three siblings, for whom Charu's theme offers hope for redemption.

Satyajit Ray, along with Tagore, is one of the most important intellectual icons of the Indian elite. Amartya Sen in *The Argumentative Indian* (2005) devotes two full chapters to eulogizing Tagore's philosophy and Ray's "universalism." Ray's neo-realism and universalism made realist claims and cannot be separated from his modernist Nehruvian zeal. Most of Ray's films and their narratives advocate a liberalism and a commitment to cultural cosmopolitanism that are central to the consciousness of the contemporary Bengali upper-caste elite. Films like *Shatranj Ke Khiladi* (1977) and *Aranyer Din Ratri* (1969), among others, play on the binary of tradition and modernity to show English as the new language of power where English is spoken, or where English words are used as signifiers of exclusion. Ray's films created a reality while claiming to represent it. *Sonar Kella* (1969), Ray's most significant film on train journeys and travel, involves a detective journeying by train to various highly exoticized parts of Rajasthan. Anderson's film uses numerous allusions to Ray, including, quite improbably, his portrait on a wall of the compartment shared by the three brothers.

The Darjeeling Limited is a nod to colonial nostalgia. With its plush and ornate interiors reminiscent of palatial splendours, the train comes with male stewards dressed in the style of the Raj who speak untainted English and supple young female stewards with pumped up exoticity serving sweet limes. Token images of Orientalist stereotypes such as the snake-catching head steward, peacock feathers that have healing qualities, the man-eating tiger on the prowl, and Rita, the kohl-lined steward, as a sexually promiscuous woman appear throughout the film. The brothers are perpetually in a drug-induced haze, which further colors their vision of India. A sense of nostalgia abounds in the film's use of 1960s technicolour, evocative of the Beatles's era (Jack, played by Jason Schwartzman, even looks like Ringo Starr or George Harrison) and the distinctive cinematography of Robert Yeoman. It is a nostalgia harvested out of the insecurities and vulnerabilities of the American materialism the Whitman brothers embody. Similarly, "Where Do You Go to My Lovely," performed by Peter Sarstedt, who was born in India and had a thick Indian moustache just like Jack's, is used as a background score for the sexual encounter between Rita and Jack.

This comedy veers into absurdist farce when the eldest brother Francis says, "I love the way this country smells. I'll never forget it. It's kind of spicy." Just like the gentleman traveler and typical of other Wes Anderson films the characters in this film allude to an elite class of people who enjoy infinite leisure—idlers with ample time and money who can embark on such spiritual journeys as and when they please. The Whitman brothers, at the end, leave behind their father's belongings and suitcases to catch the Bengal Lancer, an act of detachment steeped in materialism, for without the nostalgic value of their father's association with them the possessions are all replaceable and can be dumped out on a third-world train station platform. Anderson's hyper-realism has some basis in reality. In a land of poverty and widespread economic and social inequality, the luxury train in *The Darjeeling Limited* is based on a real train called the Palace on Wheels, a luxury train similar to the Orient Express that runs from New Delhi to Rajasthan. The luxury train's erstwhile grandeur is now fading, and has been supplemented by another such train, as Monisha Rajesh observes in *Around India in 80 Trains*:

The Indian Maharaja-Deccan Odyssey was a relatively new member to the royal family of trains. His predecessor, the Palace on Wheels, still rolled his old bones up and down Rajasthan's tracks, but had succumbed to age. Reports suggested that his skin was peeling, his insides were damaged and the sparkle in his eye had dulled. Inside the suite, it was clear that the younger model was a picture of health. Fluffy carpet sprouted from the floor and a white duvet hugged the double bed that filled the room. At the head, four pillows puffed out their chests, their corners tweaked into place and a snip of hibiscus lay in the centre of the bed with a note saying: "Welcome aboard a journey to the depths of your soul." (Rajesh 2012, 95–96)

Such exotic claims are vended to affluent tourists visiting India. The fate of the protagonists of the film is no different, as they end their spiritual journey reminiscent of the Eliotian fantasy of redemption with the chant, "Shantih, Shantih, Shantih" (Eliot 1922).

Loss of "Aura" in Paul Theroux's *The Great Railway Bazaar*

Mass travel and mass production of art, the defining features of the modern era, are distinguished by what Walter Benjamin ([1936] 1969) called the loss of "aura."[2] Both the railways and photography were nineteenth-century inventions that fundamentally changed the way humanity perceived time and space. In both, the landscape is framed and presented for consumption to a particular stationary gaze that the photographic lens and cozy railway compartment offer. Wolfgang Schivelbusch in *The Railway Journey* notes the disparity between the railroad and the landscape through which it runs: "The empirical reality that made the landscape seen from the train window appear to be 'another world' was the railroad itself with its excavations, tunnels, etc. Yet the railroad was merely an expression of the rail's technological requirements, and the rail itself was a constituent part of the machine ensemble that was the system. It was, in other words, that machine ensemble that interjected itself between the traveller and the landscape" (2014, 24). As Schivelbusch notes, the destruction of aura by means of mechanical reproduction also meant that spatial distance was no longer experienced in the same way because the railroad seemed to bring everything closer. This led to the local and the regional losing their value in terms of temporal identity (42).

I would like to equate this argument to the idea of travel losing its aura to mass tourism, and its repercussions on the genre of the modern travel book, for which we need to take into account the generic history of the modern travel book. The first attempt to ground travel writing as a literary genre was made as late as 1980, when American critic Paul Fussell (1980) classified the works of "gentlemen travellers," such as Robert Byron (1982) and Wilfred Thesiger (2007), as literature in *Abroad: British Literary Travelling between the Wars* (Fussell 1980). Contemporary travel writers like Paul Theroux and V. S. Naipaul have been accused by postcolonial critics of mimicking the trope of gentlemanliness in their author-persona. Much of contemporary travel writing seems to harp on the nostalgia of its constructed Golden Age, and blurs the conventional opposition between traveling and tourism. The audience of contemporary travel writing is not motivated by what Fussell described as "armchair curiosity" (98); indeed, the reader did not read the gentlemen travelers' narratives to recreate their journey. Rather, contemporary travel writing in the postcolonial, and later the globalized world, appears to be a valuable accessory to tourism—fast becoming one of the largest industries in the world at the time—in conjunction with the surge in the sale of travel books in the 1980s, exemplified by the bestseller status of Theroux's *The Great Railway Bazaar* ([1975] 1987).

Paul Theroux was already an established novelist before he embarked on a four-month journey by train in 1973 from London through Europe, the Middle East, the Indian subcontinent to Southeast Asia. He chronicled his return by the Trans-Siberian railway network connecting Moscow with the Russian Far East and the Sea of Japan in *The Great Railway Bazaar* ([1975] 1987). His previous novels were set in exotic locations he had lived in, in Africa and the Far East, and were narrated in an incisive prose style that he also brought to his travel writing. Theroux describes the people he meets, turning his fellow passengers into characters, most of whom he judges very harshly. The word "bazaar," in this context, then, evokes images of crowds and chaos. This word "bazaar" fits into a very Oriental stereotype about India, things beings sold for consumption by virtue of their very existence. It is as if these things exist to be consumed, and their lives have little or no ontological merit beyond props in picture postcards designed to be soaked in for their difference.

Theroux begins the book by declaring "*I sought trains, but found passengers*" ([1975] 1987, 12; emphasis added) Although he claims that that the work is not fiction—rather lamentably, since he has been a writer of novels so far—he says, "The difference between travel writing and fiction is the difference between recording what the eye sees and discovering what imagination knows. Fiction is pure joy—how sad I could not reinvent the trip as fiction" (66). However, Theroux's writing reads like well-crafted fiction, as he seeks out characters that appeal to his somewhat jaundiced vision of human nature, and charts his narrative around them.

The author narrates his encounters with random people in a series of arbitrary montages, nonchalantly devoid of any attempt at serious historical or cultural analysis. It is an intercontinental tour aboard famous trains such as the Orient Express, the Khyber Pass Local, the Frontier Mail, the Golden Arrow to Kuala Lumpur, the Mandalay Express, and the Trans-Siberian Express, from famous stations like Victoria Station in London or Tokyo Central. Theroux's perspective is that of a spectator viewing life from inside a train. He is a literary traveler who makes no-holds-barred, frequently racist observations about his fellow travelers and steps into the cities only to give prearranged lectures, assignments that funded his trip on American literature in Turkey, India, Sri Lanka, Vietnam, and Japan. Theroux's opinions on American literature seem to evolve with his travels, as he notes, "Over three months earlier in Istanbul, I had spoken on the tradition of the American novel, implying that it was special and local. In India, I contradicted most of this, and by the time I had come to Japan I had come full circle, claiming there was no real tradition in American writing that was also not European (Theroux [1975] 1987, 64).

Theroux's book is unlike the travel books of the past and has little to do with the usual themes of adventure, discovery, or exploration ubiquitous in classical travel narratives of the past. He paints a picture of the world he sees by selecting interesting characters and writing about them before abruptly forsaking them at a station; this demystifies the conventional travel experience by denuding it of any beauty or romantic ideals. Like the contemporary tourist, his priorities change with the changing landscape. Theroux's book, which seems largely in the service of mass tourism, does not extend the idea of travel by mingling with the crowd at some unfamiliar location but instead relies on an Olympian solitude and perspective of a world from behind the first-class windows of his railway compartment: "I preferred to travel for two or three days, reading, eating in the dining car, sleeping after lunch, and bringing my journal up to date in the early evening before having my first drink and deciding where we were on my map" ([1975] 1987, 166). His observations are strangely bereft of any of the sense of wonder that is generally associated with travelers.

Theroux demystifies the supposed nobility of the traveler with caustic, yet undeniably accurate, observations, such as his comments on Indian passengers and their luggage in the Grand Trunk Express: "There were trunks all over the platform. . . . They were like evacuees who had been given time to pack, lazily fleeing an ambiguous catastrophe" ([1975] 1987, 255). He describes Calcutta as a "city of mutilated people" (249) and observes that, "throughout India and Pakistan, I was to see that same body . . . [,] starvation lending a special quality of saintliness to the bony face" (158). Theroux is mostly tired, bored, and disgusted with the people he meets and the journey is not represented as a self-actualizing trip that has helped him grow as a person. His author-persona seems none the wiser for his travels and the travails that he faces. Painting a panoramic picture of our contemporary world—in which travel like the days of Robert Byron is no longer possible—the traveler can no longer afford to be a romantic, and the act of traveling no longer offers any possibility of escape. *The Great Railway Bazaar* is a document of stark ordinariness, where all grand narratives of travel have collapsed in a world changing toward an unknown postmodern future, where travel and travel writing no longer happen in the hallowed isolation of upper-class refinement. It is this precise lament that makes the author shut himself up in a first-class coach as he watches the ordinariness of the world go by, his chronicle of train journeys also bringing travel writing—as Peter Whitfield observes in *Travel: A Literary History* (2011)—up to speed with the modern world of mass tourism in the 1970s.

Theroux exposes the falsity of the notion that travel can be a medium of spiritual escape in a world increasingly commodified, and when he retraces his trip thirty years later in *Ghost Train to the Eastern Star* (Theroux 2008), he finds that the more things have changed, the more they have remained the same: "Most of the world is worsening, shrinking to a ball of bungled desolation. Only the old can really see how gracelessly the world is ageing and all that we have lost" (483). Theroux's account of train travel is a far cry from Anderson's romanticized vision of train journeys as a pathway to enlightenment and a source of endless spiritual possibilities.

Pursuit of Nostalgia in *Around India in 80 Trains*

Shifting our gaze to a twenty-first-century account of railway journeys in India, this section examines Monisha Rajesh's *Around India in 80 Trains* (2012), a travel book in the self-conscious tradition of Paul Theroux's author-persona that subverts the trope of gentlemanliness through a single woman's perspective of traveling in India. The book documents a marathon of eighty train journeys across India over five months in 2010. The book, as the author informs us at the outset, is a function of nostalgia. It arose out of the fear of losing a sense of the past—something of the authenticity of slow travel in India—to the boom of low-cost airline travel, postliberalization of the 1990s and its large-scale affordability in twenty-first-century India. The idea came to her while scrolling through an article about booming airline travel, whose network was about to reach eighty cities even in 2010, but were still not comparable to the penetrative nature of the railway network that connected the entire landmass of India. In 2017 the Indian Railways itself was slated for sweeping changes with its then Railways minister, Suresh Prabhu, proposing a digital revamp, aircraft-like premium toilets, and bullet trains. Rajesh's document of train travel in India is a document of nostalgia, and a desire to preserve the memory of the nostalgia-inducing train journeys of the twentieth century.

The book is unique because there exists no other account of a young woman undertaking train journeys across India—a country perilous for women's safety. The only other significant accounts are by Paul Theroux and Rudyard Kipling, and the New Zealand journalist Peter Riordan, whose *Strangers in My Sleeper* came out in 2005. Rajesh writes as a privileged outsider to India, who earnestly wants to discover the country and her twenty-eight-year-old-self in the process. Born and raised in England, Rajesh had spent two scarring years as a child in India in the 1990s, growing up in Madras where her parents worked as doctors. They were elite and modern, her parents drove Mercedes cars in a land of oppressing poverty, and the children struggled to fit in. Rajesh, her brother, and parents found life in the third world despairingly difficult. They soon went back to England, and the author's only happy memories of India were of train journeys that she remembers as comforting. The privilege of the author-persona is highlighted at the outset, as she is aware of her entitlement and sincerely wants to experience the country of her birth. Though a journalist by profession writing columns for *The Telegraph* and *The Guardian* in the United Kingdom—the erstwhile colonial master, and for all practical purposes the creator of the idea of India in its present form—Rajesh has all the characteristics of a literary traveler. Rajesh's literary travelogue stands in stark contrast with the trite writing style of Biswanath Ghosh's *Chai Chai: Travels in Places Where You Stop But Never Get Off* (2009), an account of the author's travels to small towns near railway junctions.

Although the genre of literary travelogue markedly differs from the novel or the romance, the modern travel book in Paul Fussell's view also offers its readers something similar to the narrative pleasure of a novel or a romance, while claiming to be something entirely different from fiction. There is already a mythic motif to the journey. The travel book invariably begins with the narrator leaving what he or she calls home to venture into the unknown, either with a specific goal or with a yearning for adventures, stories, and experiences of a defamiliarizing and unfamiliar kind. During the journey, the narrator, occupying the liminal position of a traveler, undergoes significant and potentially life-altering experiences, before returning full circle to the place he or she called home. Fussell describes travel writing—with more than a passing nod to critic Northop Frye—as a "displaced quest romance" (1980, 209).

Rajesh draws inspiration for her own displaced quest romance directly from the most famous travel-adventure novel in the canon of highbrow literature, *Around the World in 80 Days* by Jules Verne, in which Londoner Phileas Fogg and his French valet Passepartout set out to circumnavigate the world in eighty days on a wager of 22,000 pounds. While reading the novel, Rajesh discovers that Phileas Fogg would not have undertaken the journey if he had not chanced on the news that the Great Indian Peninsula Railway had been opened between Rothal and Allahabad, thereby reducing the time it would take to circle the globe, only furthering the fact that the establishment of the Indian Railways had been quintessential to global travel in the nineteenth century. She suggests that the birth of the Indian Railways had clearly been a major spur for global travel in the nineteenth century (Rajesh 2012, 15).

Rajesh undertakes her journey in collaboration with a Norwegian photographer she nicknames Passepartout, which suggests universal access. The unnamed companion, who functions as her master key as she undertakes travails in India, a country notorious for being unsafe for women, becomes her handyman, bodyguard, and squabbling partner. She writes of him,

> In *Around the World in 80 Days,* Jean Passepartout claims that his surname has clung to him due to his natural aptness for going out of one business and into another and has abandoned his own country of France for England. Passe-partout—the French phrase for "all-purpose"—seemed the perfect nickname for my new companion. Twelve years ago he had abandoned his own country of Norway for England, and had now left a job in sales to pursue a career in photography. Less manservant and more travel buddy, his remit now extended to being my personal bodyguard and friend for our journey around India in 80 trains. (Rajesh 2012, 28)

As a woman traveler in India, a country that is intensely patriarchal and conservative, she is heavily dependent on Passepartout for her journeys and wants to keep the collaboration strictly professional. Passepartout, however, attempts to kiss her, during her farewell party in England, after which she chastises him. Things go smoothly between them until one day they begin to talk about religion. Tired of explaining the nature of their relationship to curious, talkative copassengers, Rajesh allowed people to assume that "Passepartout, my barren womb and I were a family [rather] than go through the torturous process of allaying suspicions of harlotry" (2012, 295). The book is revelatory in highlighting the anxieties of a single woman traveling in India.

She begins her travels by getting a ticket on the Chennai-Kanyakumari Express using her privilege, through the connections of influential family friends in Madras. India, post-liberalization and in the twenty-first century is in a curious state of flux, such that most Indians have to negotiate their relationship with the country almost on a daily basis. She writes about her elite friends in Chennai who wedding hop to Taj hotels in their BMWs and Mercedes. This was not the India she had left behind in the 1990s. They take the first train from Chennai Egmore station and thus begin their foray into the rawness of Indian life, undertaken by few people before. In her very first journey, she observes,

> For Indians a journey is important, but it is reaching the destination that really counts. In a country where survival is priority, this applies, in a broader sense, to their every undertaking. Lying, cheating, bribing and conning are bad, but if they get you where you want, then their definitions become flexible. Buying medical degrees, flashing red lights with no VIP in the car and inviting an entire constituency to a political wedding in exchange for votes are the norm. Everyone does it and everyone knows. . . . Theoretically, this clashed wildly with the naivety of our travelling mindset, but the practicality was undeniable. (Rajesh 2012, 148)

She travels on the Indian Maharaja, a luxury train like the one depicted in Wes Anderson's *The Darjeeling Limited,* and finds herself the only person of Indian origin on board, aside from the staff. From this privileged vantage point, she reflects on poverty in India: "On a day-to-day basis, nobody really notices poverty. People go about their business, chins up, eyes fixed forward, hiding behind tinted windows or in air-conditioned homes. Beggars, pavement dwellers and sick children carrying sick babies are just a part of the landscape. On the other side of the train, a row of ladies with jasmine dangling from their plaits waited with wedding-sized garlands and a silver tray of coconut, sandalwood paste and a pot of kumkum" (Rajesh 2012, 106).

Unlike Theroux, Rajesh is sympathetic to the otherness she has come to seek, and ultimately consume, but she too falls into the traps of seeking out stereotypes and easy generalizations. Benoy, a butler on a luxury train, one day surreptitiously chats with her. He laments to her that although the country seems to be doing well from the outside, only the rich stand to benefit. However, Rajesh's indulgent train journey and her position of the privileged observer are something this man will never experience, nor fully comprehend.

As Marian Aguiar points out, the "rational utopia" (2011, 11) of integration that the railway network in India was expected to bring about never quite arrived. In twenty-first-century India, the railway journey has come to be looked down on by the nation's microscopic, but overtly visible and vociferous upper class. When Rajesh is back in Delhi near the middle of her project, her endeavor becomes a great source of amusement to the people of her class. In one of the highbrow parties she attends in the capital, people are suitably shocked to hear about her journeys in "dirty" trains. Somebody cautions her that she would get a tapeworm from cleaning her teeth with the train's tap water, while another holds forth on the benefits of a tapeworm diet.

Rajesh's narrative shows that the social and material conditions that modernity has sought to eradicate have just been airbrushed, and boundaries of class, caste, and gender have only further been naturalized within the superficial paint of economic progress. She writes, "Outside the tinted windows, the outskirts of Delhi began to slip away. Within minutes, BMWs had morphed into bullock carts, shopping malls into shacks" (2012, 144). Rajesh, Passepartout, and her friend Ed brave the experience of taking a local train in Mumbai, notorious for being extremely crowded, and after completing one journey—something locals in Bombay do on a daily basis—emerge with a touristic sense of triumph. Through the journey, Rajesh believes that she has experienced India intimately through its people, even while observing that an Indian train ticket is a permit to trespass on the intimacies of other people's lives. While it is true that the essence of India can perhaps be distilled in the mobility of its railway network, its diversity and schizophrenic relationship with modernity makes it an ever-elusive, rather unattainable object of desire for its soul-hungry foreign visitors.

However, the reality of train travel in India is that it makes one tired at the end; it is travail in the purest sense. Both Monisha Rajesh and Paul Theroux battle depression near the end of their travels. At the end of *The Great Railway Bazaar,* Theroux enters a period of depression, about which he writes, "I felt flayed by the four months of train travel: it was as if I had undergone some harrowing cure, sickening myself on my addiction in order to be free of it. To invert the cliché, I had had a bellyful of travelling, hopefully I wanted to arrive" ([1975] 1987, 191). Rajesh, too, after the many train journeys, and an ugly fight with Passepartout, finds that the sight of people and sounds of conversation have become too overwhelming. She takes Train No. 78, the Konark Express, to do a Vipaasana meditation course near Hyderabad, which entails spending ten days at a spiritual retreat in complete silence. Traveling through railway bazaars of India makes her yearn for stillness, much like Pico Iyer's shift from the celebration of the global soul to the decidedly antitravel stance in *The Art of Stillness* (2014).

Conclusion

In 2020, in the post-COVID-19 era, when nostalgia has become the new-normal and transnational travel seems to be a relic from the past, this seems to be an appropriate time to reassess how viewers and readers are meant to interpret the nostalgia of these elite travel writers. Who identifies with the representations of journeys, and who finds them laughable very well depends on the subject-position of the reader. Travel books are generally sought by readers as literature of escape, as not as guidebooks. The reader/viewer, motivated by armchair curiosity, is not looking to follow on the travel writer/filmmaker's footsteps, but to vicariously live the journey through representation.

Although the pristine idea of travel died sometime in the past century—and all that we may be left with is pedantic tourism—issues connected to travel policy and its regulation have dominated the public sphere in the twenty-first century. The 9/11 attacks on the United States in 2001 changed, among other things, the dynamics of travel forever. Stringent rules and increased security at airports, along with racial profiling of travelers from the East serve to discourage certain travelers to the West. Over the years refugee crises in different parts of the Middle East, Asia, and Africa and subsequent travel bans have made the world a decidedly more restrictive space. As the world becomes more digitally connected and its wonders seemingly accessible, the pursuit of travel of pure escape, of simply going somewhere, unmediated by intrusive technology and curated information, has become next to impossible.

Now that almost the whole of the Earth has become, in Paul Theroux's words, "a fool proof Google map" (2014, xxiv), the only kind of travel that entails hardship would be possible at places where access is a problem Theroux even lists out these dwindling places in the 2014 Introduction to *The Best American Travel Writing*: "In the fractured countries of Africa, in quarrelsome Pakistan, in the disputed parts of India, and the nations that have emerged from the old Soviet Union" (2014, xxiv). In short, travel, as opposed to tourism, in the digital age seems possible only in the realms of the forbidden, viewed through the mist of nostalgia.

This chapter has considered railway journeys in India from the gaze of the Western outsider as the travelers negotiate their nostalgic fantasies with the complex realities of contemporary India. My study of the accounts of railway journeys in India attempts to capture the sense of nostalgia that pervades railway journeys in India and is specific to the privileged elite in a land of mass deprivation where train travel is a necessity for the masses and not an exotic curiosity. However, the nature of the accounts of railway journeys discussed in this paper may soon be a thing of the past considering the pace at which digitization, globalization, and cosmopolitanism threaten to obliterate quaint Indian ways of the past—both real and imagined.

Dr. Abhishek Chatterjee is assistant professor in the Department of English and Cultural Studies at CHRIST (Deemed to Be University), Bengaluru, India. His doctoral thesis, from the Department of Indian and World Literatures, The English and Foreign Languages University (EFLU), Hyderabad, is an inquiry into the philosophy of literary traveling and the modern travel book. His current research interests lie in the intersections of cultural studies, film theory, psychoanalysis, and literature. He has published his research in various journals, including *Critical Quarterly*.

Notes

1. The film *Charulata* is Satyajit Ray's 1964 adaptation of Rabindranath Tagore's novella *Nashtanirh* (*The Broken Nest*, [1901] 1977).
2. The concept of aura and auratic art is a seminal idea that Benjamin introduces in his work "The Work of Art in the Age of Mechanical Reproduction" ([1936] 1969). As the term suggests, the "aura" an object of art is the atmosphere of detached and transcendent beauty and power, rooted in the fabric of tradition' that is on the decline in the age of mechanical reproduction. By making reproductions, the uniqueness or the singularity of the work of art is negated and the unique existence of the object is substituted by a plurality of copies. The copy functions because it replicates or, in Benjamin's words, "reactivates" the object reproduced. Thus, the reproduced object is distanced from the domain of tradition. The advent of mechanization and the disappearance of the cult alludes to the symptomatic end of auratic art.

References

Aguiar, Marian. 2011. *Tracking Modernity: India's Railway and the Culture of Mobility.* Minneapolis: University of Minnesota Press.

Anderson, Wes, dir. 2007. *The Darjeeling Limited.* DVD. Beverly Hills, CA: 20th Century Fox Home Entertainment.

Benjamin, Walter. (1936) 1969. "The Work of Art in the Age of Mechanical Reproduction." In *Illuminations*, edited by H. Arendt, 217–51. New York: Schocken.

Boccagni, Paolo. 2012. "Rethinking Transnational Studies: Transnational Ties and the Transnationalism of Everyday Life." *European Journal of Social Theory* 15, no. 1: 117–32.

Fussell, Paul. 1980. *Abroad: British Literary Traveling between the War.* Oxford: Oxford University Press.

Guillen, Michael. 2007. "2007 MVFF30: THE DARJEELING LIMITED—Interview with Wes Anderson, Jason Schwartzman and Roman Coppola." *Screenanarchy,* 10 October. http://screenanarchy.com/2007/10/2007-mvff30-the-darjeeling-limited interview-with-wes-anderson-jason-schwart.html. Accessed 17 April 2021.

Iyer, Pico. 2014. *The Art of Stillness: Adventures in Going Nowhere.* New York: Simon and Schuster.

Khagram, Sanjeev and Peggy Levitt. 2008. "Constructing Transnational Studies." In *The Transnational Studies Reader: Intersections and Innovations,* edited by S. Khagram and P. Levitt, 1–22. New York: Routledge.

Macaulay, Thomas Babington, Baron Macaulay, and George Malcom Young. 1935. *Speeches by Lord Macaulay with His Minute on Indian education.* London: Oxford University Press, H. Milford.

Rajesh, Monisha. 2012. *Around India in 80 Trains.* London: Nicholas Brealey.

Ray, Satyajit, dir. 1964. *Charulata.* DVD. Calcutta: Angel Video.

Ray, Satyajit, dir. 1969. *Sonar Kella.* DVD. Government of West Bengal, 1974.

Ray, Satyajit, dir. 1969. *Aranyer Din Ratri.* DVD. Calcutta: Purnima Pictures.

Ray, Satyajit, dir. 1977. *Shatranj Ke Khiladi.* DVD. Calcutta: Devaki Chitra.

Riordan, Peter. (2005) 2006. *Strangers in My Sleeper.* Auckland: New Holland.

Said, Edward W. 2006. *Orientalism.* Brantford, ON, Canada: W. Ross MacDonald School.

Schivelbusch, Wolfgang. 2014. *The Railway Journey: The Industrialization of Time and Space in the Nineteenth Century.* Berkeley: University of California Press.

Sen, Amartya. 2005. *The Argumentative Indian: Writings on Indian History, Culture, and Identity.* New York: Macmillan.

Sontag, Susan. 1977. *On Photography.* New York: Farrar, Straus and Giroux.

Tagore, Rabindranath. (1901) 1977. *The Broken Nest.* Madras: Macmillan.

Theroux, Paul. (1975) 1987. *The Great Railway Bazaar.* Harmondsworth, Middlesex, UK: Penguin.

Theroux, Paul. 2008. *Ghost Train to the Eastern Star: On the Tracks of the Great Railway Bazaar.* Boston: Houghton Mifflin.

Theroux, Paul. 2014. "Introduction." In *The Best American Travel Writing,* edited by Jason Wilson and Paul Theroux, xviii–xxiv. Boston: Houghton Mifflin.

Thesiger, Wilfred. 2007. *Arabian Sands.* London: Penguin.

Wordsworth, William, and Samuel Taylor Coleridge. 1798. "Tintern Abbey." *Lyrical Ballads: With a Few Other Poems,* 201–210. London.

CHAPTER 9

Memories of Trains and Trains of Memory

Journeys from Past-Futures to Present-Pasts in El tren de la memoria *(2005)*

Araceli Masterson-Algar

A treaty between Spain and the German Federal Republic on 20 January 1960 set the grounds for the mass transport of *Gastarbeiter* (guest workers), from Spain to Germany via the rail system. German companies paid the Spanish state an equivalent of $17 (2,400 pesetas) per worker, which covered the costs of his or her passport, a train ticket, and a bag of food for the journey (Sorel 1974, 21). Changes in Spain's agrarian practices due to industrialization and the economic growth in Northern Europe following World War II were central to these processes. Migration to Northern Europe, as a true "Plan Marshall *made in Spain*" (148); set the grounds for Spain's industrial growth during the 1960s. Furthermore, through an estimated $3 billion in remittances it offered a solution to Spain's high unemployment and increased social tensions, and fueled the economies of northern Europe (Muñoz Sánchez 2005; Riera Ginestar 2015, 44–48; Santos 2018). The documentary film *El tren de la memoria* (The train of memory) by Marta Arribas and Ana Pérez (2005), retells the collective memory of these events with attention to three women who took the rails to Nuremberg in the 1960s: Josefina Cembrero, Victoria Toro, and Leonor Mediavilla.

Yet, *El tren de la memoria* is hardly about the past. Marta Arribas herself describes its origin in present-day debates about migration in Spain: "Surge de los debates sobre la inmigración con los que nos levantábamos cada mañana" (it emanates from current debates about migration to which we woke up every morning) (Arribas quoted in Simón 2010; all translations in this chapter are mine). This project stands out from the larger corpus of recent Spanish films about immigration in at least two important ways: its main characters are Spanish nationals, and their journey is not one of departure, but rather of return.[1] The narrative is structured through Josefina's trip back to Nuremberg to join friends in

Figure 9.1. Promotional poster for *El tren de la memoria* (2005). Reproduced with the permission of Producciones La Iguana.

the celebration of Leonor's retirement after years of social work. Leonor's last client, Victoria Toro, is about to return to Spain after a lifetime in Nuremberg with her mother who is bedridden with Alzheimer's and no longer remembers. Through train travel, the film articulates their individual experiences into a collective act of remembering.

Drawing from Deleuze (1997) and Guattari (1994), among others, scholars in mobility studies have insisted on the physical experience of moving in space: "The body especially senses as it *moves*" (Urry 2007, 48). Through a journey, physical and imaginary—in an actual train and through trains of thought—*El tren de la memoria* is an invitation to think about memory and human mobility in a broader sense, and as inseparable from economic, social, and political processes. By favoring movement over a narrative of loss, the film disrupts the possibility of nostalgic framings of the past, thus moving space back into time, and memory back into history. Arribas and Pérez's (2005) train articulates the complex interrelation between history and memory, and between human mobility and the urban experience. Its protagonists often address the frugality of the process of remembering, marked by memories that come and go, in a journey at times smooth, but mostly marked by jolts and changes of tracks in a chain of past-presents and present-futures. Ultimately, and as the film's promotional poster announces (figure 9.1), this train is grounded in the lived experiences that make its suitcases, cars, rails, and—ultimately—Nuremberg itself.

"Un tren del año de 'catapumpum la pera'" (Returning in a train from who knows when)

La gente más elevada
Va en primera acomodada

En los coches de segunda
La gente mediana abunda.

En asientos de tercera
Va la gente bullanguera.
    (Popular fin de siècle verses, quoted in Wais San Martín 1967, 291)

(The high-society folk
ride comfortably in first class

In the second-class coaches
the middle class abounds

In the third-class seats
are all the rowdy folk.)

The rail has been amply analyzed as a recurrent metaphor in cultural expression. Under this light, rather than constituents of a grounded system, trains are often represented as a presence from the past, and as such, a means to evoke nostalgia.[2] The train in *El tren de la memoria* (Arribas and Pérez 2005) is certainly a vehicle to the past. Yet, its rails are grounded, and thus its memories are collective and embodied. On this train, the process of remembrance (a process that includes emotions and desires) takes priority over what is remembered, bringing forth the imagined and lived experiences that ultimately bind memory to space.

Drawing from Michel Foucault, Patrick Hutton highlights how, "rather than returning to some mythical beginning and working forward, the historian would do better to proceed from the present backward" (1993,

112). Such are the journeys that structure the narrative. Josefina returns to Nuremberg years after her return to Spain from Nuremberg, and Victoria is preparing her return to Spain after years in Nuremberg to fulfill the wishes of a mother who no longer remembers, or whose mind might very well be already there. People, spaces, lives, voices, and means of remembering converge via the train, which acts as both the structure of the story and material grounds for its lived experience. *El tren de la memoria* (Arribas and Pérez 2005) offers a journey for remembrance in an oral account where, as in a web of rails, memories come and go, running parallel, merging, waxing, and waning through tracks that chain the weight of the iconic *maletas de cartón* (cardboard suitcases) of the mid-twentieth century to the wheels of the latest carry-on.

The opening shots show Josefina's arrival via taxi to Madrid's Atocha train station. It soon becomes apparent that the journey is both present and past, articulated through the physical experience of travel. The abrupt sonic and visual transitions from Atocha station today to footage of the 1950s and 1960s echo both the continuities and discontinuities between the trip she is about to take and the one she sets off to remember. Thus, middle and long dolly shots in crisp color accompany Josefina's walk to the platform through sliding doors and up mechanic escalators. The diegetic sounds of the station on a calm day speak to her ease of movement as she comfortably pulls a travel-sized suitcase behind her. From the station's smooth surfaces, the narrative transitions abruptly to a foreground of loud and muffled sounds of voices and of machines accompanying black-and-white close-ups and extreme close-ups of hands and suitcases of travelers in the past, most of them low-angle shots by handheld camera. The integrity of her travel today, where the camera captures her full body, contrasts with the fragmented bodies of the archival footage, while also alluding to its continuities. Josefina's story is her own, but also that of all of the faces in the frozen images of the black-and-white footage. A low-angle shot of a train cutting through space transitions to the title of the film and to her voice in a voiceover confirming the film as a journey that *is* remembrance—"un viaje que *es* recordar el que hice hace cuarenta y dos años" (a journey that *is* remembering what I did forty-two years earlier) (emphasis added). Or, in other words, a journey of what, for the most part, is no longer present.

In effect, rather than turning to sources, the film follows Dutch historian Gustaaf Reinier (1892–1962), who called for replacing the idea of sources with that of traces of the past in the present (Burke 2001, 13). Josefina tracks her own journey through what remains: ruins, photographs, and, above all, her body. Her memories are invoked through the physical sensations of the experience of train travel, in a process that braids individual experiences into a collective memory. Victoria Toro, merging onto the track laid by Josefina, invokes via words, sounds, and gestures the physicality and sensations of the journey: "Un tren del año de 'catapumpum la pera' . . . un tren que iba dando así . . . unos zurríos ¡tac! ¡pah! . . . así ¿no? . . . Muy incómodo, olía que apestaba, mujeres veníamos muy poquininas, estábamos toas cohibidas. Teníamos mucho *miedo de movernos* de nuestros asientos" (A train from who knows when . . . and it did like this . . . moving and shaking ¡tac! ¡pah! . . . like that, right? . . . Very uncomfortable, it reeked, and only some of us were women, and we felt shy. *We were really afraid of moving* in our seats) (emphasis added). The fear of moving in a moving space reveals the contradictions of the migrant experience, showing how "movement, potential movement and blocked movement" are contingent on social hierarchies of class, gender, ethnicity, and documented status among others (Urry 2007, 43).[3]

Along these lines, the politics of collective memory speak in the film through the discontinuities between the clean narratives offered by official sources, the memories of the film's protagonists, and the historical footage from the period. These splits in the tracks move attention to the power of enunciation—"who" remembers. For instance, in the film, Alvaro Rengifo, former director of the Instituto Español de Migración describes the train journey as "muy organizado" (very organized), and business delegate Hans Peter Siber says it was "en general, muy bien" (in general, very good). The middle shots of these officials sitting comfortably in their living room and office respectively are transversed by snapshots—sonic and visual—of the actual train stations, revealing the gaps between these officials' memories and the stories that speak through the bodies in those trains.

Arriving Who Knows Where

Gastarbeiter on their way to Nuremberg arrived first in Irún (Spain), and from there to Cologne, where they were distributed to their corresponding factories throughout Germany (Riera Ginestar 2015, 95). Yet, the logistics of the journey can hardly be discerned from the protagonists' oral accounts. In their memory, itineraries are bundled up into the expressions of fear and uncertainty accompanying perceptions of an immense distance—one that cannot be measured. Josefina describes the destination to Nuremberg as "no nos podíamos hacer una idea de lo que era *aquello*" (we could not even have an idea of what *that* would be) (emphasis added), conveying thereof a distance too large even for the imagination. Leonor's voice in a voiceover also narrates her arrival to "aquello," to a "something" so far that it can only be reminisced through a narrative of forgetting:

> Me *olvidé* de mis padres, me *olvidé* de mis hermanos, me *olvidé* de mi misma porque creía que *aquello* no podía ser realidad, que era una película de de . . . *aquel* andén estaba cubierto de . . . mayoritariamente hombres, unos sentaos, otros tumbaos, montones de maletas, de cartones . . . *no sé si fueron instantes o minutos* . . . *sentí vergüenza* de mi misma, de *verme* en *aquella* situación." (Arribas and Pérez 2005; emphasis added)

> (I *forgot* my parents, I *forgot* my siblings, I *forgot* myself because I thought that *it could not be true*, that it had to be some kind of movie. . . . I mean, *that* platform was covered with mainly men, some sitting, others laying down, mountains of suitcases, of cardboard. . . . *I didn't know* whether it was *instants or minutes*. . . . I *felt ashamed* of myself, of *seeing myself* in *that* situation).

Leonor's forgetting conveys the intensity of her memories in the present, while simultaneously serving as an expression of her spatial distance from the memory she is recalling ("aquello, aquel, aquella" [that, that, that]) (Arribas and Pérez 2005), and for which she cannot provide an accurate timeframe ("no sé si fueron instantes o minutos" [*I didn't know* whether it was *instants or minutes*; emphasis added]). Her countertestimony ("aquello no podía ser realidad" [it could not be true]) overlaps with a layer of archival sounds and footage from the period that, by running parallel to her narrative, aids the tracks of their collective memory.

Victoria Toro also communicates the real and imagined distance between Alemania (Germany) and Alía, her small hometown in Extremadura through the intonation and body language accompanying her statement, "El salto era *chico*" (it was *quite* the jump) (emphasis in original) (Arribas and Pérez 2005). Her choice of the term "salto" reduces what was surely quite an itinerary to two spatial referents: her town and the nation of destination, with nothing in the middle. Similarly, Josefina describes the space between Spain and Nuremberg as a *mientras tanto* (a meanwhile): "al llegar allí era una sensación muy fuerte porque ya habías llegao. *Mientras tanto* había sido el viaje. Pero allí ya estás y a ver *ahora* qué pasa" (The sensation upon arrival was very strong because you had arrived. *Meanwhile* was the trip. But now you are there and *now* what) (emphasis added).

The editing of the film announces the arrival at the station—to the *now* of then and the *now* of now—by shortening the transitions between shots and reverse shots of the train ride from the outside in and

Figures 9.2 and 9.3. Shot of Josefina traveling in the present followed by footage of young woman making that same journey in the past. Screen captures by Araceli Masterson.

from the inside out, and through the growing visual and sonic overlap between shots from the present and footage from the past. A telling example is the close-up of Josefina looking out the window is followed by an archival shot of a young woman facing the opposite direction. The strong similarity and interplay between both shots announces both the proximity to the destination and the distance—the "mientras tanto" (meanwhile)—between Josefina's arrival in the past and her arriving at its return in the present (figures 9.2 and 9.3).

Josefina's words in a voiceover accompany the images of her arrival to Nuremberg in the present, and overlap then and now—a forty-two-year interval—onto the spatial distance between Madrid and Nuremberg. Ironically, it is precisely the distance from the past that extends the protagonists' ability to derail experiences from the past onto their understanding in the present. Victoria, for instance, reminisces about the cardboards they had to wear at the stations with the names of their factories of destination: "los cartones atrás y alante como las ovejas, y no nos enterábamos . . . *ahora*, caramba, caramba, como los judíos" (cardboards across our chest like we were sheep, and we didn't think anything of it . . . and *now* . . . well well . . . as they did to the Jews) (emphasis added) (Arribas and Pérez 2005). Leonor also denounces how, upon arrival, migrants were moved about as if they were "sacos de patatas" (sacks of potatoes). Hence, the passing of time often wears off memories while strengthening the possibilities of remembrance.

Along these lines, Leonor sums up the archival density of the journey through its traces and wounds: "Ese viaje marcó mucho" (That trip left a strong trace) (Arribas and Pérez 2005). Part of a collective history, Josefina's return and the collective memories running through those tracks follow Sarlo's characterization of remembrance as a form of healing the alienation of the migrant body (2005, 51), while ultimately reaffirming its place in the city. The luminosity and duration of long shots of Josefina's reencounter with Leonor contrast with the unsettling feelings of their first arrival in Germany—"aquello"—because, on this occasion, Josefina has purposefully arrived in a city she knows well: Nuremberg. From this point on, her collective process of remembrance extends its rails to the streets of Nuremberg, unveiling the entwinement of migrant bodies and the urban history of Germany's "capital of nostalgia."[4]

Rails, Ruins, and Two Fingers

> Nuremberg is Germany's Grail castle, its Mont Salvat.
> It is a place that permits time travel.
>   —Stephen Brockmann, *Nuremberg:*
>   *The Imaginary Capital*

Pierre Nora explains modernity as a loss of *milieux de mémoire* (environments of memory) into *lieux de mémoire* (sites of memory) through the institutionalization and materialization of the past (1989, 7). Extending this to the urban, Henri Lefebvre (1991) and others denounce the disassociation of space from the social processes that ultimately make it, resulting in cities becoming "dreamscapes of visual consumption" (Zukin 1992, 221). Nuremberg epitomizes these processes.

Stephen Brockmann describes Nuremberg as the "most powerful and prominent of German mythic cities" (2006, 7), and its place in the German imagination so vivid that "Nuremberg is more famous than Nuremberg" (2). But contrary to its medieval aesthetic, Nuremberg, as Brockmann puts it, is "in a very real sense new" (4). After World War II, only 9 percent of Nuremberg's buildings were undamaged, and its population was largely evacuees, refugees, and returning war veterans. Efforts to rebuild the city in order to preserve its medieval qualities gained particular urgency vis-à-vis Nuremberg's recent history as the symbolic center of the Nazi regime, further "underlying the tension between the invocation to remember and the urge to forget" (Gregor 2008, 3).[5] In this light, Neil Gregor asks, "What kind of a memory culture would emerge in this shattered, divided disoriented city?" (119). Josefina's lived and collective memories are set therefore against the backdrop of a city crystallized into medieval postcards of tourists' imagination and national nostalgia. Josefina and the many voices that rode those trains to Nuremberg remember the city from their lived experiences, and in so doing affirm themselves as part and parcel of its making.[6]

During a walk through the Aldstadt, Nuremberg's historical center, Josefina' in a voiceover yields to the city's carefully crafted charm, which she describes as a *maravilla* (marvelous), albeit one inaccessible during her years working in Nuremberg: "Ni te interesan las ciudades, ni te interesan los países, ni tienes tiempo para disfrutarlo . . . encerradas en las residencias . . . vivíamos en otro mundo" (you have no interest in cities, or countries, nor do you have time for any of that . . . trapped in the barracks . . . we lived in another world) (Arribas and Pérez 2005). Another former migrant and current resident of Nuremberg joins Josefina's train of thought: "*Ahora* te das cuenta que Nuremberg tiene cosas bonitas y tú llevas aquí cuarenta años y no has apreciado lo que tienes" (*Now* you realize that Nuremberg has beautiful things, and you've been here forty years and never appreciated that) (emphasis added). Thus, in the collective memory, migrants describe their time in Nuremberg as away from Nuremberg ("otro mundo" [another world]), due to a combination of living conditions, limited budget, long working hours, and, largely, their memories of fear and exclusion: "vivíamos apartados" (we lived apart), "no te atrevías" (you would not dare).

Tellingly, the protagonists identify the train station, located immediately to the south of Nuremberg's wall, as their closest approximation to the city center. Josefina describes the station as warm ("era un lugar donde había calor") (a place where you found warmth)–both in the literal and figurative sense (Arribas and Pérez 2005). To Leonor the station was a space of *posibilidad* (possibility) where one could meet

with friends, and, as Josefina adds, find job opportunities and learn how
to move about the city. Train stations, they agree, "tienen mucho sig-
nificado para nosotros" (hold a lot of meaning for us). Addressing the
embodied experience of mobility, David Bissell identifies the train station as the node between the body and the city (2009, 176).[7] Indeed,
the warmth of the station speaks to the interrelation between memory,
access to the city, and the body. Thus, Josefina's choice to return by
train to Nuremberg, and to enter the city via its station is key, and has
everything to do with the place of the railroad in Nuremberg's history.

Nuremberg was the site of Germany's first rail company in 1835, and
became the administrative headquarters of the Royal Bavarian State
Railway Company, as well as the location of its repair shops and marshaling yards. Nuremberg's recent history finds its trace in its rails, that
"Like a spider . . . spun a web of steel rail centered on herself, for by 1877
seven trunk lines linked Nürnberg [Nuremberg] to most other major
cities on the continent" (Reisser 1986, 383). In *El tren de la memoria*
(Arribas and Pérez 2005), train travel, as both metaphor and lived experience, is the vehicle to remember, to heal, and to access the right to the
city and to walk its streets.

Craig Reisser highlights the interrelation between the railroad,
transportation systems, and urban planning in Nuremberg since the
mid-nineteenth century, wherein the city is organized into zones, each
tied to a specific phase of its development. Zone 1 is the Aldstadt, the
historic core within the walls. Zone 2 is the belt of nineteenth-century
apartments distributed at the edges of Zone 3, the industrial sectors.
According to him, migrants' experience of the city was as follows: "The
daily existence of immigrant life in Nürnberg [Nuremberg] are to be
found in the cityscapes engendered by the industrial revolution, but the
venerated landscapes of the Altstadt are the city's soul and the locus of
its sense of place" (Reisser 1986, 168). Once in Nuremberg, Josefina's
journey shows her gradual displacement from Zone 3 to the Aldstadt,
and back to the train station for her return to Madrid from her return to
Nuremberg. The film's continued attention to the physical experience of
moving anchors migrant memories and bodies to these spaces.

Hence, Josefina's path rests on a "muscular consciousness" (Bachelard
[1964] 2014, 11) that reveals the entanglement between the degenera-
tion of migrants' bodies and the rebuilding of the city. In the film's closing scene, for instance, Josefina explains that, by the mid-1970s, most
Spanish migrants returned to Spain as the outcome of damaged bodies:
"nuestros cuerpos estaban gastados" (our bodies were worn out) and
because "empezábamos a sobrar" (we were beginning to spoil) (Arribas and Pérez 2005). In a way, Josefina brings her remains (embodied

memories) back to Nuremberg, confirming her place in the city that migrants helped build, gradually reinserting her body into its streets, first by train, then by taxi and, ultimately, on foot.

Upon arrival in Nuremberg, Josefina's journey continues with Leonor via taxi. This choice of transportation speaks to their increased mobility in the present, particularly as Josefina recalls aloud, "entonces siempre cogíamos el tranvía" (back then we always rode the streetcar) (Arribas and Pérez 2005). Their trajectory along Nuremberg's emblematic city wall reveals that Leonor and Josefina are sightseeing from the taxi, an expense hardly imaginable during their years as migrant workforce.

The choice of the wall as the first spatial reference for Nuremberg outside the train station is key. As summed up by Brockmann, "Nuremberg is defined by its wall" and "divides Nuremberg from everything that is not Nuremberg" (2006, 292). Namely, its medieval aesthetic around the Aldstadt, the city's historic center, "defends Nuremberg against the onslaught of time" (296). Josefina, like most migrants to the city, lived and worked outside its wall. Yet, during this return trip to Nuremberg, she will eventually cross it, while her narration serves as witness to its temporariness: "esa muralla estaba completamente destruída. La reconstruyeron estando yo aquí" (that wall was completely destroyed. They reconstructed it when I was here) (Arribas and Pérez 2005). Leonor and Josefina converse in German with the taxi driver about the city they remember through what is no longer there: "Nuremberg ha cambiado mucho" (Nuremberg has changed a lot), and make recurrent remarks on memories of its ruins: "había muchas ruinas" (it was full of ruins). Just as Josefina's journey is a following of tracks, the ruins surface as both remnant and origin of a city to which she belongs, reinserting social processes into Nuremberg's heritage sites.

The taxi continues on toward the southwest, passing Quelle, the mail catalogue and distribution center where Josefina, Victoria and many other Spanish women used to work. Nuremberg's southwest belt (Zones 2 and 3) materializes the entwinement between the rails, the factories, and Nuremberg's migrant history. Most Spanish immigrants arriving by train settled in this area. They arrived with contracts to work in factories along the railroad line, and lived either in housing (known as *barracas*) provided by those same factories or in the adjacent neighborhoods formed during the city's industrialization in the nineteenth century. The inseparability between migrants' lives and their place of employment is evident at a gathering at St. Claire's church, where Josefina and others recall each other by asking, "¿En qué fábrica estabas tú?" (in which factory were you?). Specifically, Josefina's former employment, Quelle, is near Gostenhof, also known as Nuremberg's Bronx, the neighborhood with the largest concentration of Spaniards in the city (Reisser 1986, 156). An enclave for Nuremberg's transportation arteries extending south across the railroad line and its adjoining expressway, Gostenhof holds immigrant histories that date back to Nuremberg's growing industrialization in the nineteenth century and that continue to the present (156, 228)[8].

Smets and Shannon argue that the train, and later the car, replace the experience of the landscape with its vision: "vision—rather than sound, smell, or touch—has become the primary sense through which the landscape is experienced" (2010, 122). Yet, this is not the case in *El tren de la memoria* (Arribas and Pérez 2005), where, revisiting Nora, the experience of mobility counters the reduction of *milieux de mémoire* (environments of memory) into *lieux de mémoire* (sites of memory). Thus, at the site of Quelle, Josefina reframes vision into a narrative of disbelief: "ahí, en la segunda planta trabajaba yo . . . *imagínate, no me lo puedo creer*" (I worked there, in the second floor . . . imagine, *I can't believe it*) (emphasis added). This scene, the last one inside the taxi, starts a recurrent motif throughout Josefina's time with Leonor in Nuremberg, whereby we witness the protagonists engaging with representations of themselves in the past, thus moving attention away from what is seen to *how* it is remembered.

At Leonor's home, the two friends sip wine while looking through a heap of pictures on the table. Their still lives, their absent presence, are recalled through Josefina and Leonor's mutual prompting: "¿te acuerdas?" Rather than witnessing events, *El tren de la memoria* (Arribas and Pérez 2005) opens the space to observe the process of witnessing, as Josefina, Victoria, Leonor, and others retrace their memories to the places where they used to live, share pictures and footage of themselves and others, and patch together memories.[9] Through their journey together, these images—rather than serving as sources—serve as traces of the past in the present. This becomes most evident in their memories of labor.

At the factories, speed and efficiency went on par with workers' increasing loss of movement and worsening physical impairment. Victoria describes the frantic labor at Quelle "¡chas! ¡chas! ¡chas! y correr y correr y correr y correr" (clank! clank! clank! and run and run and run and run) (Arribas and Pérez 2005), and its incarnation in open wounds in her feet, so painful she could barely walk. The film accompanies Josefina's walk through Quelle in the present. Through filmic choices that parallel those of her train ride back to Nuremberg, the camera alternates shots of Josefina walking through Quelle's installations in the present with archival footage of factory workers in the past. Like Victoria, Josefina's voice in a voiceover reminisces about the contradictions of her labor: "tocamos todo y no tenemos acceso a nada" (We touch everything, but can access nothing). Yet, the most material expression of cost of labor on its workers' integrity is Josefina's embodied memory of her roommate's accident at work. Josefina explains this episode as key in her decision to return to Spain in order to preserve what was left of her physical and mental health. During her account of this memory, Josefina' in a voiceover accompanies quick shifts between contemporary and archival images, which alternate from medium shots of factory workers to close-ups and extreme close-ups of various machine parts. The combination of Josefina's voice in a voiceover with these visual images and diegetic and nondiegetic sounds of machinery generate the anxiety that leads to the outcome: her friend's loss of two fingers to a machine. Like Nuremberg's ruins, those fingers are memories of a loss, presence of an absence, traces to a rail into memory. Ruins and two fingers—the remains—are the permanence and origin of Josefina's memories, and the traces for Josefina's journey back to Nuremberg. From this point on, the film shows Josefina walking through the streets of Nuremberg's historical center, where past-futures and present-pasts, body and city, merge to reconfigure the city's heritage into lived experience.

Streets of Nuremberg

Reisser describes how a visitor's impression of Nuremberg "is basically a filtered view of the Altstadt" (1986, 173). Yet, this is hardly the case of the protagonists of *El tren de la memoria* (Arribas and Pérez 2005), whose lives outside the city walls "detracted from its [Nuremberg's] image" (Reisser 1986, 185). Thus, nearly half a century following her departure, Josefina returns to walk her remains across those walls and into the Aldstadt. Josefina literally places her body amidst Nuremberg's sandstone medieval aura, inviting memories that reveal the porosity of the city's fortified grandeur. Indeed, "the tourist landscape of old Nürnberg [Nuremberg] conceals more than it reveals" (173), for its lineage finds its tracks in the history of its peripheries and in the lives of its many migrants.

During its industrial development in the nineteenth century, many of the Aldstadt's medieval houses were "settings of abject poverty", overcrowded and unsanitary, not unlike those of migrants' homes in Gostenhof and other peripheral neighborhoods during the 1960s and 1970s (Reisser 1986, 177–78). Above all, the fortified city holds the ruins of its absolute destruction following World War II. Its spectacle of permanence and easy access to tourism is on par with the erasure of the bodies that ultimately made it possible, and some of whom never stepped foot in it. Josefina's walk through these streets puts the migrant body back into the city, simultaneously laying tracks across pasts and presents, centers and peripheries. And, most importantly, this leg of her journey is on foot. John Urry addresses the history of walking as "the history of principally private, self-directed and endogenous action that helps to constitute the self especially through the kinaesthetic sense" (2007, 90). Forty-two years earlier, Josefina left a Nuremberg she could barely access, taking back to Spain a body worn from meager diets, strenuous working conditions, and seven surgeries: "Estaba delgadísima" (I was so skinny) (Arribas and Pérez 2005). No doubt, walking Nuremberg in the present serves to reconstitute her place in the city, while sealing the footprints of its collective memories.

During the walk through the Altstadt, the camera follows Josefina through the "colorful candy-striped tents of the Christmas market overflowing with handmade Christmas ornaments and nutcrackers," the "venerable assemblage of sandstone buildings," "the Gothic parish churches," and "footbridges spanning channels of the Pegnitz River" (Reisser 1986, 173). Middle and close-up shots of Josefina and Leonor convey their immersion in the Christmas market, while the sound transitions from diegetic German voices and Christmas tunes to Josefina's voice in a voiceover recalling the separation between migrant and German spaces: "era muy difícil entrar en el mundo alemán" (it was very difficult to enter the German world) (Arribas and Pérez 2005). But, mostly, the footage within the Altstadt consists of long shots of Josefina walking alone through Nuremberg's streets, with stops at three of its picturesque footbridges. Richard Dennis describes the significance of the bridge in urban history as a space of hopes and fears of modernity, of opportunities and threats (2008, 20). This aligns with the progression of the narrative that, from this point on, transitions to the collective memory of Spaniards' places of socialization, and the gradual paving of their political action on Nuremberg's streets.

According to Muñoz Sánchez (2005), the Spanish government prioritized guest-worker treaties with Germany partly for ideological reasons, including the latter's absence of active political opposition to the Franco regime, and its strong anti-communist stance. Quite ironically, by the end of the 1970s Nuremberg had become a rallying point for migrant political organization in Germany. For example, between June and November 1971, migrants in Nuremberg held a series of events to make demands of both the Spanish and German governments, and on 28 September 1973 migrant organizations throughout Germany met in

Nuremberg for the Primer Congreso Democrático de la Emigración Española en Alemania (Sorel 1974, 52, 113; Muñoz Sánchez 2005).[10] The film overlaps multiple voices with historical footage of migrants walking the streets of Nuremberg to call for better housing, improved labor conditions, and the end of Franco's dictatorship.[11] Pablo Guerrero's song "A tapar la calle" (Let's block the streets; 1978) is the nondiegetic track for this stream of voices and images of migrant bodies walking Nuremberg's streets. These memories further confirm the place of migrants in the city, not only as its makers, but also as actors in the political histories of both Germany and Spain.

Departures

The oil crisis of 1973 marked a turn for the worse for migrant populations in Germany. The ensuing social and economic instability led many to blame rising national unemployment on the country's migrant residents. As Josefina sums it, "sobrábamos" (we were leftovers) (Arribas and Pérez 2005). By the mid-1970s, most Spaniards in Germany were back in Spain undergoing a second journey—one of return. Their remittances had fueled Nuremberg's economy, while opening possibilities for their families in Spain. Thus, their labor financed the homes, careers, and possibilities for their families back home, but often at the cost of their own. In one of the last interviews, a former immigrant to Germany addresses these experiences as one of split bodies: "la generación de los cuerpos partidos (the generation of split bodies)." Victoria Toro, in a room packed and ready for her trip back to Spain with her mother, explains the partiality of her return: "una parte mía se queda en Alemania, otra se va" (a part of me remains here in Germany, another part leaves). Her journey therefore, and that of the voices in her collective memory, remains unfinished.

El tren de la memoria (Arribas and Pérez 2005) runs through tracks that *are* remembering, and thus, ongoing—a trip that, returning to Josefina's opening lines, *es recordar* (is to remember). The last shots follow Josefina back into the train for a departure that is simultaneously a return to a departure and a departure to a return. The camera alternates between scenes of Josefina's arrival in Nuremberg station and footage of Victoria Toro's last interview, revealing that, in fact, neither of them is returning to the same place they once left.

Victoria explains her departure as the fulfillment of her mother's dream to see her back in Spain: "La ilusión de mi madre ha sido siempre verme en España" (my mother has always wished to see me back

Figure 9.4. Last shot of the journey: A landscape of rails. Screen capture by Araceli Masterson-Algar.

in Spain) (Arribas and Pérez 2005). Yet, her mother is in the advanced stages of Alzheimer's, which hardly allows for the desired closure. And they are not returning to their former hometown in Extremadura, but to Madrid instead, a city where Victoria has never lived. Rather than a return, for Victoria, this journey is a departure from her home of nearly half a century: "Hay muchas cosas que voy a echar de menos y . . . sobretodo . . . .Nuremberg, que para mi es como si fuera mi ciudad" (There are many things I will miss, and . . . above all . . . Nuremberg, which I feel is as if it was my own). The combined hesitance and emphasis with which she addresses Nuremberg speaks to the social hierarchies underlying access to its streets, drawing attention to the ties between mobility, body, and space in the configuration of migrants' collective memory.

Similarly, Josefina, teary eyed, returns to her seat in the train for a departure from a place that holds much of her remains. Close-ups of her face looking out the window parallel those of her departure from Madrid's station some days earlier. Yet, this time around, her journey is accompanied by the nondiegetic song "Emigrante" by Pablo Guerrero (1975). Her spatial trajectory with Madrid as destination runs counter to Guerrero's lyrics, which sing of the departure from Spain to Germany. This counternarrative extends to time, given that the clock at Nuremberg's station—a parallel frame to that of the clock in Atocha in the film's opening scenes—shows an earlier time of return: Josefina left Madrid at 9:20 in the morning, but is returning at 9:00 in the morning.

Guerrero's lyrics announce the departure of the *emigrante* as a journey in time: *"un día* cambió todo" (everything changed one day), and in place: "si el Rhin fuera el Guadiana, no estaríamos *aquí"* (if the Rhin was the Guadiana we would not be here) (emphasis added). *El tren de la memoria* (Arribas and Pérez 2005) is a journey along the tracks of Josefina, Leonor, and Victoria's collective memory from that one day to an *aquí* (here). Via this undefined timetable, it does not offer a narrative of Spanish-German migration history, but rather an invitation to remember it. To do so, it follows the traces of absences, silences, and erasures, revealing historical continuities, but also splits in its tracks. Thus, the last shot of this journey (figure 9.4) offers a landscape of rails, crisscrossed and clustered, that sets the grounds for the loose stitches between places that never were, and the tracks of their lived experiences.

Araceli Masterson-Algar is associate professor at the University of Kansas. Her research is largely on migration dynamics and human mobility, with attention to the ties between transnational social processes, cultural production, and urban planning. She is author of *Ecuadorians in Madrid: Migrants Place in Urban History* (Palgrave, 2016), and coeditor of *"No vale nada la vida, la vida no vale nada": Political Intersections of Migration and Death in the U.S. Mexico Border* (University of Arizona Press, 2016). She is also associate editor of the *Journal of Urban Cultural Studies.*

Notes

1. The recent emergence of historical fiction series for public television is telling, particularly, and follows on the work of Geoffrey White, because representations of the past "are always in some ways about the present" (2006, 331). These representations include series on Spain's grandiose pasts, such as *El Ministerio del tiempo* (2015–17), *Isabel* (2011–14), and its sequel *Carlos, rey emperador* (2015), or telenovelas that appeal to the quotidian in Spain's more recent past, including *Cuéntame cómo pasó* (2001–), *Amar en tiempos revueltos* (2005–12) *Acacias 38* (2015–), and *Seis hermanas* (TVE1, 2015–). Juan Aranzadi alerts to the growth of this corpus in the national imaginary, highlighting the series *Memoria de España,* which places the origin of Spain in the Big Bang (2009, 168). Specifically on the history of migration, the documentary series *Camino a Casa* (2007) addresses Spain's history of emigration. See also Sanz Díaz (2011) for an analysis of recent exhibits on the history of Spain's migration, and Pablo Marín-Escudero (2014) for a review of Spain's recent documentaries about migration.
2. In an overview of the significance of the rail in Latin American literature and film, Reati and others address it as an "intermediary space" (Reati 2011b, 16), a "system of signification for a story" (Bracamonte 2011, 25), and an "aesthetic ex-

perience" (Menczel 2011, 119). Along similar lines, Sarah Misemer describes the train as "a metaphor for major shifts in frameworks of perception from the 19th Century to present" (2010, 19).

3. Sorel and others explain how those without the proper documentation, which is the majority of these travelers, risked their lives by taking the journey on foot, or found the means to do so by bus. Counter to what the film might convey through the choice of three female protagonists, women made up approximately 24 percent of these migrations, but most of them were undocumented, and were employed in domestic service (Riera Ginestar 2015, 47; Sorel 1974, 22).

4. Brockmann (2006) refers to Nuremberg as such throughout his book. See also Chipps Smith (2008).

5. In 2003 the Goethe-Institut and the Instituto Cervantes collaborated in a series of events addressing the common lines between Spain and Germany's construction of historical memory following authoritarian regimes. See Olmos and Kilholz-Rühle (2009).

6. See Gregor (2008) for an analysis of how Nuremberg has worked to rebuild its image as a democratic town, and Reisser (1986) for an overview of migrant populations in Nuremberg following World War II.

7. For ties between train stations and urban planning see also Chiner i Mateu (2010), López (2005), Santos y Ganges (2007), Saus (2013), Smets and Shannon (2010), and Wais San Martín (1967).

8. Gostenhof holds Nuremberg's highest and most rapidly increasing concentration of foreign-born residents (39 percent in 2019) (Köhler 2016, 42).

9. Marta Arribas describes the importance of visual footage in the process of remembering: "era fundamental tener imágenes que son nuestra memoria. No valía solo el testimonio de los emigrantes, había que verlo." Yet, denouncing the cost of these images at 6,000 euros per minute, Arribas alerts to the need to socialize the image: "Nos sorprendió que nuestra memoria en imágenes esté en manos de instituciones públicas que hacen casi imposible su uso" (we were surprised to find that the images of our memory are in the hands of public institutions that make their use nearly impossible) (Arribas quoted in Simón 2010).

10. The political action of Spanish residents in Germany has made the news to present. On 10 October 2015, for instance, *Diario Público* among other newspapers covered the presence of Spanish residents in Germany in protests against the Transatlantic Trade and Investment Partnership. One of the participants commented: "Hemos [en España] perdido la calle y en Alemania están a punto de perderla" (Cruz 2015).

11. Migrant protests also used the rail for political action. Sorel describes how residents of the factory barracks in Frankfurt laid down at night along the rails of the tram to protest bedbugs (1974, 22). [end of ch9]

References

Acacias 38. 2015–21. Boomerang TV, Televisión Española, aired on TVE1. https://www.rtve.es/television/acacias-38/. Accessed 25 May 2021.
Amar en tiempos revueltos. 2005–12. Diagonal TV, aired on TVE1. https://www.rtve.es/television/amarentiemposrevueltos/la-serie/. Accessed 25 May 2021.

Aranzadi, Juan. 2009. "Historia y nacionalismo en España hoy." In Olmos and Keil-holz-Rühle, *La cultura de la memoria,* 159–69.

Arribas, Marta, and Ana Pérez, dir. 2005. *El tren de la memoria.* Producciones La Iguana S. L., Madrid.

Bachelard, Gastón. (1964) 2014. *The Poetics of Space.* New York: Penguin Books.

Bissell, David. 2009. "Conceptualizing Differently-mobile Passengers: Geographies of Everyday Encumbrance in the Railway Station" *Social and Cultural Geography* 10, no. 2: 173–95.

Bracamonte, Jorge. 2011. "Medios de transporte, tecnificación y poéticas. O cómo revisitar clásicos narrativos latinoamericanos." In Reati, *Autos, Barcos, Trenes y aviones,* 25–46.

Brockmann, Stephen. 2006. *Nuremberg: The Imaginary Capital.* New York: Camden House.

Burke, Peter. 2001. *Eyewitnessing. The Uses of Images as Historical Evidence.* New York: Cornell University Press.

Camino a Casa. 2010. Televisión Española. https://www.rtve.es/alacarta/videos/camino-a-casa/. Accessed 25 May 2021.

Carlos, rey emperador. 2015–16. Directed by Oriol Ferrer. Diagonal TV for Televisión Española (TVE). http://lab.rtve.es/carlos-v/serie. Accessed 25 May 2021.

Chiner i Mateu, Rosella. 2010. "Estaciones de tren y ciudad." Universitat Politécnica de Catalunya.

Chipps Smith, Jeffrey. 2008. "A Tale of Two Cities. Nuremberg and Munich." In *Building Baroque Cities in Europe*, edited by Gary B. Cohen and Franz A. J. Szabo, 164–90. New York: Berghahn.

Cruz, Laura. 2015. "Masiva protesta en Berlín contra el TTIP y su expolio a los trabajadores." *Diario Público*, 10 October. https://www.publico.es/internacional/masiva-protesta-berlin-ttip.html. Accessed 17 April 2021.

Cuéntame cómo pasó. 2001–present. Written by Miguel Ángel Bernardeau. Ganga Producciones for Televisión Española (TVE), aired on TV1. https://www.rtve.es/television/cuentame-como-paso/. Accessed 25 May 2021.

Deleuze, Gilles. 1997. *Essays Critical and Clinical.* Minneapolis: University of Minnesota Press.

Dennis, Richard. 2008. *Cities in Modernity. Representations and Productions of Metropolitan Space, 1840–1930.* Cambridge: Cambridge University Press.

El Ministerio del tiempo. 2015–present. Directed by Marc Vigil. Televisión Española. https://www.rtve.es/television/ministerio-del-tiempo/la-serie/. Accessed 25 May 2021.

Gregor, Neil. 2008. *Haunted City. Nuremberg and the Nazi Past.* New Haven, CT: Yale University Press.

Guattari, Félix. 1994. "Space and Corporeity." *Columbia Documents of Architecture and Theory* 2: 139–48.

Guerrero, Pablo. 1978. "A tapar la calle." Recorded December 1977. Track 1 on *A tapar la calle.* Gatefold, vinyl.

Guerrero, Pablo. 1975 "Emigrante." Recorded 2 March 2 1975. Track B4 on *Pablo Guerrero en el Olimpia.* Gatefold, vinyl.

Hutton, Patrick H. 1993. *History as an Art of Memory.* Hanover, NH: University Press of New England.

Isabel. 2011–14. Directed by Jordi Frades, Salvador García, and Oriol Ferrer. Diagonal TV for Televisión Española (TVE). https://www.rtve.es/television/isabel-la-catolica/. Accessed 25 May 2021.

Köhler, Claudia. 2016. "Rise and Resolution of Ethnic Conflicts in Nuremberg's Neighborhoods." In *Inter-group Relations and Migrant Integration in European Studies*, edited by F. Pastore and I. Ponzo, 39–67. New York: Springer.

Lefebvre, Henri. 1991. *The Production of Space*. Oxford Oxford, UK: Blackwell.

López, Enrique. 2005. "Urbanismo y ferrocarril." *PH Boletin del Instituto Andaluz del Patrimonio Historico* 55 (October): 15–22.

Marín-Escudero, Pablo. 2014. *Cine documental e inmigración en España. Una lectura sociocrítica*. Salamanca, Spain: Comunicación Social Ediciones y Publicaciones.

Memoria de España. 2004–2005. Directed by Adolfo Dufour. Radio Televisión Española (RTVE). https://www.rtve.es/alacarta/videos/memoria-de-espana/memoria-espana-espana-libertad/1506079/. Accessed 25 May 2021.

Menczel, Gabriella. 2011. "La búsqueda del centro: viajes horizontals y verticals en los cuentos de Julio Cortázar." In Reati, *Autos, Barcos, Trenes y aviones*, 107–24.

Misemer, Sarah M. 2010. *Moving Forward, Looking Back: Trains, Literature and the Arts in the River Plate*. Lewisburg, PA: Bucknell University Press.

Muñoz Sánchez. 2005. "La emigración española a la República Federal de Alemania." In *Projekt Migration*, edited by Kölnischer Kunstverein, 523–30. Cologne: Dumont.

Nora, Pierre. 1989. "Between Memory and History: Les Lieux de Mémoire." Translated by Marc Roudebush. *Representations* 26 (Spring): 7–25.

Olmos, Ignacio, and Nikky Keilholz-Rühle, eds. 2009. *La cultura de la memoria. La memoria histórica en España y Alemania*. Madrid: Edtorial Vervuert, 2009.

Reati, Fernando, ed. 2011a. *Autos, Barcos, Trenes y aviones. Medios de transporte, modernidad y lenguajes artísticos en América Latina*. Córdoba: Alción Editora.

Reati, Fernando. 2011b. "Prólogo" In Reati, *Autos, Barcos, Trenes y aviones*, 9–24.

Reisser, Craig T. 1986. "The Residential Distribution of Italians in Nurnberg: A Case Study in Cultural Urban Geography." PhD Diss. Ann Arbor: University of Michigan.

Riera Ginestar, Joaquín. 2015. *Maletas de Cartón. Trabajadores españoles en la República Federal Alemana (1960–2007)*. Amazon Createspace.

Santos, Félix. 2018. "La emigración económica a Europa. La década de los 60: dos millones de emigrados." *Biblioteca Virtual Miguel de Cervantes*. http://www.cervantesvirtual.com/obra-visor/exiliados-y-emigrados-19391999--0/html/ffdf03e4-82b1-11df-acc7-002185ce6064_8.html. Accessed 25 May 2021.

Santos y Ganges, Luis. 2007. *Urbanismo y ferrocarril. La construccion del espacio ferroviario en las ciudades medias españolas*. Madrid: Fundacion de Ferrocarriles Españoles.

Sanz Díaz, Carlos. 2011. "Las relaciones España-Europa y la historia de la emigración española: en torno a dos exposiciones." *Cuadernos de Historia Contemporánea* 33: 297–307.

Sarlo, Beatriz. 2005. *Tiempo pasado: cultura de la memoria y giro subjetivo*. Buenos Aires: Siglo XXI.

Saus, María Alejandra. 2013. "Infraestructura ferroviaria y ciudad: su cambiante correspondencia espacial desde los paradigmas de la ciencia, la historiografía urbana y el urbanismo." *Revista de estudios sociales* 45: 144–57.

Seis hermanas. 2015–2017. Bambú Producciones for Televisión Española, aired on TVE1.

Simón, Patricia. 2010. "La mitad de los emigrantes españoles se fueron sin contrato de trabajo." 27 September. https://patriciasimon.es/migracion/la-mitad-de-los-emigrantes-espanoles-se-fueron-sin-contrato-de-trabajo/. Accessed 25 May 2021.

Smets, Marcel and Kelly Shannon. 2010. *The Landscape of Contemporary Infrastructure.* Rotterdam: Nai Publishers.

Sorel, Andrés. 1974. *4o Mundo. Emigración española en Europa.* Bilbao, Spain: Zero.

Urry, John. 2007. *Mobilities.* New York: Polity.

Wais San Martín, Francisco. 1967. *Historia General de los Ferrocarriles españoles (1830–1941).* Editora Nacional: Madrid.

White, Geoffrey. 2006. "Epilogue: Memory Moments." *ETHOS,* 34, no. 2: 325–41.

Zukin, Sharon. 1992. *Landscapes of Power.* Berkeley: University of California Press.

CHAPTER 10

Nord-Sud

The Paris Metro and Transnational Avant-Garde Artistic Mobilities and Movements in Early Twentieth-Century Paris

Scott D. Juall

In their seminal studies of railway travel in the nineteenth and twentieth centuries, Wolfgang Schivelbusch (1986) and John Urry (2007) describe the profound changes that the locomotive exerted on voyagers' spatio-temporal orientation and means of organizing, analyzing, and describing their travels by train. This new mode of transportation, which radically transformed the human mobile experience, seemed to shorten the distance from faraway lands, and inspired transnational exchanges that reconfigured interactions in sociocultural and political domains. Railway mobility also promoted transcultural exchange in nineteenth-century France, and especially in Paris, which became an important site of international exchange in artistic milieus. By the final two decades of the century, transnational collaborations accelerated among those creating in modernist artistic movements and, at the dawn of the twentieth century, the French capital became the definitive global epicenter of transnational artistic transfers, largely owing to a new form of transportation. The Paris Metro, opened in 1910 by the Compagnie du chemin de fer métropolitain de Paris (CMP; Paris Metropolitan Railway Company), motivated a significant change in the means by which Parisians traveled through the cosmopolitan capital.[1] The metro is thus a crucial element of the mobility paradigm that contributed to the transmission of incomparably rich transnational exchanges in contemporary artistic movements and literary and visual artworks in the early twentieth century. These observations exemplify how the field of mobilities studies bridges travel and physical movement, enhanced by transport technologies, and the transmission of images, information, and communications that "organise and structure social life" (Sheller and Urry 2006, 212). In the context of the mobility turn, Geraldine Clarsen emphasizes that one of the most important products of travel is what is "mediated into spoken words, written texts, and visual images that are circulated through channels of communication" (2015, 118; see also Hannam, Sheller, and Urry 2006). The mobility paradigm, as well as two of the foundational approaches to transnational studies described by Sanjeev Khagram and Peggy Levitt (2008)—the empirical and the philosophical—are joined together in this chapter, as in early twentieth-century Paris numerous international artists, many who were immigrants, frequently moved between different sociocultural spaces and transgressed conventional artistic boundaries to explore novel dimensions of modernist art and so create entirely new genres.

On 5 November 1910 a new private subway company, the Société du chemin de fer électrique souterrain Nord-Sud de Paris (North-South Society of Electric Underground Trains of Paris), commonly referred to as Nord-Sud, opened its first metro line.[2] The goal of this new line was to compete commercially with the CMP and in particular to rival its popular Line 4, opened on 23 May 1910, which connected the two major axes of artistic creation: Montmartre in the north and Montparnasse in the south. The earliest stretches of the Nord-Sud Line A connected the periphery of Paris in the fifteenth arrondissement at the Porte de Versailles station, which remained the line's southern terminus in Montparnasse for decades, with the southern edge of Montmartre on the boundary of the ninth and eighteenth arrondissements. Over the next five years, the construction of Nord-Sud Line A advanced farther northward, and by 23 August 1916 this urban railway line stretched to the Porte de la Chapelle station in the eighteenth arrondissement on the northern boundary of Paris. The Nord-Sud Line A now joined Montmartre with Montparnasse even more directly than its competitor's Line 4 (map 10.1).[3]

The northern and southern regions had a long reputation as important nexuses of artistic creation among groups of international artists hailing from all regions of Europe. Montmartre held a prestigious place in late nineteenth-century transnational artistic development since visual artists innovated there in their neo-impressionist and post-impressionist artworks. The region inspired a new generation of international avant-gardists in the first decade of the twentieth century, notably at the Bateau-Lavoir, the principal center of transnational artistic innovation. At these studios the Catalonian Pablo Picasso and his *bande* (gang)—including fellow Catalonians Juan Gris and Pablo Gargallo and the French artist Georges Braque—developed modernist artist innovations, among them fauvism and cubism, between 1904 and 1909. Other important figures who frequented this space were writers Guillaume Apollinaire, Max Jacob, Jean Cocteau, and the American Gertrude Stein, who also promoted avant-garde art in her circles, as well as the German

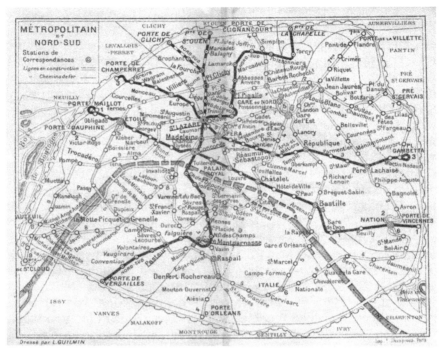

Map 10.1. L. Guilman, map of the Paris Metro in 1921, showing both the CMP and the Nord-Sud metro lines; the Nord-Sud lines are emphasized. "Métropolitain et Nord-Sud," *Plan de Paris par arrondissement, Bois de Boulogne, Métropolitain, avec Répertoire* (1920–1921). Provided by Steve Trussel: https://www.trussel.com/parismaps/gui20_-03.jpg.

dealer of modernist art Daniel-Henry Kahnweiler. Restaurants, dance halls, and cabarets located on the Place Pigalle and in its immediate vicinity were centers of lively exchange among manifold notable international avant-garde writers and visual artists, including Apollinaire, Braque, Pierre Reverdy, and Italians Amadeo Modigliani and Gino Severini.

During this period Montparnasse held the central place in the development of transnational exchanges in avant-garde literature. The burgeoning literary cafés in this region attracted international artists from both Montparnasse and Montmartre. Visual artists and poets such as Picasso, Severini, Apollinaire, and Paul Fort were among those peripatetic artists who traveled south from Montmartre to the Left Bank and congregated at the popular Montparnasse cafés to exchange ideas in transnational intellectual and artistic settings. International émigré painters and sculptors also lived and worked together at the artistic colony La Ruche, a southern counterpart to Montmartre's Bateau-Lavoir, located near the Convention station of the Nord-Sud Line A in the fifteenth arrondissement. These artists, who were some of the central figures in what was named The School of Paris, regularly traveled the Nord-Sud Line A northward to exchange ideas with fellow artists in Montmartre.

These studios, cabarets, and other gathering places in both Montmartre and Montparnasse—and the movements between them on the Nord-Sud Line A—correspond to the new mobilities paradigm, in which "places themselves are seen as travelling . . . within networks of humans and nonhuman agents. Places are about relationships, about the placing of peoples, materials, images, and the systems of difference that they perform" and, as a result, there is an intricate relationship between "places and persons connected through performances" (Sheller and Urry 2006, 214). Through the second decade of the twentieth century, the Nord-Sud Line A played an integral role in developing early twentieth-century literary and visual arts in Paris by facilitating transnational relationships, physical movements, and artistic exchanges among avant-garde writers, painters, art theorists, and art dealers participating in the dynamic avant-garde artistic milieus in these two artistic centers of the French capital. The relationship between movements along the newly constructed Nord-Sud Line A, literary and visual arts, and art criticism that developed in the second decade of twentieth-century Paris is reflected in a number of artworks of the period that directly refer to the Nord-Sud metro and were created in the very artistic esthetics being explored and developed in Paris at that time. Artworks created by some of the principal figures of the contemporary transnational avant-garde developing in the French capital, such as Severini, Apollinaire, Pierre Albert-Birot, Reverdy, Joan Miró, and Braque, call attention to the direct links between the mobility enhanced by the Nord-Sud metro line and transnational artistic movements in modernist Paris. The Nord-Sud dynamic, in both its transportational and artistic contexts, is thus an overarching concept that served as a major network of physical and artistic movements guiding and orienting some of the most dynamic transnational cultural exchanges leading to significant transformations in modernist art and literature in Paris between 1910 and 1920 and that also had international repercussions. This chapter addresses how and why the Nord-Sud Line A is represented in the literary and visual arts and how it has "symbolic consequences at the spatial level well beyond the immediacies of the technologies themselves" (Divall and Revill 2005, 108–9).

Severini and Parisian Futurism in Montmartre

At the end of the first decade of the twentieth century, as painters Picasso and Braque were developing cubism in Paris, Italian futurists, based in Milan, drew on the cubist esthetic of portraying fragmented, multiple perspectives of objects to introduce speed and dynamic movement into art. Beginning with Filippo Tommaso Marinetti's founding manifesto "The Founding and Manifesto of Futurism," published in French in the Parisian daily newspaper Le Figaro on 20 February 1909, theoretical works written by the futurists initially explored the influences that modern developments in science and technology would exert on art. Futurists portrayed new rapid forms of transportation such as automobiles, racing cars, motorcycles, airplanes, and especially, as Alessio Lerro (2012) argues, locomotives.[4] They also depicted major developments in the spaces of the European city, focusing frequently on crowded urban spaces and forms of urban public transportation such as tramways and autobuses.

Severini, who had moved from Rome to the Montmartre region of Paris in 1906, officially joined the futurist movement shortly after Marinetti published his first manifesto in Paris, the contemporary center of international intellectual and artistic creation, where the leader of futurism would attract the greatest amount of attention to his new movement. In 1910, when Severini signed two of the earliest futurist manifestos related to painting, he laid the foundation for the Parisian branch of futurism—now a transnational Franco-Italian artistic movement.[5] Frequent travel by rail between Italy and France led the futurists to keep in contact with artistic developments in Paris and exchange ideas with avant-garde artists there as they transgressed national artistic borders. In January 1911 Severini moved into a studio at 5, passage Guelma (eighteenth arrondissement) where his neighbors were some of the most influential figures in contemporary modernist art, including Braque, Raoul Dufy, and Suzanne Valadon. The Guelma studio was located only twenty meters from the lively Place Pigalle, where cosmopolitan artists gained access to the dynamic nightlife in the northern region of the city. Spirited exchanges among those participating in the cosmopolitan artistic milieus of Paris also incessantly took place at the Moulin de la Galette, located near the Bateau-Lavoir, and also near dance halls and cabarets including Le Moulin Rouge, Le Monico, Le Pigall's, and others.

On 8 April 1911 the Nord-Sud Line A reached the southern edge of Montmartre, when its northern terminus was extended from Notre-Dame de Lorette (ninth arrondissement) to the Pigalle station, located on the border of the ninth and eighteenth arrondissements and adjacent to the Place Pigalle.[6] That year was crucial for establishing new connections and inspiring exchange among modernist artists of a variety of nationalities. Severini met Picasso through his neighbor Braque and, at the Bateau-Lavoir, Picasso introduced Severini to Apollinaire. The poet, at that time living in Auteuil, in the southern sixteenth arrondissement, took the Nord-Sud Line A almost daily to visit his friends in Montmartre.

Once the Nord-Sud reached Montmartre and Severini broadened his social and artistic circles in an international context, his art underwent a distinct change. He first created two neo-impressionist paintings with a more fragmented divisionist esthetic, including *Le Boulevard* (*The Boulevard*, 1911), which depicts the exciting city streets in Paris, and *La Danse du Pan-Pan au Monico* (*The Pan-Pan Dance at the Monico*, 1911), featuring the spirited scene inside the popular dance hall. During this period, Severini and his cohort frequently traveled southward on the Nord-Sud Line A to the crowded Montparnasse literary cafés Les Deux Magots and Le Flore, located on Boulevard Saint-Germain, and Le Coupole, Le Dôme, and La Rotonde, situated in the sixth and fourteenth arrondissements. Symbolists met at La Closerie des Lilas, which drew a particularly important and influential international clientele of writers, and Severini's future father-in-law Fort held his famous Tuesday poetry-reading soirées. Severini stated that the importance of exchanging ideas on the literary and visual arts among international artists at the Parisian cafés in the south was "infinitely more functional than any academy could be"—and was an essential factor in the development of modernist art that "could only have taken place in Paris" (1995, 77).

On 31 October 1912, the Nord-Sud A line reached the heart of Montmartre when its terminus was extended to the Jules-Joffrin station in the eighteenth arrondissement. During the two years that followed, Severini, who created numerous transportation works depicting Parisian trains, tramways, and autobuses, was the first artist to depict the Paris Metro. The most significant—and most numerous—of the metro works focus explicitly on the Nord-Sud Line A. Severini held his first solo exhibition, "The Futurist Painter Severini Exhibits His Latest Works," at the Marlborough Gallery in London in April 1913, where he gained exposure outside of continental Europe. He exhibited nearly twenty new artworks showing nightlife in cabarets and dance halls in Montmartre; the artistic milieu in London was also the first public to view Severini's innovative urban transportation works at this exhibition, including three paintings titled *L'Autobus* (*The Motor Bus*) and three with "Nord-Sud" in their titles.

Severini's painting *Il Treno Nord-Sud* (*The Nord-Sud Railway*) of 1912 is situated in a metro car in the recently created Pigalle metro station

Figure 10.1. Gino Severini, *Il Treno Nord-Sud* (1912). Oil on panel. 49 × 64 cm. Pinacoteca di Brera, Milan. © 2017 Artists Rights Society (ARS), New York / ADAGP, Paris.

(figure 10.1). The painting features cubist fragmentation and futurist interests in rapid modes of urban transportation and various kinds of movement associated with them, qualities that reflect innovative spatio-temporal research undertaken by contemporary mathematicians, scientists, philosophers, and psychologists.[7] The vivid sensations of modern transport appear through a simultaneous and multi-perspectival vision created by the proliferation of intersecting planes that the futurists promoted in their manifestos of that era.

The sign identifying the Pigalle station is portrayed in the distinctive shape and colors of the deluxe Nord-Sud subway tiles. But the misspelled "PIGALLLE" suggests the deformation of words perceived by passengers as the rapid metro car passes through the station and the Bergsonian concept of the relationship between perception and memory and the indivisibility of humans—especially those in movement—and their surroundings. The work also reinforces the futurist concept that objects are never distinctly separate entities, but rather that their interior forces interact with each other in dynamic attraction. The overlapping images of the passengers and their glances through the windows, the metro tunnels, platforms, stairwells, and corridors accentuate the interpenetration (named *"compénétration"* by futurists) of planes and blur the distinction of spaces inside and outside of the metro car. Additional signs—"METRO," "1 CLASSE, "SORTIE," and DIRECTION S^t. LAZARE"—emphasize vectors of movement and perception, resulting from multidirectional viewpoints of passengers in the metro car and the crisscrossing of passengers' physical itineraries in the train, on the platforms, in the staircases and hallways, and through entrances and exits.

The painting reflects many ideas introduced in the "(Technical) Manifesto of the Futurist Painters," cosigned by Umberto Boccioni, Carlo Carrà, Luigi Russolo, Giocamo Balla, and Severini and published in Milan as a leaflet in *Poesia* on 11 April 1910, which emphasizes the notions of the dynamic movement of passengers in public transportation. In the manifesto, the futurists state, "The gesture that we would reproduce on canvas shall no longer be a fixed *moment* in universal dynamism. It shall simply be the *dynamic sensation* itself. Indeed, all things move, all things are rapidly changing. . . . Moving objects constantly multiply themselves; their form changes like rapid vibrations" (Apollonio 1973, 27–28).

The faint images of the passengers also reflect the futurist esthetics of simultaneity and compression of time specifically related to movement in modern public transportation: "The sixteen people around you in a rolling motor bus are in turn and at the same time one, ten, four, three; they are motionless and they change places; they come and go, bound into the street, are suddenly swallowed up by the sunshine, then come back and sit before you, like persistent symbols of universal vibration" (Apollonio 1973, 28).

In this painting, Severini thus develops these ideas in the setting of the Paris Metro, a new spatiotemporal experience in modernist Paris that transcends Schivelbusch's concept of the annihilation of traditional space-time continuum that trains imposed on travelers (1986, 36). The metro was an even more complex form of transportation, with its underground labyrinthine passageways, platforms, and stairways, and the dynamic interactions occurring within the spaces of the metro car—and into spaces exterior to it—as it travels from station to station. In the Marlborough catalogue Severini pointed out the unique esthetic of *Il Treno Nord-Sud,* stating, "The idea of speed with which a lighted body spins through dark or lighted tunnels, is conveyed by means of colours, tones and forms. The great notice boards placarded in the stations enter the compartments in motion. The letters written on the placards act upon

Figure 10.2. Gino Severini, *Nord-Sud* (1913). Oil on canvas. 45 × 33 cm. Galleria d'Arte Moderna, Turin. © 2017 Artists Rights Society (ARS), New York / ADAGP, Paris.

the memory through their literary significance at the same time as they act upon the eyes by means of their colour" (Marlborough Gallery 1913, 8).

Severini's description of *Il Treno Nord-Sud* highlights in particular the lettering and color of the subway signage in his transportation works, topics that he and other futurists would develop in their theoretical writings on modernist art. Moreover, the objects seemingly deformed as the metro car speeds by resemble some of the modernist paintings that contemporary avant-garde artists were creating at the time; such rapid movements among artists traveling in the Paris Metro certainly contributed to the developing modernist esthetics of both futurism and cubism.

After Severini painted a work titled *Nord-Sud* (1912), which also depicts the Pigalle station of the Nord-Sud Line A and shares many elements of *Il Treno Nord-Sud,* he created a third painting titled *Nord-Sud* in 1913 (figure 10.2), around the time that he was writing his independently penned theoretical works. In this work, he develops his concept of planar interpenetration and simultaneity. While the painting is again situated in the "[PI]GALLE" station (eighteenth arrondissement), Severini includes a fragment of a sign indicating "S^T. G[EORGES]" (ninth arrondissement), another Nord-Sud station situated near Pigalle but in an adjacent arrondissement. This feature, Severini's boldest expression of spatiotemporal and phenomenological simultaneity, amplifies and accelerates the aesthetic of dynamism found in the other *Nord-Sud* paintings and dismantles clearly designated concepts of time and space. Another Nord-Sud work of 1913, a charcoal drawing *Ferrovia Nord-Sud* (*North-South Railway*), develops this notion even further. Severini situates the action in "PIGALLE," "S^T. GEO[RGES]" and "[TRI]NITE"—three successive metro stations on the Nord-Sud Line A. "NORD-SUD" written in the lower-left corner explicitly identifies this line of the Paris Metro for the first time.

Around two months after Severini's three *Nord-Sud* and other works received remarkable acclaim in England, he returned to Paris and moved into the studio of Félix Del Marle, a French adherent to this transnational branch of futurism based in Montmartre and in contact with Apollinaire, Picasso, Braque, and other cubists. As a result of Severini's influence—social and artistic—on Del Marle, the French futurist crafted an aggressive manifesto in which he commented explicitly on the role that Parisian public transport would play in modernizing the region. In the "Futurist Manifesto against Montmartre," first published in *Paris Journal* on 13 July 1913, Del Marle comments on the importance of the Paris Metro and other urban transportation: "When we established, in Paris, the solid pedestal of Futurism, we thought of you, Montmartre. . . . Your Moulin de la Galette will disappear ineluctably into a metro station. Your flea-ridden Place du Tertre will be crossed by autobuses and tramways. . . . You will seek . . . to release all of the novel beauty of geometric constructions, of train stations, electric machinery, airplanes, all of our tumultuous life constructed of steel, excitement, and speed" (Lista 2015, 552–53; my translation). Shortly thereafter, Del Marle created his own work portraying the Parisian underground urban train system titled *Métro* (1913), in the materials—pastel and charcoal—and style clearly influenced by one of Severini's contemporary works, *Métro-Grande Roue-Tour Eiffel* (*Metro-Ferris Wheel-Eiffel Tower*, 1912–13), which the Italian completed while living at Del Marle's studio. And indeed, working alongside the Frenchman, Severini completed two additional metro works: *Sortie Nord-Sud* (*North-South Exit*, 1913), situated at the exit of an unidentified metro station on the Nord-Sud Line A, and *Figure dans le métro* (*Figure in the Metro*, 1913), an ironic title for the non-figural image of a passenger in the metro car.

In the mid-summer of 1913, Severini moved out of Del Marle's studio, and out of Montmartre, when he moved to the Rue Sophie-Germain (fourteenth arrondissement) in the southern region of Montparnasse. The success of his exhibition at the Marlborough Gallery, and chiefly his *Nord-Sud* works, led him to develop an increasingly independent and peculiar perspective shortly thereafter. Severini continued to work on his futurist artworks and independently wrote two highly relevant theoretical texts commenting on his concept of time, space, and movement in futurist art, demonstrating the importance of the constant interplay of artistic creation and theory. In one of these, *The Plastic Analogies of Dynamism—Futurist Manifesto* (September–October 1913), the most comprehensive of the futurist manifestos heretofore written, Severini adds a new concept of plastic analogy leading to a chain of signifiers that enhances the dynamism in his futurist art. His examples in this manifesto include rapid modes of modern transport and their movement and he mentions the significance of the metro: "a complex of dynamic elements like an aeroplane in flight + man + landscape; a tram or an automobile travelling at speed + boulevard + passengers; or carriages in the Métro + stations + poster + light + crowd, etc., etc. and all the artistic analogies which they arouse in us, offer us sources or feeling and lyricism which are much deeper and more complex" (Apollonio 1973, 125).

Modernist Artist Mobilities:
From Montmartre to Montparnasse and World War I

By mid-1914 Montmartre's dominant artistic influence was beginning to wane. On 24 June 1914 Apollinaire published an article "Montparnasse" in *Paris Journal* in which he describes the shift in artistic interest from Montmartre, which was "difficult to climb" and "full of false artists," to Montparnasse, where "true artists" are found (Apollinaire 1960, 497; my translation). Apollinaire stated that, more than ever, artists exchanged ideas on the terraces at the cafés, which were the "oases where Montparnasse would be both the organ of speech and the weekly gazette where art and literature would come to fruition" (497–98; my translation).[8]

But the outbreak of World War I on 28 July 1914 had the most profound effect on the Parisian art scene and, by extension, on the Nord-Sud dynamic. Dozens of the most important avant-garde French artists in the North, among them Apollinaire, Braque, Fernand Léger, and Jean Metzinger, enlisted in the war. International School of Paris artists working at La Ruche, including Polish painter Moïse Kisling, Lithuanian sculptor Jacques Lipschitz, Russian sculptor and painter Ossip Zadkine, among others, enlisted in the French Foreign Legion and constituted an allied international military contingent. Many other international modernist artists such as Robert and Sonia Delaunay, Marie Laurencin, Francis Picabia, Albert Gleizes fled Paris to seek refuge in neutral Catalonia; in Barcelona they frequently met at Josep Dalmau's avant-garde gallery where they interacted with Catalonian painters who were in touch with the transnational modernist artistic scene developing in Paris through letters and artistic reviews sent by fellow Catalonian artists working in the French capital.[9]

Those who stayed in Paris gravitated to Montparnasse, where writers and artists initially frequented the famous cafés more assiduously—ostensibly to discuss their initial reactions to the war more than to create art. But artists quickly noted a significant change in this new dynamic as the war progressed. Severini stated, "Before the war, solid cliques had formed at the Montparnasse cafés—the Café Rotonde and the Dôme—but most of the participants had gone to war" (1995, 150); as a result, the international contingent, so crucial to transnational exchanges in avant-garde art, had been dispersed.

On 20 November 1914 Marinetti sent a letter to Severini that urged him to participate in the war in his own way by living "the war pictorially, studying it in all its marvelous mechanical forms (military trains, fortifications, wounded, ambulances, hospitals, parades, etc.)" (quoted in Martin 1981, 310). This statement inspired Severini to create several important works in 1914 and 1915 that portray the war in his own unique esthetic—now locomotives traveling across the above-ground spaces of the French countryside as a counterpart to his underground metro works. Paintings such as *Train de la Croix Rouge traversant un village* (*Red Cross Train Passing through a Village*, 1915) and *Train des blessés* (*Train Transporting the Wounded*, 1915), portray trains as crucial elements in movements associated with World War I (Severini 1995, 156).

Wartime stresses and worsening physical and mental health led Severini to travel southward to seek convalescence in Barcelona (May–June 1915), where he interacted with the exiled French and Catalan modernists who met at Dalmau's gallery—experiences of lively multinational artistic exchange that assuredly influenced the creation of his artworks. After returning to Paris in August 1915, Severini rented a studio in southern Paris at 37, Rue de la Tombe Issoire (fourteenth arrondissement),

Figure 10.3. Gino Severini, *Nord-Sud / Apollinaire Alcools* (ca. 1915). Charcoal on paper. 53 × 42 cm. Private collection. © 2017 Artists Rights Society (ARS), New York / ADAGP, Paris.

where he created several new Nord-Sud works, including the *Nord-Sud (Le Métro)* in pastel on paper and *Le Wagon de Ière classe Nord-Sud (North-South First Class Car)* in oil on wood, both of which, while reprising the style of the earliest metro works, portray an increasing number of interpenetrating planes, situating the scene of both works in five different metro station on both the CMP Line 2 and the Nord-Sud Line A.

Severini's *Nord-Sud/Apollinaire Alcools* (figure 10.3), presents a novel link between the Nord-Sud metro line and the movement of avant-garde artists and their thought. This charcoal drawing brings together the Nord-Sud metro, Apollinaire, who exerted one of the greatest influences on modernist art, and his inventive poetry, shown in the female passenger reading a book "APOLLINAIRE ALCOOLS." The picture also features the names of two metro stations, adjacent to each other in the eighteenth arrondissement but on two different metro lines: "BLANCH[E]" on the CMP Line 2, and "PIGAL[LE]", which provided a metro correspondence between that line and the Nord-Sud Line A.

Literary reviews *SIC* and *Nord-Sud*:
Artistic, Social, and Textual Mobilities in Paris

In January 1916 Severini and his wife moved into a studio at 51, Boulevard Saint-Jacques (fourteenth arrondissement), located in the same building as the home and office of the modernist writer Pierre Albert-Birot, who had just published the first issue of a monthly review that attempted to inspire renewed interest in the avant-garde arts during the war. *SIC: Sons, Idées, Couleurs, Formes,* consisting of fifty-four eight-page issues published through December 1919, was one of the most important avant-garde literary reviews of that era.[10] It exerted a tremendous influence on the Nord-Sud dynamic, since it brought together manifold international writers, visual artists, and art theorists representing futurism—the review's particular artistic slant—as well as cubism, orphism, dadaism, and proto-surrealism. Severini suggested that Albert-Birot enlist Apollinaire by inviting him to contribute to *SIC,* and the editor equally sought Severini's participation in the review. The move to this region of Paris also brought Severini into closer proximity to Apollinaire, who was then living at 202, Boulevard Saint-Germain (sixth arrondissement), adjacent to the Montparnasse cafés and within walking distance of Severini's and Albert-Birot's residences.

After Severini's first solo exhibition in Paris, "Gino Severini: Première exposition futuriste d'art plastique de la guerre et d'autres œuvres antérieures" ("First Futurist Exhibition of the Plastic Arts of the War and Other Previous Works"), held 15 January–1 February, 1916 at the Galerie Boutet de Monvel, Albert-Birot wrote a review of the exhibition, "Exposition futuriste," in the second issue of *SIC* (February 1916). In his review, which includes a reproduction of an oil painting by Severini titled *Train arrivant à Paris* (*Train Arriving in Paris*) (Albert-Birot 1973, 12), Albert-Birot revives the importance of Severini's works portraying the Parisian underground trains by analyzing Severini's *Métro-Grande Roue-Tour Eiffel,* which he found to be particularly interesting and influential. Severini stages the scene on Line 5 of the CMP, showing two metro stations simultaneously: Cambronne and Sèvres Lecourbe, both above-ground stations in the seventh arrondissement, as well as fragments of Paris's magnificent Ferris wheel and the monumental Eiffel Tower.

Albert-Birot identifies the work as marking a major turning point in avant-garde art, celebrating the work's innovative spatiotemporal qualities by portraying several locations simultaneously from multiple perspectives. He states that, before Severini, paintings portrayed only a "fraction of space" but with the creation of this *Nord-Sud* work, Severini's paintings now depict a multitude of events taking place in a "fraction of time" (1916, 15; my translation). Albert-Birot also remarks on the success of the innovation in portraying the subjective nature of the human experience: "I believe that it would be interesting to push to the extreme the consequences of the principal of subjective realization, to aim for the maximum amount of integrality, in order to reach the greatest expression of realism" (1916, 15; my translation). Inspired by Severini's exhibition, Albert-Birot then urges the futurists, now led by Severini's unique brand of futurism, to move forward with their project: "Futurists, thrust yourselves towards this unknown that draws you inexorably; your enthusiasm, alone, already, is beautiful; your faith is regenerative and nurturing; we must all hold you as precious stimulators of intellectual activity" (1916, 15; my translation). Albert-Birot's critique demonstrates the manners in which Severini's depiction of the Paris Metro were an exercise in a new avant-garde approach to painting. The metro, as portrayed in the visual arts, was now recognized by modernist artists and critics as the ideal vehicle of transporting international artists and their ideas. Severini's artistic portrait of the Nord-Sud metro, which marked a unique development in avant-garde art, was the dynamic result of such artistic exchanges—one that epitomizes this stage of transnational artistic creation linked with mobility and movement of such artists.

In issue 4 of *SIC* (April 1916), the same issue as Apollinaire's first contribution—a poem titled "L'Avenir" ("The Future"), which projects to a new innovative future in avant-gardist literature and visual arts—Severini published an important India ink drawing. The work, *"Dans le Nord-Sud": Compénétration Simultanéité d'idées-images* (*"In the North-South": Interpenetration Simultaneity of Ideas-Images*) (Albert-Birot 1973, 28) is situated in the Nord-Sud's Montparnasse metro station during World War I (figure 10.4). Located on the boundary between the sixth and fourteenth arrondissements, Montparnasse was one of the busiest Paris Metro stations, where four different metro lines intersected, including the Nord-Sud Line A, and it was also an important hub for trains traveling between Paris and the warfront. Numerous connections and correspondences at this station would have added to the dynamic and lively exchanges taking place among avant-garde artists traveling on the Nord-Sud line.

The name of the metro station, "MONPARNASSE" [*sic*], is one of the most prominent and suggestive aspects of the drawing. In addition to deforming the sign's shape and design of its letters, Severini replaces the substantive *mont* (hill) with the possessive adjective *mon* (my) suggesting the 'futurists' emphasis on the subjective perspective of the human experience at the station. The artist's subjectivity is further emphasized by the name "SEVERINI" written in a clockwise spiral at the center of

Figure 10.4. Gino Severini, *"Dans le Nord-Sud" Compénétration Simultanéité d'idées-images* (1915; *SIC* 4 [April 1916]). India ink on paper. 22.5 × 17 cm. © 2017 Artists Rights Society (ARS), New York / ADAGP, Paris. Provided by the International Dada Archive, Special Collections, University of Iowa Libraries: http://sdrc .lib.uiowa.edu/dada/Sic/4/index.htm.

the work, and from which emanate numerous written messages that express planar interpenetration and simultaneity in a very different manner compared with Severini's *Nord-Sud* paintings. The verbal messages are primarily phenomenological in nature, describing numerous sensorial experiences—sights, sounds, smells, and touching—most exceedingly unpleasant in the overcrowded metro. Others that express psychological states such as suspicion, paranoia, and mental disarray dominate the spaces during the politically charged atmosphere of the war, which exerted a tremendous effect on the political and sociocultural dimensions of life in Paris. These onomatopoeic ideograms that display shapes of transforming typography increase the dynamism of the painting. Although there is one figure visible, there are no seats explicitly shown; everything swirls around within the metro car—and in the station. Uncontainable chaos has invaded the Nord-Sud trains and metro stations, much as the war has shaken up both Western European civilization and modernist art in Paris.

The mobility of these artists and the development of artistic movements that *SIC* inspired are also highly significant, since Albert-Birot contributed directly to the Nord-Sud dynamic. Because Albert-Birot's office was located at 37, Rue de la Tombe Issoire in Montparnasse (fourteenth arrondissement), within walking distance of La Closerie des Lilas and just south of literary cafés such as La Rotonde and others, he had unlimited access to a wide array of international artists—and their ideas—who contributed to *SIC*. The first four issues of the review announce that Albert-Birot held biweekly meetings in two different locations. Artists met on Tuesdays from 5:00 to 6:00 in the evening at 11, Rue Maubeuge (ninth arrondissement), located within walking distance of both the Notre-Dame de Lorette and the Saint-Georges metro stations on the Nord-Sud Line A; on Saturday evenings at 8:00 Albert-Birot held meetings at the office of *SIC*. This inspired members of the international artistic milieus in Paris to travel in the Nord-Sud Line A to reach each other's regions, which encouraged new exchanges "created through networks spreading across geographically and socially extended spaces" (Divall and Revill 2005, 100). The activities taking place at these meetings correspond to an important aspect of the mobility paradigm to the extent that they "are not separate from the places that happen contingently to be visited" and such meetings bring together socio-artistic groups that "produce certain performances in certain places at certain times" (Hannam, Sheller, and Urry 2006, 13).

SIC reached a very wide public—in Paris, elsewhere in France, and more broadly in Europe. At the height of its local distribution in early 1917, the review was sold in twenty-one bookstores in several locations adjacent to the Nord-Sud stations—eight in the northern ninth arrondissement of Montmartre and thirteen in the sixth and fourteenth arrondissements of Montparnasse. Moreover, beginning with the triple issue 8-9-10 (August-September-October 1916), the review announced that "one may procure [*SIC*] in bookstores at all of the Parisian train and metro stations" (Albert-Birot 1973; my translation). It was also sold regionally and internationally, primarily in Italy and Spain and, as announced in the sales panel of the wartime issues, all soldiers fighting in the war received the review gratis. Members of the military fighting for France in World War I submitted contributions from the international warfront, as issues 1 and 2 (published January and February 1916) request mobilized troops' responses to the crucial inquiry "the influence that war might exert on art" (my translation), which were published in issues 2, 3, and 7 (February, March, and July 1916). Since these soldiers—French and foreign—fought in France and along borders with Belgium, Luxemburg, Austria, and Germany, clearly nationalist discourse is at play during World War I, but the allied forces transgressed national boundaries in their military collaborations, which would have strong implications on the transformation of transnational avant-garde artist innovations both during the war and after the armistice of 11 November 1918.

Over the following four years, *SIC* published works, primarily poetry and essays but also visual arts, by an international who's who of modernist literary, visual, and musical artists, including the fauvist André Derain; exiled Israeli sculptor Chana Orloff and her Polish husband, poet Ary Justman; Italian futurists Balla and Luciano Fulgore; emerging dadaist poets Paul Dermée and Franco-Romanian Tristan Tzara; Russian composer Igor Stravinsky; proto-surrealists Philippe Soupault, André Breton, Louis Aragon, and Jean Cocteau; among many others. Manifold works by Apollinaire appeared in *SIC*, including ten poems in five issues and an interview by Albert-Birot—all produced in the Val-de-Grâce Hospital in Paris while he was recovering from a head wound that occurred while he was fighting in World War I.

Transformations in the artistic milieu during World War I led modernist poet Reverdy, who published poetry in *SIC*, to create his own review, *Nord-Sud: Revue littéraire* (Reverdy [1917–18] 1980); the lettering of its title page was identical to the tickets of the Nord-Sud line (figure 10.5). Published in sixteen issues between March 1917 and October 1918, *Nord-Sud*, primarily a cubist review, featured poetry and essays on esthetics and artistic movements contributed by avant-garde poets, visual artists, and art theorists from both the northern and the southern regions of Paris. Immersed in the artistic and political atmosphere of Western Eu-

NORD-SUD

REVUE LITTÉRAIRE

N° 1   15 Mars   1917

SOMMAIRE

▼ ▼ ▼

UN NUMÉRO
PAR MOIS

0,50

G. APOLLINAIRE. La Victoire (poème).

M. JACOB .... Poème.

—   .... Histoire de don Juan.

P. REVERDY...... Sur le Cubisme.

—   ,.... Poème

P. DERMÉE....... Quand le Symbolisme fut mort.

Adresser tout ce qui concerne la Revue, 12, rue Cortot (18ᵉ)

Figure 10.5. Pierre Reverdy, *Nord-Sud* (issue 1, 15 March 1917). Printed media. 28 × 19 cm. Not in copyright. Provided by the Blue Mountain Project, Princeton University: http://bluemountain.princeton.edu/exist/apps/bluemountain/title.html?titleURN=bmtnaaw.

rope during the final years of World War I, writers and artists from all of the developing artistic movements rallied around Apollinaire, who had returned to his residence on the Boulevard Saint-Germain. Apollinaire had become both the undisputed architect of the review's philosophy and objectives and the central figure in the development of the avant-garde poetry and art criticism central to the Nord-Sud dynamic.

The first text in issue 1 (March 1917), signed by "N.S."—presumably Reverdy—sets the *Nord-Sud* in the context of World War I and projects to a future artistic impulse: "The war continues. But we know in advance the way out. Victory is certain from now on. This is why it is time, we believe, to ignore no longer letters and to reorganize and revive them among us, between us" (Reverdy [1917–18] 1980, 1, 2; my translation). The text announces that the group will be organized under Apollinaire, who had fought in the war and was leading the pursuit of so many new artistic pathways leading to innovative connections. The content of the first issue, which features Apollinaire's poems "La Victoire" ("The Victory"), "1914," and "La guerre" ("The War"), and texts by Jacob, Reverdy, and Dermée, introduces the strong focus on World War I and the somewhat militant avant-garde approach of these *Nord-Sudistes.* The emphasis on the politics of World War I in *Nord-Sud* demonstrates the importance of textual representations of physical and related political movements, reflecting the tendency of artistic representations of mobility in culture to "gather and distribute heterogenous materials in ways which are highly politicised in terms of both formal and cultural politics" (Divall and Revill 2005, 109).

As had Albert-Birot, Reverdy created a physical Nord-Sud dynamic of exchange by organizing regular meetings in both the northern and the southern regions of Paris. Ever since the first issue, Reverdy had announced that he would hold meetings at his headquarters, which were located at 12, Rue Cortot in the eighteenth arrondissement of Montmartre, between the Abbesses and Lamarck-Caulincourt stations of the Nord-Sud Line A. The review also declared that Apollinaire would host his meetings on Tuesday evenings at 8:15 at the famous Le Café de Flore, at 172 Boulevard du Montparnasse, situated on the boundary of the sixth and fourteenth arrondissements, and close to the Montparnasse metro station. For this reason, a number of the most important artistic figures from both regions of Paris regularly traveled along the Nord-Sud metro to exchange ideas at these cafés. During the nineteen-month run of *Nord-Sud,* with Reverdy and Apollinaire remaining at the center of its creation and inspiration, important international artists who collaborated were many of those who also contributed to *SIC,* including Tzara, Dermée, Breton, Soupault, and Aragon, now joined by Jacob, and cubists Léger and Braque, who created illustrations and composed art theory for the review.

Nord-Sud's International Movement toward the South: Joan Miró's *Nord-Sud*

Similar to Albert-Birot's *SIC,* Reverdy's *Nord-Sud* was sold in Paris at numerous bookstores all over Paris—two in Montmartre and eight in Montparnasse, especially around the Notre-Dame-des-Champs and Vavin regions in the south—precisely where the important literary cafés were located. Reverdy also announced in every issue that *Nord-Sud* was also available to artists and writers on the war front. The review reached an international readership and established a new transnational Nord-Sud dynamic—now between France and Spain. Catalonian artists who had sought creative inspiration in the French capital—in addition to Parisian modernists exiled in Catalonia—returned to neutral Barcelona during World War I. These Catalan artists, who brought back copies of numerous avant-garde reviews, including *SIC* and *Nord-Sud,* as well as stories of the artistic dynamism of Paris, made a great impression on the young Catalonian painter Joan Miró.

Miró was an avid reader of *Nord-Sud;* in the spring of 1917, after reading the first two issues of the review,[11] he completed *Nord-Sud,* a futurist-inspired and very lively still life begun at his family home in rural Montroig and completed in Barcelona, where Miró shared a studio with Ricart (figure 10.6). In the painting, the eye is drawn immediately to the folded copy of *Nord-Sud,* around which Miró includes an apple—a conventional element of a still life—and, most important, a vibrant blue *botijo* (water jug), a brightly colored change purse, and a potted plant—all representing Miró's rootedness in Catalonian culture. A book with the name *Goethe*—the influential philosopher, art critic, and proponent of world literature and world citizenship—a goldfinch in a birdcage with an open door, and a pair of scissors suggest the artist's desire to cut ties with Catalonia and pursue a blossoming artistic sensibility outside of his homeland. The circular movement of the objects, which spin in a whirlwind of radiant colors in a *counter*clockwise direction, simultaneously pushes the objects outward toward the edges of the painting as it pulls them toward a center—recalling the futurist focus on opposing—and attracting—centrifugal and centripetal forces. These elements emphasize the central place that the literary and theoretical works in the review held in motivating Miró's—and so many other artists'—developing artistic sensibility. The image of *Nord-Sud* in the painting thus represents

Figure 10.6. Joan Miró, *Nord-Sud* (after March 1917). Oil on canvas. 70 × 62 cm. Private collection of Paule and Adrien Maeght, Paris. © Photo Galerie Maeght, Paris 2021 / Successió Miró / Artists Rights Society (ARS), New York / ADAGP, Paris 2017.

the review as the eye of a transnational artistic storm accelerating in Paris and the influence that the review had on Miró's artistic interests; it also reflects Miró's repeatedly expressed desire to work among the international cohort of avant-garde artists in the French capital as he stated with increasing intensity in manifold letters written to Dalmau and other Catalonian colleagues between 1917 and 1920 (see Miró 1992, 52–72).[12]

Severini's and Braque's homages to Nord-Sud's artistic transfers and collaborations

The expanding transnational Nord-Sud dynamic, now including the Nord-Sud metro, Severini's *Nord-Sud* works, Albert-Birot's *SIC,* Reverdy's *Nord-Sud: Revue littéraire,* and Miró's Catalonian *Nord-Sud,* was further developed once again by Severini. The Italian futurist referred explicitly

Figure 10.7. Gino Severini, *Nature morte à la revue littéraire* Nord-Sud: *Hommage à Reverdy.* Paper collage, gouache, chalk, pencil, paper (after September 1917). 56.3 × 78 cm. Private collection. © 2017 Artists Rights Society (ARS), New York / ADAGP, Paris.

to all of these factors in his autobiography, and he commented on the important influence of *Nord-Sud: Revue littéraire* at that time (Severini 1995, 185–86, 195). Still living at his residence in Montparnasse, Severini created *Nature morte à la revue littéraire Nord-Sud: Hommage à Reverdy* (*Still Life with the Literary Review Nord-Sud: Homage to Reverdy*) two months after Miró completed *Nord-Sud* (figure 10.7). The dynamic transnational exchanges in Paris among different artistic esthetics introduced by physical movements and exchanges among international artists transformed Severini's art. Clearly influenced by collages created by synthetic cubists Picasso, Braque, and Gris, the work portrays items typical of still lifes such as a bottle and fruit, which are placed on a multimedia pedestal table made in glued construction paper, wallpaper, and cardboard for increased texture, with drawings in India ink, pencil, charcoal, and chalk. Three playing cards add to the realia tied explicitly to the social interactions and artistic collaborations of these artists, who all traveled along the Nord-Sud, a source of movement—physical and artistic alike—to meet frequently and exchange innovative ideas related to avant-gardist art.

Severini's multimedia and multifaceted work actually renders homage not only to Reverdy, but also to three of the other central members of the Nord-Sud dynamic. As opposed to Miró's painted copy of Reverdy's review, Severini's work is a papier collé that includes the actual cover page of a double issue of *Nord-Sud* 6–7 (August–September 1917). The collage also includes two fragments from that issue glued onto the surface of the work. The first consists of the last four lines of "À Luigi Amaro: Poème liminaire de son 'Ode à Gallieni'" ("To Luigi Amaro: Introductory Poem for His 'Ode to Gallieni'"), a poem by Apollinaire that celebrates the joint efforts of France and Italy against the Germans during World War I. In his poem, Apollinaire addresses Italian dada artist Amaro's elegy to Joseph Gallieni, French general and military governor of Paris who orchestrated the French victory in the First Battle of the Marne in 1914, saving Paris from the onslaught of Germans; Gallieni had since died in 1916:

> France oh Peaceable
> Oh sweet, oh beautiful France
> Amaro you know that I love you
> And both of us love France and Italy
> (Reverdy [1917–18] 1980, 6–7, 9; my translation)

The poem's fragment thus reflects Apollinaire's celebration of Franco-Italian transnational efforts against the Germans and both nations' reactions to Gallieni's proclamation of victory to Parisians in 1914.

The second text from *Nord-Sud* 6–7 glued onto Severini's collage is a diagonally torn fragment of "Atlas," a poem by Alberto Savinio that addresses the contemporary state of Italian art, which was in dire need of renewal through the influence of the international avant-garde based in Paris. Savinio praises neither Italy nor any war heroes; instead, the prose poem obliquely and ambivalently addresses Italy's participation in the war. The torn fragment—a sort of dismantling of war that requires the reader's reference to the text published in the review for full comprehension, reads,

> The vicinity of Greece, in its figuration of the le[af of the grape vine,]
> symbol of hypocritical obscenity—developed our m[oral sense.]
> The most ancient wisdom—since t[he Hindus up until the old man from]
> Tarente—advises us n[ot to look for happiness through the]
> flowerbeds of tranquil[ity of sovereignty. How, therefore, would happiness
> live in]

Italy, where ea[ch purchase of salt and tobacco yields under the weight of its tragedy.]
(Reverdy [1917–18] 1980, 6–7, 31; my translation)

Savinio thus states that modern ideology and culture have replaced traditional Italian lifestyle, and he implies that it is impossible to find happiness without tranquility, which is absent during wartime. Savinio continues his poem by reflecting a new kind of futurist modernity that praises the destruction of traditional Italian art and culture; this is similar to the futurists' declarations in their manifestos in which war is praised for its cleansing effects and leading to renewed political and sociocultural ideologies. Severini's collage therefore demonstrates a richness of social meaning generated through a diversity of artistic mediums representing different artists creating in a variety of artistic genres and esthetics, an important concept of the mobility paradigm, and it further emphasizes the political dimensions of artistic representations of culture (see Divall and Revill 2005, 101, 109).

Braque, a long-time friend and collaborator of so many of the important avant-garde artists, is the final figure in the decade's Nord-Sud dynamic. Having returned to Paris after suffering a head wound on the war front, he moved back to Montmartre and lived at Rue Constantin Pecqueur near Reverdy's office in the eighteenth arrondissement. In issue 13 (March 1918) of *Nord-Sud,* Reverdy published two of Braque's original semi-cubist ink "original plates" created specifically for the review, as well as a series of his maxims on art titled *Pensées et réflexions sur la peinture,* focusing primarily on contemporary avant-gardist calls for improvisation, innovation, and renewal in modernist arts. In his autobiography, Severini comments on the importance of Braque's contributions: "Braque exercises a sort of spiritual influence over that publication [*Nord-Sud*]: two drawings of his were published in *Nord-Sud* as were some of his axioms related to art" (1995, 228). Issues 13 and 14 (March and April 1918) of *Nord-Sud* also advertise Reverdy's *Les Ardoises du Toit* (*Roof Slates,* published 15 March 1918), a collection of cubist poems written between 1916–1918,[13] which includes two additional original India ink drawings by Braque.

One of the illustrations, which shows a copy of the *Nord-Sud* literary review (figure 10.8), is found on the first page of Reverdy's volume of poetry and it places the entire collection into the context of the Nord-Sud dynamic (Reverdy 1918). Although reminiscent of a still life, the objects on the table are reduced to the copy of the influential *Nord-Sud* and a lamp. The soft light of the lamp and subtle shadows on the nightstand suggest a peaceful, contemplative nighttime reading. The drawing thus

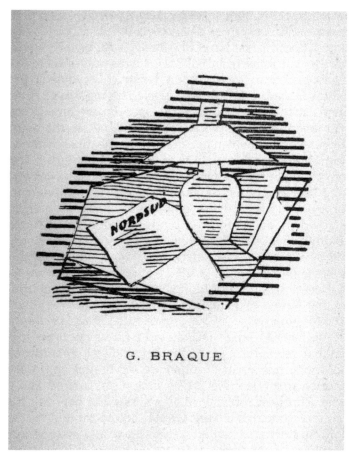

G. BRAQUE

Figure 10.8. Georges Braque, untitled (1918) for Reverdy's *Les Ardoises du toit* (15 March 1918). India ink on paper. 28 × 19 cm. © 2018 Artists Rights Society (ARS), New York / ADAGP, Paris. Provided by the Internet Archive: https://archive .org/details/lesardoisesdutoi00reveuoft.

seems to forecast the end of World War I, which Reverdy and fellow contributors to *Nord-Sud* had fervently anticipated since the first issue of the review was published. Both *Nord-Sud* and *SIC* advertised Reverdy's collection of poetry, reaffirming the link between the three works.

Seven months after Braque's illustration appeared in Reverdy's poetry collection, the principal factors motivating the later stages of the Nord-Sud dynamic were coming to an end. Reverdy had ceased publishing his review in October 1918 after sixteen issues, Apollinaire died of influenza on 9 November 1918 only three days before the armistice for World War I was declared, and the last issue of Albert-Birot's review, whose raison d'être was the war (Albert-Birot 1972, 53), was published in December 1919. But a new stage in the Nord-Sud dynamic would begin in the next decade when, in January 1920, Miró fulfilled his dreams of visiting Paris. After a brief visit in 1920, he decided to spend more time in the city. In 1921 Miró moved into a studio at 45, Rue Blomet, in the southern fifteenth arrondissement, which became one of the most dynamic sites of transnational artistic exchange in twentieth-century Paris.[14] This studio, located next to that of André Masson and frequented by Robert Desnos, Gris, Roland Tual, and others—known today as the Groupe Blomet—was located only one block from the Volontaires metro station on the Nord-Sud Line A which, as Miró stated in an interview titled "Souvenirs of the rue Blomet" (Miró 1992) continued to play an exceedingly crucial role in the development of modernist art. Miró states that this line of the Paris Metro promoted "an exalted exchange and discovery of ideas among a marvelous group of friends" who traveled along "the famous Nord-Sud that served as a link between the Montmartre of the Surrealists and the Montparnasse [of our group]" (101). Travel on the Nord-Sud Line A of the Parisian urban railway would thus continue to facilitate movement between artists at the Blomet studios in Montparnasse and a group of modernist artists grouped around Breton on the Rue Pierre Fontaine, once again near the Pigalle station of the Nord-Sud Line A in Montmartre. This new mobility of artists traveling between the northern and southern regions of Paris would set into motion the next stage of the Nord-Sud dynamic, when surrealism would emerge as the next major vehicle of avant-garde artistic expression in twentieth-century Paris that broadened the transnational reverberations of modernist art movements in all of Western Europe, throughout Central and Eastern Europe, and to North and South America.

Scott D. Juall is professor of French at the University of North Carolina Wilmington. He works on transnational avant-garde artistic movements in twentieth-century Paris and depictions of early modern European imperialism in the New World in writing, cartography, and visual culture. He was a consultant for *45/47 Rue Blomet: Adresse d'artistes* (Blomet Paradiso, 2009) and the exhibition *Surrealism and the Rue Blomet* held at Eykyn Maclean Gallery in New York City in 2013. He edited *Early Modern French Travel Writing and Encounters with Alterity* (*Esprit créateur*, 2008) and coedited *Cultural Exchanges between Brazil and France* (Purdue University Press, 2016).

Notes

1. For a thorough study of the political, economic, and sociocultural complexities related to the planning and construction of the Paris Metro, see Soppelsa (2012). For historical studies of the construction and development of the Paris Metro, see Bindi and Lefeuvre (1990), Collectif (1996), Hovey (1991), Jacobs (2001), Larroque, Margairaz, and Zembri (2002), Ovenden (2008), and Tricoire (2004).

2. For a history of the construction of the Nord-Sud metro lines in particular, see Fontaine (2013).

3. On 9 April 1911 the northern terminus of Nord-Sud Line A reached the Pigalle station, and on 30 October 1912 it reached the Jules Joffrin station.

4. See Lerro (2012) for a study of the futurists' interests in exploiting trains, as both vehicles of physical transportation and transformations in modernist linguistic and artistic innovation, in their artworks and theory.

5. The "[First] Manifesto of Futurist Painters" was published as a leaflet in Milan in the Italian futurist review *Poesia* on 11 February 1910 and the cosignatories were futurist painters Umberto Boccioni, Carlo Carrà, Luigi Russolo, Aroldo Bonzagni, and Romolo Romani. This manifesto was reprinted after Bonzagni and Romani left the group, and their names were replaced by Giacomo Balla and Severini. See Apollonio 1973, 24–26. The "Technical Manifesto of Futurist Painters" was published as a leaflet in *Poesia* on 11 April 1910. The signatories were Boccioni, Carrà, Russolo, Balla, and Severini. See Apollonio (1973, 27–30).

6. The Pigalle station was originally opened on 21 October 1902 as part of an extension of the CMP's Line 2.

7. See Frontisi (2008) for a discussion of the role of cultural and scientific actors such as Albert Einstein, Max Planck, Henri Bergson, Friedrich Nietzsche, Johann Wolfgang von Goethe, and Sigmund Freud, who "converged together to undo the perspectives of Euclidian geometry related to spatio-temporality" and influenced contemporary visual artists whose works created "a renewed sensibility of the world" (2). For the influence of the sciences on the artworks and theory of Severini in particular, see Lukach (1974).

8. For a thorough study of the shifting intellectual and artistic influences among writers, artists, and other thinkers in Montmartre, Montparnasse, and Saint-Germain-des-Prés during the first three decades of twentieth-century Paris, see Hewitt (1996).

9. For a book-length study of the influence of dadaism on the development of modernist art in Barcelona, see Richard de la Fuente (2001).

10. For a detailed study of the relationship between *SIC* and Parisian modernist literary and visual arts, see Kelly (1997), especially chapter 2: "Pierre Albert-Birot, *SIC*, and the Avant-Garde: Collective Adventure and the Voyage of Self-Discovery" (1997, 58–122).

11. Miró possessed issue 2 (April 1917) and the double issue 4–5 (June–July 1917) of *Nord-Sud: Revue Littéraire*. See Labrusse (2004, 285, n18).

12. In a letter written to Enric Cristòfol Ricart in Barcelona on 10 November 1918, Miró states, "The war will be over at any moment and we do not have to put on a show in the provincial theaters . . . and we will be able to appear in the Capital (of Europe). . . . During the current offensive Foch said, *fight, fight, fight!* We can say PARIS, PARIS, PARIS" (1992, 60, emphasis in original). Subsequent letters written before his departure for Paris express similar anticipation (61–66).

13. For extensive studies of the cubist nature of Reverdy's poetry, see Howe (2014), Pap (1996), Rexroth (1969), and Rothwell (1988).
14. For a detailed study of the interactions among the international artists congregating at the Blomet studios and their transnational—and transgeneric—collaborations, see Juall (2013).

References

Albert-Birot, Pierre. 1916. "Exposition futuriste." *SIC: Sons, Idées, Couleurs, Formes* (2, February).
Albert-Birot, Pierre, ed. 1973. *SIC: Sons, Idées, Couleurs, Formes.* Facsimile reprint. Paris: Editions de la Chronique des Lettres Françaises. First published 1916–1919.
Apollinaire, Guillaume. 1914. "Montparnasse." *Paris Journal,* 24 June 1914.
Apollinaire, Guillaume. 1960. *Chroniques d'art.* Paris: Gallimard.
Apollonio, Umbro, ed. 1973. *Futurist Manifestos.* Translated by Robert Brain, R. W. Flint, J. C. Higgitt, and Caroline Tisdall. New York: Viking Press.
Bindi, Armand, and Daniel Lefeuvre. 1990. *Le Métro de Paris: Histoire d'hier à demain.* Rennes, France: Ouest-France.
Boccioni, Umberto, Carlo Carrà, Luigi Russolo, Aroldo Bonzagni, and Romolo Romani. 1910. "[First] Manifesto of Futurist Painters." *Poesia* [Milan], 11 February 1910. (Reprinted, replacing Bonzagni with Giocomo Balla and replacing Romani with Severini.)
Boccioni, Umberto, Carlo Carrà, Luigi Russolo, Giocamo Balla, and Gino Severini. 1910. "(Technical) Manifesto of the Futurist Painters." *Poesia* [Milan], 11 April.
Clarsen, Georgine. 2015. "Ideas in Motion: Frontiers in Mobilities Studies." *Transfers* 5, no. 1: 114–21.
Collectif. 1996. *Le patrimoine de la RATP.* Paris: Editions Flohic.
Del Marle, Félix. 1913. "Futurist Manifesto against Montmartre." *Paris Journal,* 13 July.
Divall, Colin, and George Revill. 2005. "Cultures of Transport, Representation, Practice and Technology." *Journal of Transport History* 26, no. 1: 99–111.
Fontaine, Astrid. 2013. *Le Peuple des tunnels.* Paris: Ginkgo.
Fraser, Benjamin, and Steven D. Spalding, eds. 2012. *Trains, Culture, and Mobility: Riding the Rails.* Lanham, MD: Lexington Books.
Frontisi, Claude. 2008. "Mouvement, vitesse, dynamisme. L'espace-temps futuriste." *Images Re-vues* 1: 1–17.
Hannam, Kevin, Mimi Sheller, and John Urry. 2006. "Editorial: Mobilities, Immobilities and Moorings." *Mobilities* 1, no. 1: 1–22.
Hewitt, Nicolas. 1996. "Shifting Cultural Centres in Twentieth-century Paris." In *Parisian Fields,* edited by Michael Sheringham, 30–45. Chicago: University of Chicago Press.
Hovey, Tamara. 1991. *Paris Underground.* New York: Orchard Books.
Howe, Elizabeth. 2014. "The 'Cubist' Poetry of Pierre Reverdy." *French Review* 87, no. 3: 145–60.
Jacobs, Gaston. 2001. *Le Métro de Paris: un siècle de matériel roulant.* Paris: Éditions La Vie du Rail.
Juall, Scott. 2013. "*L'Oiseau lunaire*: Joan Miró's Memorial to 45, rue Blomet." *Public Art Dialogue* 3, no. 1: 6–38.

Kelly, Debra. 1997. *Pierre Albert-Birot: A Poetics in Movement, a Poetics of Movement.* Cranbury, NJ: Associated University Presses.

Khagram, Sanjeev, and Peggy Levitt. 2008. "Constructing Transnational Studies." In *The Transnational Studies Reader: Intersections and Innovations*, edited by Sanjeev Khagram and Peggy Levitt, 1–18. New York: Routledge.

Labrusse, René. 2004. *Miró: Un feu dans les ruines.* Paris: Hazan.

Larroque, Dominique, Michel Margairaz, and Pierre Zembri. 2002. *Paris et ses transports XIXe et XXe siècles: deux siècles de décisions pour la ville et sa région.* Paris: Éditions Recherches.

Lerro, Alessio. 2012. "Futurist Trains: Aesthetics and Subjectivity in Italian Avant-Garde." In Spalding and Fraser, *Trains, Literature, and Culture*, 77–94.

Lista, Giovanni. 2015. *Le Futurisme: Textes et manifestes, 1909–1944.* Ceyzérieu, France: Champ Vallon.

Lukach, Joan. 1974. "Severini's Writings and Paintings, 1916–1917, and His Exhibition in New York City." *Critica d'Arta* 138: 59–80.

Marinetti, Filippo Tommaso. 1909. "The Founding and Manifesto of Futurism." *Le Figaro,* 20 February.

Marlborough Gallery. 1913. *The Futurist Painter Severini Exhibits His Latest Works.* "Exhibition Catalogue." London: The Marlborough Gallery.

Martin, Marianne W. 1981. "Carissimo Marinetti: Letters from Severini to the Futurist Chief." *Art Journal,* Special Issue on "Futurism," 41 no. 4: 305–12.

Miró, Joan. 1992. *Selected Writings and Interviews*, edited and translated by Margit Rowell. New York: Da Capo.

Ovenden, Mark. 2008. *Paris Metro Style in Map and Station Design.* London: Capital Transport.

Pap, Jennifer. 1996. "'Entre quatre murs': Reverdy, Cubism, and the Space of Still Life." *Word* and *Image* 12: 180–96.

Reverdy, Pierre, ed. (1917–18) 1980. *Nord-Sud: Revue Littéraire.* Facsimile reprint, 1980, edited by Etienne-Alain Hubert. Paris: Jean-Michel Place.

Reverdy, Pierre. 1918. *Les Ardoises du Toit.* Paris: Birault.

Rexroth, Kenneth. 1969. "The Cubist Poetry of Pierre Reverdy." In *Selected Poems* by Pierre Reverdy, translated by Kenneth Rexroth. New York: New Directions. http://www.bopsecrets.org/rexroth/essays/reverdy.htm.

Richard de la Fuente, Véronique. 2001. *Dada à Barcelone: 1914–1918.* Céret, France: Éditions des Albères.

Rothwell, Andrew. 1988. "Cubism and the Avant-Garde Prose-Poem: Figural Space in Pierre Reverdy's 'Au soleil du plafond.'" *French Studies* 43, no 2: 302–19.

Schivelbusch, Wolfgang. 1986. *The Railway Journey: The Industrialization of Time and Space in the 19th Century.* Berkeley: University of California Press.

Severini, Gino. 1995. *The Life of a Painter: The Autobiography of Gino Severini*, translated by Jennifer Franchia. Princeton, NJ: Princeton University Press.

Sheller, Mimi, and John Urry. 2006. "The New Mobilities Paradigm." *Environment and Planning A* 38, no. 2: 207–26.

Soppelsa, Peter. 2012. "Urban Railways, Industrial Infrastructure, and the Paris Cityscape, 1870–1914." In Fraser and Spalding, *Trains, Culture, and Mobility*, 117–44.

Tricoire, Jean. 2004. *Un Siècle de métro en 14 lignes: de Bienvenüe à Météor.* Paris: Éditions La Vie du Rail.

Urry, John. 2007. *Mobilities.* Cambridge, UK: Polity Press.

Mind the Gap

Benjamin Fraser and Steven Spalding

As a way of thinking through what this volume has accomplished and what still remains to be done, we invoke a cinematic metaphor. What follows is a brief, comparative analysis of two short films featuring the train, shot with the cinematograph machine and separated by a gap of one hundred years. Taken together, these films become a metaphor for interdisciplinary scholarship on the railway, and also for that vast terrain implicated in transnational analysis. After a concise presentation of each film, we use the notion of the gap as a way of thinking through the limitations and possibilities of scholarship crossing the humanities and social sciences.

The first short film was shot by brothers Auguste and Louis Lumière, known as the Lumière brothers, at the close of the nineteenth century, and the second—also using the original cinematograph machine—was shot at the close of the twentieth century as part of a series of experiments bringing together a number of distinguished filmmakers from across the globe. The second is a direct commentary on the first.

The Lumière brothers' film *L'Arrivée d'un train à La Ciotat* (*The Arrival of a Train at La Ciotat*) (1896) is certainly one of the most renowned of early cinema, if not also the most storied. Making use of their cinematograph, the brothers recorded images of a train pulling into a railway station in Bouches-du-Rhône, France, and coming to a complete stop, allowing passengers to disembark. The cinematograph was one specific type of a handful of novel cinema machines that were modeled in the late nineteenth century on prior moving-picture technologies such as the zoetrope, of which accommodated bourgeois families were fond. Given the limitations of the machine itself and the film it used, *L'Arrivée* lasts under a minute. Films of the period were black-and-white and soundless, and in this case editing was not used. Famously, reports of the film's screening dramatized the ensuing reactions of the public suggesting that they were in fact afraid of being hit by the lifelike image of the arriving locomotive. True or not, the short film has become an iconic example of the spectacular appeal of early cinema.

Approached as a subject of early cinematic representation, this arrival of the train takes the pulse of an increasingly industrialized and urbanized society that was very much—as evoked in the title of Tim Cresswell's philosophical, historical, and theoretical treatise—*On the Move* (2006). The passengers spilling off the train function in filmic terms as a visual metaphor for a modern mobile society. The hustle and bustle, their movements to and fro, are to transportation history what Baudelaire's writings on the flâneur and the crowd were for urban literary history. Thus, they are at once a symbol for the role played by technology in the larger social shifts that would later fascinate Leo Marx in his locomotive-centered historical-literary study *The Machine in the Garden* ([1964] 2000), as briefly covered in the introduction to this book.

The second film is Patrice Leconte's *La Ciotat 1996*, which as mentioned was shot with the original cinematograph one hundred years later. More important still, is the fact that it captures images of the very same train station captured in the early cinema work of the Lumière brothers. Soundless and in black and white, the film is less than one minute's duration. The train that approaches is, of course, strikingly modern by comparison with that filmed by the brothers Lumière, but equally striking is the absence of passengers and bystanders on the platform. The locomotive does not come to a complete stop, nor does it seem to slow down, instead continuing on through the station to another destination. From a transportation and mobility perspective, this moving image—and the contrast it produces with its antecedent from early cinema—becomes a symbol of the constant movement, the acceleration of certain aspects of contemporary mobile societies. Yet it also exposes the stagnation that arises as a consequence of this perpetual movement. That is, if the train—and its commercial passengers, business travelers, and tourists, if not also packages and deliveries—symbolizes the modern mobile society, then the platform by consequence symbolizes those spaces that persist: they are neglected, underused, or rather used up, the gaps in the narrative of a fluid ever-shifting modernity.

Leconte's film showcases the power of what Wolfgang Schivelbusch called "the machine ensemble" ([1977] 1986, 24) to shape and mold the natural landscape, and with it, to construct and reproduce social terrain. The construction of stations along the path of the nineteenth-century railway supported, or even prompted the formation of, new population centers. Yet at the same time this activity held the power to cause the demise of a town if it was bypassed by the railway. In the same way, the never-ending reproduction of express-train schedules and the establishment of new routes can cause or assist in the decline of a given population center. It is this power of the train as a social technology that is so well captured in the contrast between these two short films. This is the power to promote or sever connections.

Here is our point of entry into the broader metaphor we seek to establish through the comparison of these two films. Just as there is a gap between the frames of any film shot with the original cinematograph technology, there is a gap between railway stations. Cinema theory has long been fascinated by the cinematic illusion produced through the motion of images. The feeling we have as viewers is that we are seeing a continuous slice of time. Yet these frames are not continuous. Rather, it is in the act of viewing that continuity is produced. Similarly, the construction of the railway makes it seem as if two points on its line are inherently connected. Yet this feeling of continuity is only present in the act of travel at a particular time. Taking into account Waldo Tobler's first law of geography—which held that "everything is related to everything else, but near things are more related than distant things" (1970, 236)— the railway can be understood as a social technology that constructs, reconstitutes, rearranges, and erases relationships of distance. These relationships become to some degree naturalized for many, until that is—as with Leconte's locomotive—the train passes us by.

All this has likely been said before, and certainly more perspicaciously.

This book has not been comprehensive, nor totalizing. The contributions to this volume—just as the contributions to our previous books *Trains, Literature, and Culture: Reading/Writing the Rails* (Spalding and Fraser 2012) and *Trains, Culture, and Mobility: Riding the Rails* (Fraser and Spalding 2012), and the special section of *Transfers* (Spalding 2014)—are incredibly varied in their approaches, geographies, and themes. Still, there are gaps throughout in terms of treatments and material that are methodological, geographical, and thematic. These gaps are the necessary byproduct of a group of self-selecting authors working at a particular time on original material destined for a shifting network of publishing possibilities. Nonetheless, to work in an interdisciplinary area in general, and in this interdisciplinary area in particular, is to accept gaps for what they are. Gaps signal possibilities for further inquiry. Gaps are shifting absences, standing out in relief from the written inscriptions that reflect a certain moment in disciplinary motion, rather than any timeless appeal to some immobile or perfect form. If you encountered this book, it is likely you were standing at the station when it arrived, and that your station is midway between the humanities and the social sciences. Please, mind the gap.

Benjamin Fraser is professor in the College of Humanities at the University of Arizona. He is the founding editor of the *Journal of Urban*

Cultural Studies and coeditor, with Steven Spalding, of *Trains, Culture, and Mobility* (2012) and *Trains, Literature, and Culture* (2012). He is the author of ninety articles and book chapters and ten single-authored books, including *The Art of Pere Joan* (2019), *Visible Cities, Global Comics* (2019), *Toward an Urban Cultural Studies: Henri Lefebvre and the Humanities* (2015) and *Digital Cities: The Interdisciplinary Future of the Urban Geo-Humanities* (2015). His publications have appeared in *Catalan Review, Transfers: Interdisciplinary Journal of Mobility Studies, Cultural Studies, Social and Cultural Geography, Environment and Planning D: Society and Space,* and *Emotion, Space and Society.*

Steven Spalding holds a PhD from the University of Michigan and a D.E.A. from the Université de Paris VIII. He is editor of the special section on "Railways and Urban Cultures" (2014) in *Transfers: Interdisciplinary Journal of Mobility Studies* and coeditor of the books *Trains, Culture, and Mobility* (2012) and *Trains, Literature, and Culture* (2012). After more than twenty-five years of teaching at colleges and universities in the United States, France, and Switzerland, he is an independent scholar who writes about French cultural studies, mobility studies and urban studies. His interests involve twentieth- and twenty-first-century French and francophone novels, films, and comics.

References

Cresswell, Tim. 2006. *On the Move: Mobility in the Modern Western World.* New York: Routledge.

Fraser, Benjamin, and Steven D. Spalding, eds. 2012. *Trains, Culture, and Mobility: Riding the Rails.* Lanham, MD: Lexington Books.

Leconte, Patrice, dir. 1996. *La Ciotat 1996.* Included in *Lumière et compagnie,* original idea by Philippe Poulet. France: Pierre Grise Distribution.

Lumière, Auguste, and Louis Lumière, dir. 1896. *L'Arrivée d'un train à La Ciotat.* Included in *Lumière et compagnie,* original idea by Philippe Poulet. France: Pierre Grise Distribution.

Marx, Leo. (1964) 2000. *The Machine in the Garden: Technology and the Pastoral Ideal in America.* New York: Oxford University Press.

Schivelbusch, Wolfgang. (1977) 1986. *The Railway Journey: The Industrialization of Time and Space in the 19th Century.* Berkeley: University of California Press.

Spalding, Steven, ed. 2014. "Railways and Urban Cultures." Special section of *Transfers* 4, no. 2: 42–130.

Spalding, Steven D., and Benjamin Fraser, eds. 2012. *Trains, Literature, and Culture: Reading/Writing the Rails.* Lanham, MD: Lexington Books.

Tobler, Waldo. 1970. "A Computer Movie Simulating Urban Growth in the Detroit Region." *Economic Geography* 46, supplement no. 1: 234–40.

Index

Lightning Source UK Ltd.
Milton Keynes UK
UKHW012030041221
395064UK00004B/243